Getting on Track

CRITICAL PERSPECTIVES ON PUBLIC AFFAIRS
Series Editors: Duncan Cameron and Daniel Drache

This series, sponsored by the Canadian Centre for Policy Alternatives and co-published by McGill-Queen's University Press, is intended to present important research on Canadian policy and public affairs. Books are by leading economic and social critics in the Canadian academic community and will be useful for classroom texts and the informed reader as well as for the academic specialist.

The Canadian Centre for Policy Alternatives promotes research on economic and social issues facing Canada. Through its research reports, studies, conferences, and briefing sessions, the CCPA provides thoughtful alternatives to the proposals of business research institutes and many government agencies. Founded in 1980, the CCPA holds that economic and social research should contribute to building a better society. The centre is committed to publishing research that reflects the concerns of women as well as men; labour as well as business; churches, cooperatives, and voluntary agencies as well as governments; disadvantaged individuals as well as those more fortunate. Critical Perspectives on Public Affairs will reflect this tradition through the publication of scholarly monographs and collections.

GETTING ON TRACK: Social Democratic Strategies for Ontario
Daniel Drache, Editor

Getting on Track

Social Democratic Strategies for Ontario

EDITED BY

DANIEL DRACHE

WITH THE ASSISTANCE OF
JOHN O'GRADY

Canadian Centre for Policy Alternatives, Ottawa
Centre canadien de recherche en politiques de rechange

McGill-Queen's University Press
Montreal & Kingston • London • Buffalo

ISBN 0-7735-0895-3 (cloth)
ISBN 0-7735-0897-X (paper)

Legal deposit first quarter 1992
Bibliothèque nationale du Québec

Printed in Canada on acid-free paper

Publication has also been supported by Canada Council through its block grant program.

Canadian Cataloguing in Publication Data

Main entry under title:
Getting on track: social democratic strategies for Ontario
(Critical perspectives on public affairs)
ISBN 0-7735-0895-3 (bound). –
ISBN 0-7735-0897-X (pbk.)
1. Socialism – Ontario. 2. Ontario – Politics and government – 1985- . I. Drache, Daniel, 1941- . II. Series.

HN110.05G48 1992 320.5′315′0971 C91-090635-1

This book was typeset by Typo Litho composition inc. in 10/12 Baskerville.

Contents

Tables

Figures

Contributors

ELAINE BERNARD is director of Harvard University's labour studies program.

GORDON BETCHERMAN is an economist with the Economic Council of Canada and specializes in employment and industrial relations.

HAROLD CHORNEY teaches public policy at Concordia University in Montreal and is an economist.

MARCY COHEN is completing her PHD in the Sociology Department of OISE at the University of Toronto.

DANIEL DRACHE teaches political economy in the Department of Political Science at Atkinson College and York University. He is co-author with Meric Gertler of *The New Era of Global Competition: State Policy and Market Power* (Montreal: McGill-Queen's University Press, 1991).

GOSTA ESPING-ANDERSEN is a professor in the Department of Political and Social Sciences at the European University Institute in Florence, Italy. His latest book is *The Three Worlds of Welfare Capitalism* (Princeton: Princeton University Press, 1991).

SAM GINDIN is research director of the Canadian Autoworkers Union.

PATRICIA MCDERMOTT teaches in the Department of Social Science at York University and has written extensively on pay-equity plans.

HUGH MACKENZIE, formerly the research director of the United Steel Workers, is presently the executive secretary of the Ontario government's Fair Tax Commission.

LEON MUSZYNSKI is a public sector consultant on social policy, welfare rights, and labour market poverty.

JOHN O'GRADY, formerly the director of research for the Ontario Federation of Labour, is now completing his doctorate at the University of Toronto.

DAVID ROBERTSON is in charge of the CAW technology project.

GUY STANDING is labour market research co-ordinator at the ILO and is currently co-chairman of the basic income European network.

DAVID A. WOLFE is a professor of political science at the University of Toronto.

ARMINE YALNIZYAN is planning director of labour market research for the Social Planning Council of Metropolitan Toronto.

Acknowledgments

This volume grew out a series of seminars on Ontario and the global economy organized by Daniel Drache and John O'Grady in 1990 in Toronto. The planning and development of the seminars were generously supported by president Harry Arthurs of York University, Atkinson College, the Premier's Council of Ontario, and the Executive of the Ontario Federation of Labour. Many of the chapters of this book were originally presented in draft form at that time. We are particularly grateful to all who participated and to those who made many helpful suggestions in the preparation of this book: Duncan Cameron, Andy Ranachan, Terry Maley, Philip Cercone, Arthur Donner, Fred Lazar, Ricardo Grinspun, and Armine Yalnizyan. Special thanks are also due to Judith Turnbull for her excellent editing of the entire manuscript and her wise counsel. A special thank you is owed to Rita Marinucci, Hazel O'Loughlin, and Amy Altomare for typing the manuscript and for their patience and support. Needless to say, we accept all responsibility for the errors that remain.

D.D.
J.O'G.
June 1991

Introduction

The global pressure to compete raises difficult questions for the Rae NDP government elected in the fall of 1990 in Canada's largest and wealthiest province. With the federal government pursuing orthodox deflationary policies, what scope is there for the Ontario government to pursue a full employment strategy? How large a deficit can it afford? How much labour market flexibility is compatible with the goals of security and labour stability? How can the drive for efficiency be reconciled with the need to maintain high levels of social welfare?

Addressing questions like these is anything but academic for the Rae government if it expects to keep its momentum and direction. This collectively inspired book attempts to provide a modern framework of analysis for a social democratic administration intent on exercising power in the nineties. The hope is that the essays and articles will push the Rae government to fight hard for the program that won it the confidence of Ontario's electorate. The way ahead, however, will not be easy. Faced with a bracing recession, the government needs to be both intellectually resourceful and politically resilient if it hopes to make it in the big time.

AN ECONOMY UNDER PRESSURE

By any standard, the economic challenge facing the Ontario NDP government is daunting. Ontario's industries are being battered. One industrial job in seven has been lost to the recession. So far over

250,000 jobs have disappeared. What is more serious, however, is that unlike the job losses in the recession of 1981–82, close to half of the current job losses are permanent. This underscores the fact that this recession is a structural recession. Its signature is the unprecedented rate of partial and complete closures.

At the heart of Ontario's economic problem is the imperative to restructure secondary manufacturing. The high-wage economy and the province's public sector can only be sustained if higher rates of productivity growth in the manufacturing sector are institutionalized. There are two sets of determinants of productivity growth. The first is technical: finding ways to produce differently – that is, without cutting wages or making labour markets more competitive than they already are. The second is social: creating new instruments and changes to Ontario's institutional structure so as to produce different outcomes for workers, for industries, and for entire sectors. In the present conjuncture, the social determinants of productivity are keys to a different future. The question is, how does the NDP intend to generate wealth in addition to reducing social inequality?

AN AGENDA FOR SOCIAL DEMOCRACY IN ONTARIO

The central message of the contributors is that Ontario needs new policy instruments to tackle the five principal agendas of social democracy. These are social welfare policy, labour market adjustment, employment equity, industrial strategy, and environmental recovery. The challenge is to define a coherent industrial strategy for Canada's largest and wealthiest province that would require the state to act as a different kind of regulator.

Social democrats have always understood that business will act differently if the rules are different. Scandinavian businesses do not invest in the skills of their workers because they share social democratic values; they do so because those are the rules. Scandinavian employers do not pay women workers wages that are virtually the same as those of male workers because they share a commitment to gender equality; rather, they do so because those are the rules. Scandinavian companies do not choose to compete on a basis of quality and technology because they reject a low-wage strategy; they do so because those are the rules. Thus, social democrats must devise rules and develop institutional arrangements that will change the way firms behave, the way corporations invest, the way labour markets function, and the way companies compete. Governments have to look at a range of solutions to get their economies back on track and to increase their leverage in a highly unstable economy.

In Part 1, "Rethinking Ontario's Industrial Strategy," the contributions of Mackenzie, Wolfe, and Gindin and Robertson take the first report of the Ontario Premier's Council, *Competing in the New Global Economy*, as their point of departure. That report stressed the strategic role the traded-goods sector would play in Ontario's economic future. It urged the government to adopt a high-tech industrial policy premised on Ontario firms' producing higher value-added goods. The contributions by the above authors share a perspective with Budget Paper E in the recently tabled Ontario Budget. This paper calls for an economic strategy based on social partnerships, a highly skilled work force, and the transformation of industrial production relations through investments. Unlike the Premier's Council's policy framework, with its trade-centred approach, the contributors to Part 1 attach more weight and greater strategic importance to making changes to the province's institutional and social infrastructure.

They take as their working premise the view that a flourishing traded-goods sector can only exist within the context of a flourishing society. Piecemeal measures are not going to make Ontario's industries more efficient. This approach has been tried in the past and it has not given Ontario's industries the clout to increase their presence in foreign and domestic markets. The debate between Mackenzie, Wolfe, and Gindin and Robertson highlights the fact that the rush to develop market niches has contradictory implications not only for firms but also for the future of Ontario. With deregulation, large and small businesses have the power to decide whether to compete on their own, combine forces with other businesses through mergers, acquisitions, leveraged buyouts, joint ventures, or strategic alliances, or organize production by becoming specialized subcontractors to mammoth global corporations.

Part 1 demonstrates that the switch from inert mechanical systems of production to electronics-based technologies has made possible a new array of managerial practices not attainable earlier. These new sophisticated technologies have opened new vistas of flexibility for business. However, as goods production becomes uncoupled from employment, governments must deal with a chronic shortage of jobs and falling incomes. The search for flexibility has brought with it a revolution in workplace practices. While some workers will find themselves upgraded, many face another reality. Many of the new production technologies require less skill and less aptitude. This raises the question, what sort of alternative industrial strategy should Ontario adopt?

Parts 2 and 3 analyze the new initiatives needed to address a broad range of issues stemming from the feminization of work, the rise of the service sector, the restructuring of labour markets, and the decline of the welfare state. Standing addresses the urgent need for income security for workers in highly fragmented labour markets. Esping-Andersen proposes a new conceptual framework for the welfare state. Both initiatives would be a response in large measure to the entry of women into the labour market in unprecedented numbers. The feminization of both welfare state services and the labour market is now recognized as the most far-reaching development of the last three decades. (See the contributions by Cohen, Betcherman, and Yalnizyan.) Workplaces, however, have done little to respond to the family-related needs of both female and male employees issuing from this development. Child care is underfunded and not available to many who badly require it. There are other gaps in the delivery of services for women, and many programs do not meet women's needs. In addition, labour standards are low in Ontario and enforcement uneven; to a considerable degree, they have been and remain unresponsive to women's needs. Paradoxically, this remains the case despite the fact that Ontario's Pay Equity Statute is often touted as the most progressive legislation of its kind in Canada. These extensive changes in both labour markets and industrial relations practices require a forward-looking response from the NDP.

Part 4 spells out different kinds of new policy directions for the NDP. Closing the gender gap, reforming the social welfare agenda, providing new services for women, overhauling the employment-equity statute, strengthening union representation, separating fact from fiction regarding the size of the Ontario deficit – all these measures are analyzed in detail in this section. (See the contributions by O'Grady, Muszynski, Chorney, and Bernard.) The challenge to the Rae government is not only to be proactive but to fashion policy instruments that will require firms and employers to produce differently. Particularly in the area of pay equity and industrial relations, Ontario badly needs forward-looking and effective legislation to empower its citizens. Yet, few of its programmatic initiatives will get off the ground if the NDP government does not get its head around the question of the deficit. As Chorney cogently argues, the deficit is not an economic problem but principally a political one. He makes the powerful case that Ontario's deficit is well within the safe limits of past practice and that if Ontario expects to have both a high standard of living and competitive industries, the government has to take the lead in investing in infrastructural activities such as training and the like.

The final article in the book, "The Way Ahead for Ontario," proposes a framework whereby Ontario could survive the current recession and rebuild its shattered industries. It makes the case that a social democratic government needs to reconcile its traditional commitment to social equity with a strong economic performance. Depending on the kinds of policy instruments that it adopts, the Rae government can transform the way economic space is used and production relations are reorganized. Today in Ontario new forms of competition demand a new institutional framework for business and labour. This final article details the kinds of new policy instruments that will cause firms and sectors to change their investment horizon and the way they treat their work forces. Such policy instruments include a development bank, a powerful restructuring commission, and an institutional mechanism that would require firms to invest in their work forces.

In the abstract, it is easy to talk of the goal of having people from all sectors become more involved in their communities and in their workplaces as they strive to produce differently. In reality, the Rae government needs to use all the power at its disposal to counter the dislocative effects of global and local change. The government faces an array of financial institutions that are less and less rooted in any national context, a business community that demands empowerment at the expense of other groups in society, and an economic system that is increasingly characterized by less economic security for the majority. Confronted with these policy constraints, the NDP government has to exploit the new possibilities for change. This is not easy to accomplish, but the economic shortfall from trade-centred growth and the political and human costs of market-favouring strategies may indeed support the emergence of a new political consensus reflective of a highly diverse but fragmented electorate. But if the Rae government expects to reach out to people and broaden their access to the state, it needs more than good intentions. It has to find ways to exploit the contradictory tendencies of the new order if it wants to build a society founded on the principle of social solidarity rather than global competitiveness.

Practical problems require practical solutions. The rapid deterioration in Ontario's economic position is creating new pressures on the Rae government to act with speed and determination to halt the province's industrial decline. Time is running out. If the NDP government expects to succeed, it will need to be bold in both word and deed.

D.D.
J. O'G.
3 May 1991

Getting on Track

PART ONE

Rethinking Ontario's Industrial Strategy

1 Dealing with the New Global Economy: What the Premier's Council Overlooked

HUGH MACKENZIE

INTRODUCTION: PRODUCTIVITY VERSUS COMPETITIVENESS

Over the past ten years, a subtle change has taken place in the language used by the business community to describe Canada's economic position relative to that of the rest of the world. Whereas the talk used to be about *productivity* and how we needed to continue to improve it to maintain Canada's standard of living, it is now about *competitiveness* and how we need to improve it to maintain the job security of Canadian workers.

If the words carried no real difference in meaning, the change could easily be ignored as an exercise in semantics driven by ideology. It is easy to understand why a business community steeped in the enthusiastic ideology of the 1980s might prefer the word "competitiveness," which speaks directly to that ideology, to "productivity," which sounds vaguely technical and unattractive. Unfortunately, we are not dealing with an innocent exercise in semantics. The two concepts contemplate radically different economic futures for Canada – and radically different economic circumstances for Canadian working people.

Increased productivity, by definition, implies increases in standards of living. How those increases are distributed is determined by unions through the collective-bargaining system and by governments through the tax system. *Increased competitiveness* implies driving input costs down to the level of the lowest common denominator. And since no one would ever suggest that such costs as interest on borrowing should ever be driven down at the expense of such deserving institutions as the banks, then inevitably it is the wages, benefits, rights, and social entitlements of working people that are driven down.

The prevailing emphasis on competitiveness is justified largely on the basis that in an increasingly open world economy, production costs have to be kept down so that export markets remain open to our producers and imports don't drive out domestic production for the domestic market. What the apostles of competitiveness do not acknowledge is that they have chosen an approach based on perpetuating weakness (a competitive, open economy that forces working people to accept lower living standards in return for tenuous and temporary job security) rather than an approach based on economic strength (a productivity-oriented economy that raises living standards and promotes employment security).

While many of the consequences of this shift – the introduction of the goods and services tax (GST), unemployment insurance cuts – have been the subject of intense political debate, even within Canada's political mainstream, the idea of competitiveness that forms the basis for these changes has for the most part been challenged only from the left.

In Ontario the 1988 report of the Premier's Council, *Competing in the New Global Economy*, stands virtually alone as a mainstream challenge to the idea that lowest-common-denominator competition is a given against which we must measure our expectations and according to which we must be prepared to trim our living standards.

THE REPORT'S ANALYSIS VERSUS THE BUSINESS PERSPECTIVE

The analysis in the report is based on the proposition that living standards can only continue to improve if the rate of growth in value-added in the economy exceeds the rate of growth in population. In a closed economy, it is at least in principle possible to sidestep the issue of productivity by shifting production from existing low value-added activities to higher value-added activities. Whether value-added is increasing or decreasing in any given activity is irrelevant as long as the value-added in those sectors that are growing exceeds that of those sectors that are not growing or are in decline. In a closed economy, this kind of economic base could in theory be sustained because high value-added activities can be protected in the domestic market from lower-cost alternative sources.

In an open economy, according to the council's analysis, only improved production-cost performance can protect domestic productive activities and/or permit them to expand. The Premier's Council avoids the three key conclusions drawn by the right-wing business community in its criticisms of the Canadian economy in the past decade: that wage increases are pricing us out of the international marketplace; that Canada can no longer afford to maintain its high level of social entitlement; and that Canada cannot afford to maintain a regulatory environment that generates costs here that are not borne by our competitors.

Instead, the Premier's Council report advances the bold proposition that increasing living standards can be sustained in an open economy through a process of continuous productivity growth. It argues strongly against low-wage strategies that depend for their success on lowering living standards. It finds that these are inherently self-defeating and that in the absence of explicitly interventionist economic policies, the low-wage/reduced-living-standards strategy is a kind of industrial strategy by default.

Precisely because the council's conclusions were so clearly out of step with the conventional business wisdom of the Reagan 1980s, the report makes some important contributions to the debate on industrial policy; the most germane of these are as follows:

- The emphasis on high value-added, "traded" products and services as the basis for an economic strategy

In this formulation, the concept of a traded product or service includes both traditional export industries and import-competing industries. The report does not dismiss the importance of non-traded commodities.[1] Rather, it argues that production in these sectors will not drive economic change. It places little importance on low value-added products and services on the basis that they cannot in the long run support a high-wage, high-living-standard economic structure.

However, the identification of high value-added traded commodities and services is two-edged. On the one hand, such identification reinforces the importance that we have traditionally attached to manufacturing (wealth-creating activity) in industrial policy. On the other hand, it takes as a given the openness of the economy and the necessity of trade.

- The importance of corporate strategies as opposed to traditional macroeconomic or microeconomic approaches for analysis and policy

The report notes that the global reach and integration of the corporate sector implies that if the focus is to be on economic results, the government's policy approach must directly address the corporation's internal decision-making process, since the corporate decisions taken produce these economic results.

The analytical emphasis on corporate strategies underlines their importance, but it leaves to be resolved the question of whether these strategies can be influenced or controlled by any national government.

- The concept of the "indigenous corporation"

In the report's schema, a corporation is "indigenous" if it has a self-contained economic position in Canada, regardless of its country of ownership. Transnational corporations whose Canadian subsidiaries have "world product mandates" would qualify as "indigenous." The report cites Pratt and Whitney as an example of a foreign-owned corporation that qualifies as indigenous because its operations encompass the full scope of R & D and manufacturing at its Montreal location. At the same time, a Canadian-owned corporation could fail to qualify because it is not capable of standing on its own. For example, a business that consisted of stamping parts from dies designed and produced outside Canada might not qualify as "indigenous" in this definition.

The concept of an indigenous corporation has some resonance with those of us who have felt uncomfortable with the argument that Canadian capitalists are inherently better for the Canadian economy than other kinds of capitalists. But it is such a slippery concept. How do we recognize an indigenous corporation? And once we have identified one, how do we keep it that way?

- The concept of the "threshold corporation"

The best way to describe what the report means by a threshold corporation is to describe what it is not. It is not a large company in a mature business, regardless of the scope of its market. It is also not a company prevented by its size and scope from contemplating an involvement in markets outside Canada. Rather, it is a company "poised" for rapid growth.

The threshold corporation concept is an interesting one, but such corporations are easily identified only after the fact – one can't expect politicians to be any smarter than stockbrokers. Important questions remain regarding what powerful public policy tools could be put in place to turn the threshold corporations of today into the significant Canadian employers of tomorrow.

In addition, in making its central point about finding industries and companies poised for rapid growth, the report effectively writes off "mature" industries like auto and steel, as if these industries are both technologically backward and somehow isolated from the cutting edge of the economy. In taking this position, the report makes a major mistake. As far as technology is concerned, the report falls into the common trap of assuming that because the product of an industry has been around for a long time, the industry itself must be backward. The fact is that in both the steel and auto industry the pace of change in process technology is extremely rapid and the components of such change utilize every aspect of leading-edge technology. In assuming that mature industries make only a limited contribution to the pace of change in the wider economy, the report ignores the complex backward and forward linkages that extend the influence of even an industry with shrinking overall employment, such as steel.

- The central role of technological capacity in economic development

The report makes the point that in a rapidly changing world in which technology is diffused extremely rapidly and very few products enjoy protected local markets, the chief factor that distinguishes success from failure will be a firm's ability to reach and stay at the leading edge of technology in a specific field.

- The identification of target industries and corporations – specifically "high-growth and emerging industries"

The report makes it very clear that government support that is not targeted (or is targeted in the wrong places) is wasted. It rejects the idea of public assistance for service sector industries that function in a domestic market (e.g., no funding for strip clubs or shopping malls). It also debunks the idea that small business per se should be a specific target for government assistance. Small business tends to be technologically backward, services-oriented and/or not in the traded sector, dependent on low wages as a competitive base, and quite clearly not in the threshold category.

Clearly, each of the above ideas raises controversial issues that must be resolved in any consistent approach to economic policy in an open, mixed industrial economy in the last decade of the twentieth century.

A BREAK WITH TRADITIONAL NEO-CLASSICAL THINKING: THE CONTRIBUTION TO ECONOMIC POLICY DISCUSSION ON THE LEFT

Beyond these critical issues, however, there is a great deal more either in the Premier's Council report or in what it implies that supports positions traditionally taken by the left vis-à-vis the role of the state in guiding economic development, the role of small business in economic growth, and the impact of wage levels and social entitlements on competitiveness. Given that its contents are the result of a kind of social bargaining with the business sector in Ontario, the report makes a number of remarkable points in calling for a conscious industrial strategy very much like the Swedish model of economic development for Ontario and, by implication, for Canada in the dynamic sectors of the economy.

The left will find that a number of the ideas in the Premier's Council exercise are of real value to a labour movement strategy. In particular, the report's emphasis on corporate strategy is critical in the world of stateless corporations, intra-corporate trade, and internal (market independent) investment decision-making. It is impossible to understand much of what takes place in the real economy without a realistic analysis of corporate strategy, broadly defined. It follows that domestic economic policies must both take into account and attempt to influence corporate strategic behaviour. This means a successful economic strategy must involve social bargaining.

The identification of traded sectors as key for future development is critical in an economy in which 40 percent of output is traded directly and even more is trade-impacted in a world environment in which economies are becoming more open. Economically, there are two ways to maintain a high-wage economy with high living standards in an open trading system: (1) by increasing value-added in domestic production and (2) by raising living standards in the rest of the world trading system. As much as we might wish to achieve our goals through the latter, the reality is that we have to try to do both, knowing that our prospects for success with the second are limited in the short term.

The concept of the indigenous corporation, even given the definitional problems referred to above, is potentially a useful one. Characterizing corporations by their structure and behaviour is much more promising as a basis for economic policy than limiting the characterization to country of ownership. The concept also helps governments deal effectively, at the level of policy development, with corporations like Northern Telecom, which is becoming less "indigenous" every day, notwithstanding the fact that its shares continue to be held in Canada.

SOME FUNDAMENTAL WEAKNESSES

As stimulating as the report's analysis may be, however, it also suffers from major flaws that unquestionably have direct implications for the policy proposals in the report.

The most important is that the report ignores the real reasons for the growth in some of the key sectors in Ontario that it holds up as success stories to be emulated. These are factors that should have been folded into both the analysis and the recommendations. For instance, the aerospace industry and Northern Telecom are cited as shining examples without reference either to the role of the Canada-US defence production–sharing agreement and the acquisition by the federal government of de Havilland for aerospace or to the status of Northern Telecom as a captive supplier to a regulated industry (Bell). A decline in US military spending will have a direct impact on the former; the Canada-US Free Trade Agreement (FTA) already precludes a duplication of the latter.

In addition, the recent behaviour of the most important success stories cited in the report undermines much of the logic. Northern Telecom's "rationalization" decisions, for example, raise questions about just how stable the "indigenous" designation of a corporation is. The report implicitly assumes that once a corporation has achieved "indigenous" status, it will maintain that status. Therefore, it has nothing to say about how the contribution of these "indigenous corporations" to our economy can be maintained when they begin to migrate.

Northern Telecom, with its rapidly growing assembly operations in the American deep south, highlights another problem. Industries cannot be neatly divided into value-added competitors and wage-based competitors. At the margin, every company becomes a wage-based competitor.

The problems with these examples notwithstanding, the report makes a key point that echoes the arguments that leftist critics of the branch-plant economy have been making for twenty-five years: corporations whose Canadian operations are not truncated make a more significant contribution to the economy than foreign branch plants that cannot stand alone.

Having reached that point in the analysis, however, the report does not recommend the creation of policy instruments strong enough to exercise the kind of influence over corporate strategies that is required to achieve its goals. In particular, it avoids recommendations that would either significantly alter existing institutional arrangements or inject the public sector into the corporate decision-making process.

The report also blissfully ignores the fact that, as attractive as the idea of developing high-productivity, high-growth indigenous firms in new areas of economic activity may be, the vast bulk of Ontario's manufacturing activity takes place and will continue to take place in branch-plant firms that will never be indigenous or in industries that the report classifies as mature and therefore of little interest.

The report's impact is further weakened by the fact that the most powerful policy levers are under federal jurisdiction – trade policy, banking policy, exchange rate and interest rate policy, foreign investment review (whose purpose is to protect and nurture indigenous firms), and competition policy. However, the report ignores key policy instruments potentially available to an Ontario government – most notably pension fund investment policy but also securities regulation, resource policy, labour relations policy (the creation of solidaristic wage policies through a decree system, for example), and training policy.

Further, it fails to address the question of a functioning planning framework for industrial development. Successful industrial economies have all had an industrial planning framework of some kind within their countries' institutional context. Japan's industrial planning framework is tied to the banking system and the role of the giant trading companies in the economy. Germany's consists of the banking system combined with the process of co-determination established after the Second World War. In the United States, NASA and the Department of Defense in combination comprise the framework. In Sweden, a combination of central tax and economic development policies, driven by planning goals, and an active labour market policy serve this purpose.

While many of the report's practical implications are favourable, its narrow emphasis on a concept of "competitiveness" remains a problem. It leaves open the question of which market-driven influences we accept as given and not subject to control (or as legitimate) and which influences we might attempt to modify or ignore. And in the absence of any actual interventionist policies designed to avoid the lowest-common-denominator trap that the report so clearly rejects, much of the report serves as a rationalization for lowering real wages and reducing expectations as much as it serves as the basis for an effective alternative. The report accepts competitiveness as a goal when competitiveness should more properly be seen and judged as an instrument towards the achievement of higher living standards for the population as a whole.

Finally, by linking productivity improvements to improved living standards, the report implicitly assumes that productivity gains will be equitably distributed. With capital even more mobile than goods and services in the "new global economy," there is no reason to assume that the same lowest-common-denominator process that puts downward pressure on wages will not push relative returns on investment capital to the highest common denominator, thereby enhancing inequality.

In sum, the report's recommendations fall far short of what is needed to achieve the objectives set out in the analysis.

PRACTICAL POLITICAL PROBLEMS WITH THE PREMIER'S COUNCIL EXERCISE

Despite the report's aggressive promotion of an activist role for the provincial government, it was virtually ignored by both the Liberal Party and cabinet and by the Queen's Park bureaucracy for the life of that government. It is not hard to see why the Liberals were reluctant to embrace their own report. Many of its recommendations would, if carried to their logical conclusion, be recognized by the business community as interventionist. To paraphrase Margaret Thatcher's view of the European Social Charter process, the Canadian business community didn't defeat the forces of intervention through free trade only to invite them in the back door in Ontario. These were difficult folk for an establishment-based party to ignore.

The report's repudiation of support for small business and of policy positions taken by small business on issues like the minimum wage was another political problem for the Liberals. A traditional Liberal government (as the Peterson government most certainly was) would consider acting on such recommendations to be pure folly.

Finally, the report was introduced into a decidedly hostile economic policy environment at the federal level. Indeed, one unintended accomplishment of the report was that it highlighted the limitations on the economic policy capacity of even a powerful provincial government when a federal government really wants to set the economic agenda, as the current Conservative government most certainly does. The free trade agreement either prohibits or imposes strict limitations on the kinds of policies needed at both the provincial and federal levels of government to support the council's proposed strategy. It is perhaps a measure of its limited influence on the Liberal government (or of the government's limited interest in opposing the free trade agreement) that the report was never formally reassessed. Furthermore, public macroeconomic policies at the federal level (unemployment insurance, interest rates, and exchange rates, in particular) are actively hostile to a strategy for Ontario manufacturing as envisaged in the report.

The combination of free trade with the United States and the extremist interest and exchange rate policies pursued by the Bank of Canada brings into sharp focus one of the unfortunate realities of economic policy activity at the provincial level in Canada. There is very little that even the Ontario government can do that cannot be *totally* frustrated by federal government policy.

It is not just the fact that it is difficult to implement an expansionist economic policy at a time when federal policies are creating a depression. The report contemplates a trade-driven strategy focusing on increasing value-added through technological change. However, exchange rate movements brought about by Bank of Canada monetary policies have had a devastating effect on the cost position of Canadian exporters in the US market. As compared with average US tariffs of about 6.5 percent on dutiable Canadian products entering the United States before the free trade agreement, the Canadian dollar has appreciated by 23 percent since 1985. If exchange rates stay at current levels, the combined effect of the FTA and exchange rates will produce costs for Canadian exporters selling into the US market 17 percent higher than before the FTA negotiations began. US exporters to Canada have already gained more from exchange rate movements than they will eventually gain from the removal of Canada's average 12 percent tariffs on dutiable imports from the US. The combined effect of the FTA and exchange rate movements will reduce the costs of selling into the Canadian market for US exporters to Canada by over 35 percent.

High interest rates have an independent impact on this kind of strategy. High interest rates discourage the capital investment needed to increase the value-added potential of the goods-producing side of the economy. And with the length of the payback period required for an investment reduced, they tend to discourage expenditures with longer-term payoffs, such as research and development expenditures.

CONCLUSION: THE PREMIER'S COUNCIL REPORT AND ONTARIO'S NDP GOVERNMENT

The Premier's Council report has been a useful document in ways that those who commissioned the work in the first place would neither have predicted nor desired. Although it had virtually no impact on the economic policy of the Liberal government that commissioned it, it is now in the hands of a social democratic government, one that was elected on a vaguely expressed mandate for change and is attempting to cope with what is likely to be a very serious recession.

A few months ago, the value of the report would have been measured by the fact that it put onto the agenda a number of concepts that can play a useful role in progressive thinking about the economy in Canada. It now has the potential to inform actual government policy in Canada's largest and most sophisticated provincial economy.

These potentially influential ideas include the following: the distinction between traded goods and services and non-traded goods and services; the emphasis on corporate strategy as a determinant of economic activity; the concept of the indigenous corporation; the role of technology development in economic growth; and the implicit imperative for a country like Canada to take a strategic approach to economic development. Some of these elements are important because they reinforce things that we on the left have always believed. Others are important because they flag issues that must be the subject of debate within the left if we are to have any hope of developing a credible response to the policies of the right.

At the same time, it is important that the new government avoid the traps created by the obvious weaknesses in the analysis and recommendations noted above. Many of the ideas behind the report's analysis are themselves fatally flawed. The task will be to take that analysis in more fruitful directions. In the immediate future, the change in Ontario's government may mean that the process that produced the report is as important as its content. First, because the report represents a consensus that involved the highest levels of the business community, its central ideas can be claimed by the new government to be a consensual springboard for a new economic policy direction. Second, as long as we operate in a mixed economy in Canada, it is inevitable that there will be elements of social bargaining in the development of economic policies. The outcome in this case was limited by the fact that the sponsoring government quite obviously had no strong agenda of its own and no particular commitment to the results of the process. Different participants would undoubtedly have produced a different bargain. Something like this process, however, with a clear government agenda and much higher stakes, is an inevitable component in the implementation of a progressive economic policy in Canada. That task now falls to the newly elected New Democratic Party government.

The report has given the new government of Ontario the advantage of a starting point for this exercise in social bargaining that is some distance ahead of the mainstream view that dominates economic thinking in this country. At the same time, the serious flaws in the council's "blueprint," together with the lack of commitment of the NDP's predecessor in office to the implementation of its own exercise, will create difficulties both for the consensus itself and for its implementation.

It is not cynical in the least to suggest that one of the things that lubricated the consensus reflected in the report was an understanding by the business participants that much of it would never actually find its way into government policy. Business participants who bought into the original exercise may be less inclined to follow the lead of the new government.

At the level of implementation, it is clear that the powerful bureaucracy in Ontario mobilized effectively to keep the ideas in the report from infiltrating economic policy at Queen's Park. The Ministry of Industry and Trade in particular was extremely effective in its resistance. Having fought the ideas in the report under the Liberals, the bureaucracy will be in fine fighting form for any successor. The NDP government will have to be equal to the battle.

NOTES

1 Domestic goods that are not exported and do not face competition from imports.

2 Technology and Trade: Finding the Right Mix*

DAVID A. WOLFE

INTRODUCTION

Social democratic economic policy traditionally has been predicated on a strong commitment to the role of a democratic political authority in directing and managing the national economy. In the period up to, and including, the Great Depression, this commitment was associated with a belief in the need for greater public ownership and control over the supply of essential commodities. These fundamental tenets of socialist orthodoxy were undermined by Keynesian ideas during the latter part of the 1930s and the Second World War. As a result of the Keynesian revolution in economic thinking, the commitment to the democratic management of capitalist economies became detached from the belief in expanded public ownership. The traditional social democratic concerns with income redistribution, greater equality, and improved social welfare measures were blended with Keynesian demand management policies to constitute the new orthodoxy of the postwar period.

A strong belief in the national economy as the relevant seat of action for the assertion of democratic control over the activities of private capital was central to the Keynesian synthesis. Keynesianism,

* This is a revised version of an article published in S. Rosenblum and P. Findlay, eds., *Debating the Future of Socialism in Canada* (Toronto: Lorimer, 1990).

in both its progressive liberal and social democratic variants, was based on "an economic theory of the national economy, in which abstract propositions are formulated in terms of a coherent set of economic aggregates."[1] In the mode of growth that prevailed throughout the postwar period, the maintenance of a harmonious balance between domestic levels of production and consumption was the key to economic stability. To the extent that international trade contributed to the expansion of demand, it played a distinctly secondary role. The underlying economic transformation of the past decade renders this strategy infinitely more problematic. If the effectiveness of the domestic economy as a site for asserting this authority has been weakened by developments in the global economy, how can our traditional goal of subjecting the private economy to democratic control still be realized?

THE CHALLENGE OF THE 1990S

This question presents a challenge for the right and left alike. The neo-conservative and business agenda that has dominated economic policy in Canada, the US, Britain, and other countries for the past decade represents one response to this challenge. The national variations of this agenda share a common goal of responding to increased global interdependence by freeing the market from state intervention. An essential element of this strategy has included the push towards freer trade. This was a key part of Reagan's electoral platform in 1980, and the United States has fought hard to ensure that the current Uruguay round of GATT (General Agreement on Tariffs and Trade) negotiations reduces trade barriers to the export of goods and services in which it remains competitive. It is an important factor (though far from the only one) behind the move towards Europe 1992. Canada's own contribution to this agenda was to seek a bilateral trade agreement with the United States, ostensibly to guarantee access for Canadian exporters to the US market. The strategy of the Canada-US Free Trade Agreement (FTA) is predicated on the economic wisdom of the 1950s – that the realization of larger economies of scale is the principal source of productivity and profit increases and that Canada can only attain these economies through guaranteed access to the larger US market.

The democratic left's response to the dilemma of how to assert democratic control over a weakened domestic economy has largely been framed in reaction to the neo-conservative agenda. For the most part, the democratic left has argued that the growing integration of the global economy represents a fundamental threat to traditional socialist values. The economic restructuring prompted by the adoption of microelectronic-based technologies is leading to a form of de-industrialization that is eliminating many of the jobs that sustained the expansion of middle-class incomes during the postwar decades. Further, the rise of the newly industrializing countries, which have a plentiful supply of relatively cheap labour, is undermining the power of organized labour in the industrialized countries. More people are working in lower-paying, poor-quality, service sector jobs or working part-time because of their inability to find full-time jobs. If left unchallenged, the new global trade imperative will result in a continuing downward spiral of incomes and living standards for the majority of workers, while capital becomes more detached from any commitment to its domestic economic base.

The principal policy response that follows from this perspective has been one of planned trade as an alternative to the pressures for increased international competition. Only through realizing some degree of insulation from the world economy can a national economy free itself from the tyranny of international capital mobility and the multinational corporations' power to relocate investment and jobs on a global basis. A strategy of planned trade is seen as a necessary and logical complement to the implementation of an industrial strategy. This position was articulated most cogently in the submission by the Canadian section of the United Auto Workers (CAW) to the Macdonald Commission (the Royal Commission on the Economic Union and Development Prospects for Canada):

> Canada will not achieve security for its citizens by playing the game of international competition. There are too many players now who have a manufacturing and technological base superior to our branch-plant economy. There are too many governments that are determined to play the same game and too many countries that will invite in multinationals to combine the most advanced technology with Third World wages.[2]

The CAW position is qualified with an extensive discussion of the distinction between free trade and planned trade. The CAW argues strongly in favour of an expanded role for government in mitigating the effects of international competition for Canadian workers and ensuring that we gain the greatest benefits possible from our trading relations with other nations. In themselves, these policies are valuable and should constitute part of a social democratic economic agenda. The problem is that the overall discussion is framed in terms of a false dichotomy between domestic economic development on the one hand and increased international trade on the other.

The Technology Factor in International Trade

The CAW position presumes that relative cost differences remain the primary basis of comparative advantage in international trade. While this may still be true for a number of industries, there is mounting evidence that costs in general, and wage costs in particular, are no longer the critical determinant of success in international trade. Technological innovation, product design, product quality, and overall productivity levels are increasingly important determinants of success in international trade. This conclusion is supported by a stream of empirical and theoretical work in international trade theory over the past two decades that stresses the role of non-price factors in accounting for international trade performance. While price may be a determining factor for trade in homogeneous primary commodities or bulk chemicals, this is not the case in most capital markets and for many consumer goods. The factors cited above, as well as others, such as technical service, marketing, and the availability of credit, play a critical role.

The current technological trends accentuate this tendency. The latest developments in process technology are diminishing the significance of unskilled labour in production costs, thus reducing the incentive to relocate manufacturing and assembly operations on the basis of wage differences alone. Furthermore, the greater value attributed to customized production increases the incentive to locate activities in close proximity to the primary markets for industrial and advanced service products. While some lower value-added manufacturing may continue to be shifted to low-wage economies, there is growing reason to question the scenario presented by the CAW.[3]

THE PREMIER'S COUNCIL REPORT

If this perspective has been overlooked by social democrats, it was not by the Liberal government in Ontario. The Premier's Council report released in May 1988 presented the most coherent vision of an industrial and technology strategy espoused by either of the two mainstream parties in this country. Rather than viewing international competition as a threat to workers' wages, the Premier's Council depicted effective international competition as the key to a high-wage economic strategy and higher standards of living:

> When nations cannot maintain productivity growth in their internationally traded goods and services at rates equal to their competitors, they have only one alternative to remain viable in international markets: they must reduce

their wages. The usual method for this is a currency devaluation. Devaluations boost exports because they reduce costs, but they do so at the expense of a nation's living standards.

The Premier's Council counterposed to this a strategy of achieving higher value-added per employee either by achieving higher productivity in the existing mix of goods and services or by shifting the industrial structure of the province towards goods and services that are inherently higher value-added per employee activities. They term the process of shifting production towards higher value-added per employee activities "industrial restructuring." In direct opposition to the position espoused by the CAW, the Premier's Council argued that Ontario can best pursue this strategy by focusing its economic policies on traded businesses – those exposed to world trade and competition. Gains realized through improvements in traded goods and services will generate increased prosperity that will diffuse throughout the provincial economy. Hence, "the traded sectors must be viewed as the fundamental drivers of our future wealth and prosperity."

The report outlined an economic strategy based on these initial premises. Much of the report is open to criticism. For instance, it targeted traded businesses to the exclusion of non-traded businesses, both in manufacturing and in services, thus excluding the non-traded segments of the provincial economy. It focused on the role of large, indigenous firms to the exclusion of smaller, often more innovative firms. It said little about the growing convergence of manufacturing and service industries. Finally, most of the specific recommendations in the report focused on increased incentives for capital – a recapitalization incentive plan, incremental R & D tax incentives, a risk-sharing fund, early-stage venture capital incentives, and initial public support incentives, redirecting government research to industry. The report ignored many things that social democrats would want to include, and the focus on incentives for private industry largely ignored the role to be played by the public sector.

AN ALTERNATIVE TRADE STRATEGY

This discussion suggests the need for an alternative trade strategy for social democrats, one which, to date, has gained much less currency than the one discussed above. This alternative should view the current wave of technological and social change as an opportunity to progress beyond the gains of the past four decades and create a new array of social and political institutions capable of supporting increased levels of social productivity and a higher standard of living. It ascribes no less important a role to the nation-state in directing the course of national economic development than does the strategy that supports planned trade. It accepts the reality of the growing interdependence of the global economy, but sees this as a challenge to progress up the ladder of technological learning. It involves a cumulative process of expanding the knowledge and skill base at every level of society – increasing our capacity for social learning and improving our collective standard of living.

The rationale for this alternative trade policy is predicated on an understanding of the link between technological innovation and international trade. As was noted above, neo-classical theorizing about the role of natural advantages, or price competition, is inadequate to explain long-term shifts in shares of world export trade among the leading industrial countries. This is because neo-classical theorizing tends to conceptualize comparative advantages in largely static terms to the exclusion of the dynamic effects that flow from technological innovation. Technology defined very broadly plays a critical role in explaining the shifts that have occurred over time in the shares of world export trade.

Theories that link international trade with technological innovation argue that shifts in leadership are not randomly distributed across industrial sectors or between countries. These theories maintain that technology is not a freely, instantaneously, and universally accessible good, as was assumed by many of the background studies prepared for the Macdonald Royal Commission. Trying to adapt industrial and technology policy on the principle of catching up to the technological leaders may prove difficult. Innovation and technological leadership are dynamic processes. The innovation process itself involves a cumulative pattern of learning within the individual firm, across industrial sectors, and throughout society at large. This cumulative pattern of learning is characterized by dynamic effects that allow production efficiency to increase and product quality to improve over time. By the time a follower attains the position of the technological leader, the leader will likely have long since moved on.

From this perspective, it is not natural advantages in resources or comparative price advantages that determine the basis of international trade flows, but national differences in innovative capacity. The recent experience of the Canadian forest products industry compared to that of Sweden and Finland illustrates this point. There is a dynamic relationship between early innovative leads, economies of scale, learning by doing, oligopolistic exploitation of these advantages, and international trade. The trajectories of economic development experienced by individual nations are determined by a mix of the production profile of the existing economy and the individual and collective choices made in a nation about how to develop and exploit technology in the future. The choices made at any point in a nation's development do not create a singular set of gains or losses in the economic well-being of that country, but fundamentally affect its future well-being through their dynamic effects over time.

The relationship between innovation and future levels of economic growth is critical. The potential benefits that flow from an individual set of technology and production choices are strongly determined by the potential demand for those technologies or products in world markets – or what economists refer to as the income elasticities of demand. The faster the demand increases in world markets for a country's products, for instance, the greater will be the net benefits, in terms of growth, that flow to that country. The choices made individually by firms, or collectively through public agencies, about the product mix that a country specializes in will strongly affect its future well-being.

Available evidence suggests that technological competition tends to be pre-emptive and produce irreversible results. The initial advantages that accrue to the technological leader in an area allow it to retain that lead for a period of time and to undermine the efforts of its competitors. The benefits of technological leadership allow a firm to recover its research and development costs, as well as realize a higher than average return on its investment. In effect, success breeds success.

Central to this notion of dynamic changes in the long-term trading position of nations is the process of technological innovation. The prevailing notion sees innovation as closely linked to basic scientific research. Research involves the process of generating new scientific breakthroughs in the laboratory that lead inevitably through the stage of application to the development of innovative new products or processes that gain a significant share of world markets. Certainly, there are some examples of new products that conform to this view. The development and application of laser technology probably corresponds most closely. But there are numerous other illustrations that call this view into question. The problems that have plagued the Canadian telidon system illustrate the complex relationship between supply and demand factors in the innovation process.

Detailed studies of the innovation process reveal that it is not something that necessarily originates in the laboratory and is then transferred to the factory. Effective innovation is largely a social process that is integrally tied to every phase of activity of the firm, as well as a complex set of relationships that exist between firms and external sources of knowledge, such as universities or government laboratories. It is an output of both the production process and the laboratory. Technical knowledge accumulates in the activities of scientific researchers, in the designs and blueprints of engineers, and in the complex set of skills, knowledge, and techniques shared by communities of production workers.

The source of technological knowledge and insight is not separable into discrete product categories; it is cumulative and dynamic. Insights gained by scientists, engineers, and production workers in the design and manufacture of one product may transfer into significant new insights and comparative advantages useful in the production of others. An ability on the part of the firm to respond quickly and effectively to suggestions from product users on how to stretch existing technologies or meet new needs may prove critical. This relationship further increases the dynamic consequences that may flow in the future from choices made about the allocation of resources today.

A sustained innovative capacity requires the effective co-ordination of policy at three different levels – that of the firm, networks of firms, and the nation.

The Firm

At the level of the firm, technical expertise constitutes a stock of knowledge that accumulates through a process of learning by doing in the layers of engineers and skilled workers that comprise the firm. It is not limited to firms located in the manufacturing sector of the economy. In today's integrated and interdependent economy, the information-processing component of many activities associated with service sector firms is every bit as important for innovation as that associated with manufacturing firms. Given the pace of diffusion of microelectronics, it is becoming increasingly difficult to distinguish a purely manufacturing from a purely service activity. The roles of each are crucial to successful innovation.

The implications of this conception of the innovative process for the role of workers and the reorganization of production are significant. New manufacturing and service processes based on microelectronic technologies are rapidly altering the skills/production nexus. Rather than viewing production workers as a source of costs to be controlled, a dynamic conception of the innovative process sees them as an asset whose creative potential must be optimized.

The new information technologies, because of their more malleable qualities, do not lead a priori to a determinant set of skill effects. A number of studies indicate that the same technology may have very different effects on the nature of work and skill levels in different firms, sectors, and countries. Overall, the progressive application of new technologies in the work process necessitates a shift in emphasis from physical to mental demands.

The spreading application of microelectronic technologies has made way for new manufacturing strategies – strategies that might find a balance between those applied to traditional forms of craft production and those applied to the form of standardized mass production that prevailed during the postwar boom. The enhanced flexibility of these technologies increases the ease with which equipment can be reprogrammed, allowing firms to introduce a wider degree of variety in the scope of products that can be manufactured economically. Microelectronic technology makes it possible to undertake small-batch, even custom, production and to phase in and phase out products as changes in market conditions dictate. This new manufacturing strategy has been termed "diversified quality production": "Industrial restructuring towards diversified quality production is now generally regarded as a highly promising strategy for old industrial, high wage economies striving to remain competitive in more volatile and crowded world markets, while at the same time trying to protect their employment in manufacturing."[4]

On balance, the managerial trends associated with the new technologies are towards higher and broader levels of skill and greater flexibility in the way that skills are deployed in the labour process. Despite the resistance of many employers in North America to the logic of this new best-practice frontier, a growing body of evidence from case studies in Canada and other countries suggests that flexible technology is most effective in an organizational setting that reflects the values associated with greater autonomy for workers.[5] The overall emphasis is on flexibility in the use of new technology through all levels of the firm and across all sectors of the economy.

Networks

The effective implementation of these more innovative production strategies also depends on the quality of relationships that exist between networks of suppliers. Innovative capabilities are sustained through national or regional communities that share a certain base of knowledge and the increments to that knowledge base. Technological knowledge, in the collective and cumulative sense described above, is often highly local in nature, in contrast to scientific knowledge, which is grounded in a broad international community of scholars and researchers. The cumulative technical knowledge necessary to transform new scientific possibilities into innovative products or processes grows out of the myriad of relationships built up among research laboratories, networks of suppliers, and a collection of innovative firms.

One reason for this is that contemporary products and production processes are so complex that no individual producer can deliver all the necessary capabilities. More and more cases can be found of emerging co-operative relationships between networks of producers – between large assemblers and smaller suppliers in the auto industry, between networks of small producers, such as exist in the Emilia-Romagna industrial district of Italy, and even between large producers in the computer and telecommunications industries, which make up the core of the new information technologies. The growing costs of R & D, as well as the increasing complexity and knowledge intensity of new scientific research and product development, make the challenge more forbidding for individual firms – hence the growing importance of regional agglomerations of innovative firms in the collective advance of technical knowledge.

Government Policy

These concerns lead back to the third level of analysis – the appropriate role for national or provincial policy with respect to innovation and international trade. An insistence on recognizing the reality of global interdependence in framing economic policies does not mean that we must bow to the logic of the neo-conservative argument and accept the dictates of laissez-faire. Experience indicates that market forces alone cannot promote the desired set of production relations at the firm or regional level. While the neo-conservative advocates of freer trade may recognize the changed reality of the global economy, they completely fail to understand the necessary link between technological innovation and international trade. It is the failure of such laissez-faire strategies to fully recognize the gains possible from a dynamic innovation strategy that necessitates a more formalized role for national and subnational policies.

The reasons for this failure of laissez-faire strategies are many, but fundamentally, their assumptions concerning the effectiveness of markets as providers of information about the timing and direction of technological change are inadequate. The effective acquisition of knowledge about technological trends and future product development is an information-intensive and time-consuming process, often well beyond the capabilities of individual firms. Furthermore, it is often difficult to perceive potential connections between scientific breakthroughs and future technological developments. Even leading-edge firms such as Northern Telecom rarely operate with a technological horizon that extends beyond three to five years.

A critical role for the public sector involves the process of gathering information, targeting potential high-growth areas in the economy, and effectively allocating public resources to a range of activities, from basic scientific research to the educational system in the critical areas. This was the approach adopted by the Japanese state towards information technologies in the early 1970s, and it is the approach currently being adopted towards biotechnologies. The process of targeting sectors for technological development is fraught with difficulties. Examples abound of countries that misdirected substantial resources in failed efforts to target high-growth sectors. Despite these failures, most countries are redoubling their efforts in this area. The growing knowledge intensity of industrial production makes it infinitely more difficult for individual firms, or even industrial sectors, to mobilize the resources needed to focus the innovation process successfully. Only the public sector can play this role.

Furthermore, massive infrastructural investments are essential to ensure that nations are able to take full advantage of new computer and communications technologies. Just as the railways and hydroelectric grids constituted the necessary infrastructures for the technologies of the first and second industrial revolutions, so telecommunications networks constitute the essential infrastructure for the third industrial revolution. Public policies are needed to ensure that the appropriate networks of fibre optic cables are installed (although the advanced state of development of these industries in Canada may mitigate the need for massive commitments of public funds).

Active public policies are also essential in the regulation of telecommunications and standards setting. This is particularly problematic in Canada, given the existing federal/provincial division of responsibilities.

The effective cost for firms to enter potentially high-growth areas may be prohibitive; firms may also be inhibited by a lack of skilled labour power to facilitate their transition. The public sector has a crucial role to play in this respect in funding pre-competitive R & D, organizing research consortia to encourage this type of development, providing alternative sources of investment for higher-risk activities, establishing public enterprises to play a lead role in the development of new technologies, and improving the educational and skill base of the work force. Indeed, there is growing evidence of an integral link between national policy orientations towards science and technology and the relative prosperity enjoyed by individual economies through the different stages of industrial development. The degree to which individual nations have improved their relative shares of world trade through successive phases of economic and technological development has been a function in large measure of the extent to which the disparate elements essential to innovation have cohered in a "national system of innovation."[6]

Such a system of innovation comprises a specific set of economic, social, and political institutions that identify the need to overcome specific problems and channel the collective resources of the society towards their solution. A national system of innovation signifies the collective institutional capacity of a society to assume certain tasks. It embodies a comprehensive approach throughout the society to the development of technology and its social and economic use. The existence of a coherent national system of innovation depends on the presence of the following elements:

the formulation of a consistent set of policies by national and subnational levels of government designed to acquire and disseminate the most up-to-date information about developments in science and technology, as well as to co-ordinate a national strategy to promote technological innovation and diffusion throughout all sectors of the economy;

a commitment by firms in both the private and public sectors to a long-term innovation strategy based on indigenous research and development programs and the effective integration of R & D with all the relevant aspects of product and process development;

the existence of developers, suppliers, and customers in sectoral and regional networks of firms that can generate a sustained innovative capacity;

the adoption of a national framework for education and training policies that ensures the provision of a work force with the fundamental skills and technological literacy required, as well as an ongoing commitment by firms to training as an integral part of the innovative process.[7]

Periods of dynamic technological innovation marked by the emergence of new interrelated sets of technologies, such as the current mix of information technologies, present unique opportunities for individual nations to improve their level of social productivity and their collective standard of living. The state of a national system of innovation may prove the determining factor in realizing these opportunities. Canada would currently rank low along all of the dimensions outlined above by any accepted standard of measurement. Despite a sustained flow of rhetoric over the past two decades, governments of both major parties have failed to rectify this situation. This presents social democrats with a unique opportunity to articulate a progressive and forward-looking economic alternative.

The elaboration of an effective national system of innovation is essential, not just to develop a narrow range of high-tech industries, but to revitalize a wide range of medium- and low-tech ones as well. The growing interpenetration of the global economy means that a range of sectors across the domestic economy with varying degrees of technological intensity are vulnerable to competition from abroad. The prospective impact of the Canada-US Free Trade Agreement accentuates this vulnerability. The same policies geared to sustaining dynamic innovation in the high-growth industries can also help revitalize or sustain lower-growth industries, such as the fashion industry or food processing. Certainly, the dramatic revitalization of the Italian fashion industry suggests that there may be significant scope for future growth in those industries previously consigned to the sunset dustbin.

Much of the literature on innovation implies that it is driven by technological imperatives beyond the control of social or political institutions. Yet technological trajectories are very much the outcome of social and political choices. The major impetus in the trend towards miniaturization in microelectronics was provided by the demands of the US space program in the late 1960s. There is every indication that political choices will remain equally important in determining technological trajectories in the future. The most pressing issue for many governments in coming decades will be the question of sustainable development. New technologies with their energy- and material-saving potential can contribute significantly to this process. A challenge for social democratic policy will be to frame technology policies that contribute the most to this objective.

CONCLUSION

There is strong reason to believe that investments in enhancing technological knowledge at all three levels outlined above will pay significant dividends in the future. The key to our future level of economic well-being involves the cumulative technical knowledge base of the enterprise, regional communities of productive relationships, and a national system for co-ordinating innovative capacity.

The adoption and diffusion of new microelectronic technologies are influenced by factors that go far beyond the development or purchase of a new product or process. The political and social relations of production are key elements in determining the outcome. New technologies have the potential to radically alter the existing skill mix in many industries, but the exact outcome will depend on organizational and other choices made in their implementation. There is increasing evidence that these choices with respect to production relations may also affect the benefits that flow from the technology.

Overall, the key to success in the emerging technological era appears to be a commitment to training and a willingness to empower workers with skills and greater autonomy. This is an argument that should hold intuitive appeal for social democrats. The organizational logic of the new system of diversified quality production accords with some of the values associated with the radical project for workers' control in the 1960s and 1970s. In many ways, current developments in global markets and production technology serve to vindicate the insistence by earlier generations of socialists and labourists on the intrinsic link between democratic control of the workplace and the broader goals of social democracy. However, what seemed a utopian goal in an earlier period may prove to be a vital necessity in today's interdependent economy.

The current wave of radical changes in the economy and technology represents the most significant challenge faced by social democrats since the 1930s. We are confronted with two options – to sound a cautionary note about the destructive and unsettling aspects of these changes and try to preserve and protect the benefits of the past four postwar decades; or to seize the opportunity that the current wave of innovation presents to improve the quality of life in the workplace through a democratization of production relations, to increase our overall standard of living, and, ultimately, to expand the realm of freedom by exploiting productivity gains to reduce necessary work time.

NOTES

1 Hugo Radice, "The National Economy: A Keynesian Myth?" *Capital and Class*, no. 22 (Spring 1984), 121.

2 United Auto Workers, "Can Canada Compete?" in Daniel Drache and Duncan Cameron, eds., *The Other Macdonald Report* (Toronto: Lorimer, 1985), 31.

3 Manuel Castells, "High Technology and the New International Division of Labour," *Labour and Society* 14 (1989): 20.

4 Arndt Sorge and Wolfgang Streeck, "Industrial Relations and Technical Change: The Case for an Extended Perspective," in Richard Hyman and Wolfgang Streeck, eds., *New Technology and Industrial Relations* (Oxford: Basil Blackwell, 1988), 31.

5 Robert H. Hayes and Ramchandram Jaikumar, "Manufacturing's Crisis: New Technologies, Obsolete Organizations," *Harvard Business Review*, September-October 1988; and Ken Hansen and Elaine Bernard, "Management Resistance to Change – Case Study Results in the Introduction of Computer Information Systems" (Vancouver, 1986, Mimeographed).

6 Christopher Freeman, *Technology Policy and Economic Performance: Lessons from Japan* (London: Pinter, 1987), 31.

7 Guy P. Steed, *Not a Long Shot: Canadian Industrial Science and Technology Policy*, Background Study No. 55 (Ottawa: Science Council of Canada, 1980), 28; and R.B. Freeman, "Canada in the World Labour Market," 32.

3 Alternatives to Competitiveness

SAM GINDIN AND
DAVID ROBERTSON

REJECTING COMPETITIVENESS

Whatever kind of society we envision, socialist or social democratic, we certainly want it to be productive. Under capitalism, the achievement of economic growth is accomplished in a very particular way: through private companies that compete to maximize their profits. This competition between firms – international or domestic – includes as a fundamental element a parallel competition between workers.

Competitiveness is, therefore, not just a mechanism for wealth creation. Its logic brings with it very powerful implications for other aspects of society – from the distribution of income and power, to definitions of freedom, to the content of our culture. Competitiveness is an expression of capitalist ideology – an instrument for reinforcing the interests of the economic establishment and limiting the inroads the rest of us can make.

There are those who acknowledge this problem but believe that by taking advantage of recent technological developments and having the proper "political will," we can have our cake and eat it too. They believe that we can take on the challenge of competitiveness *and* retain our socialist values; indeed, they believe that competitiveness will create the very economic success essential to sustaining social programs.

They are mistaken. In the first place, they are wrong because, in the particular case of Canada, there is no capitalist class with the interest or capacity to develop a strong domestic industrial base. (The free trade debate certainly raised and answered questions surrounding the "Canadian" nature of Canadian business.) Further, even if there is such a class, even if the Ontario Premier's Council's so-called "indigenous firm" (i.e., a foreign firm acting as if it were Canadian) is something more than a theoretical illusion, our industrial structure is so dependent, so underdeveloped, that playing catch-up when other countries are already so far ahead and certainly not standing still would require the sacrifice of too much.

But they are more than just mistaken. The framework of competitiveness they invite us to accept is ultimately dangerous for Canada. Once it is accepted, its hidden aspects – for example, its solutions for economic problems, such as attacks on social programs – quickly reassert themselves. Once we decide to play on the terrain of competitiveness, we cannot then step back without paying a serious price. Having legitimated the importance of being competitive (when we should have been mobilizing to defend our social values), we would be extremely vulnerable to the determined attacks that will inevitably come in the name of "global realities." As the prime minister of Singapore was recently paraphrased, "Either you have a vital competitive economy or you have a social policy."

That is why, for socialists, competitiveness is not a realistic alternative to the status quo. Capitalist economics and its expression in competitiveness is fundamentally undemocratic. Under the guise of satisfying the "needs of the market," a few subjugate the capacities and override the needs of the rest of us. As the guiding principle of the economy, competitiveness leads nowhere. We must unambiguously reject it. In taking this position, we are not arguing that competitive pressures will disappear simply because we do not like them. But if we develop our own ideological perspective, we will at least be in a position to negotiate and survive the inevitable compromises that will arise. But more than this, there is even the possibility that we can begin to change the political culture of this country to one based on a different model of economic development. What would constitute the principal elements of such an alternative strategy?

THE DEMOCRATIC DEVELOPMENT OF OUR PRODUCTIVE CAPACITIES

The starting point of an alternative perspective – a socialist economics – is the democratic development of our productive capacities. By using the word "democratic," we are not only emphasizing popular control over the economy, but also equal access to participation in the economy (democracy must be universal) and the development of individual capacities (democracy must achieve each individual's potential). It is from this perspective that we approach the issue of advancing our productive capacity, the goals of which are

- to create a strong industrial base (in factories and offices; machinery, engineering, and research and development capacities). This increases our wealth, our options, and our skills.
- to build a comprehensive social infrastructure (transportation, housing, communications, health, child care, environmental protection). This not only sustains and supports the industrial structure but is also fundamental to removing barriers to universal participation.
- to strengthen individual economic rights and the basic rights to productive employment, education, and training. That package of rights, together with the development of cultural potential, is a fundamental socialist goal, central to the extension of democracy and a critical aspect of increasing the community's productive capacity.
- to sustain and rejuvenate the natural environment. Sustainable development is the fundamental precondition for the survival of all our capacities and potentials.

Let's consider, by looking at some examples, how this focus on the democratic development of our productive capacities might differ from a competitiveness-centred agenda. Obviously, the examples are meant to be illustrative rather than exhaustive and to indicate only a direction. The objective is to help clarify differences between a strategy driven by competitiveness and one driven by its alternative. We start by exploring the differences at three levels of generality, from the vantage point of the sector, the individual company, and the workplace. Here the comparisons revolve around the themes of industrial policy and technological development. Later we outline a series of differences between the two strategies, albeit in a much briefer manner, on a range of issues.

The Sector

Industrial policies differ considerably depending on whether their starting line is competitiveness or the development of productive capacity. In Canada, the report of the Ontario Premier's Council, entitled *Competing in the New Global Economy*, is perhaps the most sophisticated articulation of a competitive strategy. The Premier's Council supposedly builds the case for an innovative competitive model. It does so by picking up some old industrial strategy themes (reminiscent of the Science Council) and repackaging them. But after some expression of support for high wages, value-added restructuring, and technological leadership, the report develops a logic that can be summarized as follows: Canada is a trading nation in a global economy. In this highly competitive environment, there are new realities – international market forces whose effects we cannot escape. Participating to any extent in today's global marketplace means running at the head of the pack, because there is no backfield. You are either a winner or you are out of it. And it is the marketplace that picks the winner. Industrial policy should encourage and support those who can jockey for position.

From that foundation the Premier's Council constructs an economic platform, the scaffolding of which rises as follows:

- first, a focus on traded business ("those companies that are exposed to world trade and competition");
- then, an assessment among traded sectors of those that are the high-growth industries;
- next, a rejection of resource-based and mature industries because, while they are important at present, they have limited potential for high growth in international terms;
- then, the problem: Canada's high-growth sectors are "tremendously uncompetitive";
- then, an answer: within the high-growth sector, there are emerging technology-intensive industries that, for a variety of reasons, are capable of international growth;
- finally, the revelation of government's role: it should back those "threshold firms" that have the potential to become "new, world scale competitors."

Industrial policy becomes a series of supportive initiatives for these threshold firms. Government should underwrite marketing and international risks, support prototype development, provide venture capital, foster a culture of entrepreneurship, and so on.

A progressive competitiveness that starts by advocating high levels of employment, high wages, and high value-added production ends with a few hundred "threshold" firms at the public trough.

If we approach the issue differently, industrial strategy necessarily takes a different shape. Our analysis shares the Premier's Council's assessment of the current importance of the resource-based (i.e., forest and food) and mature industrial sectors (auto, steel, chemical). It also recognizes the opportunities for development in high-growth manufacturing sectors (telecommunications, aerospace, medical equipment). Where it parts company with the competitive model is in its approach to these high-employment, high value-added sectors. Whereas the Premier's Council passes them by, we, in an effort to increase opportunities for larger numbers of workers in more communities, focus on them.

Each industrial sector is composed of what could be considered core and foundation firms that operate in a complex relationship as customers and suppliers. The core firms are the dominant companies – the General Motors, the Boeings, the Northern Telecoms. The foundation firms are the supplier industries – the tool, die, and mould companies; suppliers of components and intermediate parts; the equipment vendors and installers; and the cluster of service providers. The ties between the core and foundation firms are critical for economic development.

In the automotive sector, for example, the few core companies (the Big Three and the new transplants) are the hub of a network that includes literally hundreds of foundation firms – over 400 companies whose primary activity is manufacturing automotive parts – with another 1,500 companies involved in the sector. The magnitude of production is tremendous. In 1988, Canadian vehicle production was valued at $27 billion, parts production amounted to $14 billion, and direct employment was in excess of 150,000.

From a perspective of industrial strategy, it is important to understand the linkages among firms and to focus on existing supplier and customer links. The linkages are opportunities for deepening and broadening our productive base.

Take the case of motor vehicles. It is wrong to characterize this sector as producing mature products. Rather, Canada's strategically important car industry is at the forefront of the application of new process and product technologies, including computer automation, electronics, and advanced materials. The challenge is to find ways to deepen our productive base by using the links to move product and process design and engineering functions, material development, process innovations, and the adoption of new technologies "downstream." By this strategy, it is possible to broaden the base by developing the multiple capacities of producers and the aggregation of production (jointly or serially).

The relationships between core and foundation firms are also important leverage points. At present, the core firms in the various sectors exercise that leverage. This can be problematic but it can also be a key to building a dynamic economy. General Motors is a case in point. It has fairly explicit expectations of its suppliers (though it obviously doesn't care whether these suppliers are in Canada or elsewhere). In its supplier manual, GM outlines its specific requirements and the procedures for satisfying them. In the section on technology, for instance, the manual reads: "A supplier is expected to have computer-aided design (CAD) capability." And in the section on research and development, it stipulated: "R & D activities shall appear as a budgeted item. At a minimum, funds for these activities shall equal 1% of total sales."

Canadian governments continue to wring their hands about how to increase private sector R & D expenditures, whereas General Motors simply makes it a requirement of doing business. Clearly, there are lessons for public policy in the way GM imposes requirements on its suppliers.

One of the important differences between a competitive strategy and its democratic alternative concerns the focus of effort. In the competitive model, the target is the individual firm. In a model whose goal is the democratic development of productive capacity, the focus is on sectors or on clusters of firms within sectors. The goal is to develop production networks rather than world-class entrepreneurs. Such a framework recognizes the central role of workers and their unions as well as the importance of community input. In the firm-specific approach, it is necessary to generate shared values between workers and managers, to align the goals of the work force with the requirements of the company; in the development of production networks, it becomes more important to build solidarity and negotiate among different interests. In the threshold firm approach, the role of public policy is to facilitate and support private entrepreneurs, while in the democratic development model, public policy involves economic planning and co-ordination. In developing productive capacity, there is a determination to work locally, in contrast to the international emphasis of the competitive model.

In the competitive model, policy issues centre around how companies can be encouraged to invest here. If the focus is shifted to our democratic rights to maintain and strengthen our productive capacities, policy turns to enforcing job and investment commitments from the corporations if they want to share in our market (e.g., the managed trade of the Auto Pact).

There is nothing inherently democratic in an effort to develop productive capacity. But the elements suggested above – the determination to work locally, the focus on production networks, the need for co-ordination and planning, the regulation of corporate investment, the recognition that economic activity is a social process, and the opportunity to strengthen labour – combine to make democratic development possible and to provide opportunities for workers and popular action. In the competitive model, these opportunities are summarily foreclosed.

The Firm

In the view of supporters of competitiveness, Northern Telecom operates as a model firm – moving up the value-added ladder, spinning off "niche" producers, maintaining technological leadership, and going global to take advantage of international markets. But Northern's success story is actually quite different. The lesson to be learned from Northern's past is that *regulated* development is of key importance in building productive capacity within Canada (i.e., the fact that a regulated telephone industry offered Bell a market monopoly, along with financial support, was central to Northern's commitment to research and development and to Canadian regional production). The competitive model threatens regulated development. Now that Northern has built a strong domestic base, the logic of competitiveness directs the company towards the international marketing of its products. The issue isn't the international sharing of Northern's impressive achievements. Instead the concern is with the domestic consequences of a corporate strategy that is shaped by global competitiveness.

Northern is regarded as the leading company in technology in Canada. But the role of technology in market leadership is shifting. Intense international competition, according to the company, is forcing Northern to respond by changing its strategy from a focus on maintaining its technological superiority to a new emphasis on service and marketing. As the emphasis shifts from technology to marketing, there is a corresponding risk that Northern's technological intensity will decrease or at least that its technological focus will narrow. In addition, as Northern's product mix shifts from hardware to software, the consequent dematerialization of production will intensify competition among countries over a declining number of production jobs. Northern's already alarming shift of production (employment growth) out of Canada and away from union membership, together with its rapid Americanization, suggests the threats are real.

It has been argued that the converging technologies of computers and telecommunications are reshaping production and the base of economic activity. Some suggest that the silicon chip and information-driven technologies have combined to form a new heartland technology, one whose impact will be as far-reaching as those in earlier periods, such as steam power, railways, electricity, and the automobile. Northern is situated at that point of convergence, but the challenge is to ensure that its potential addresses Canadian needs. If the knowledge and skills that have emerged at the Northern labs aren't used for reducing our productive dependency, how else can it happen? If the critical mass in research and development isn't used to expand our general capacities – from telecommunications, to computer hardware and peripheral devices, to software, to spin-offs in fields other than telecommunications – how else do we take advantage of the new heartland technology? If the production and design skills of Northern's Canadian work force aren't reinforced and developed, then what meaning does value-added production have?

Rather than by the competitive positioning of Northern, our productive capacity would be better served by its continued regulation (financial support, joint agreements, enforced commitments).

The Workplace

Some of those who support a competitive model based on high wages and high value-added production are attracted by the degree of innovation required by such competition. In fact, the centrality of innovation accounts for much of the appeal of the model. The argument suggests that technological innovation and the cumulative ability to incorporate scientific knowledge and technical know-how into products will determine our competitive edge. The "discovery" that innovation occurs at all levels of the firm and includes the production skills and knowledge of the work force serves to reinforce the case. The key to our economic future in a global economy is working smarter, and that sets the stage for a "win-win" situation – greater competitive success and an opportunity to improve workers' skills and the quality of working life.

But what happens to the process of innovation when it is shaped by competitiveness? Innovation, at the level of the workplace, is recast as a process of continuous improvement. Phrased differently, continuous improvement is the competitive expression of innovation. In the context of competitiveness and the maintenance of managerial control, this process is systematically converted into one of cost cutting. General Motors, borrowing from Toyota, has clearly articulated this view. The company explains that the highly competitive world market requires a new economic model for generating profits. In the past, the traditional formula of *cost + desired profit = price* worked. It no longer does. Business, it is argued, has to adopt a different formula: *price − costs = profits*.

This competitive formula is unambiguous in categorizing the object of effort as reducing cost. Its success depends on tapping the skills and knowledge of the work force. Such a goal, GM argues, means adopting a continuous improvement process that differs from innovation in that it focuses on the incremental reduction of waste and costs. In turn, the war on waste is waged against all that is unnecessary in the workplace, with unoccupied time and non-essential workers emerging as prominent targets – a worker waiting for a machine to cycle, a worker waiting for material, a worker operating only one machine, a worker walking two unnecessary steps, a worker talking, three workers when two could "theoretically" do the job, and so on. The war on costs is waged in much the same way, with the added inducement of imposed price restraints on suppliers and the requirement that they too embrace continuous improvement. In the context of competition, working smarter becomes a new justification for working harder.

This is not just one company's particular and warped approach to innovation. In fact, one survey, whose results were released at the recent forum on global competitiveness, reported that for the majority of companies the "critical factor" in maintaining a competitive edge was "cost reduction." In sector after sector, the agenda is being set. As one analyst put it, "Cost and flexibility will become the dramatic competitive battlegrounds of the nineties."

Marshalling the skills and knowledge of the work force in a corporate campaign to reduce cost and eliminate waste in order to better take on the competition does not add up to a strategy for innovation. A more dependable framework for innovation is one in which the skills and knowledge of the work force are directed at improving working conditions and developing productive capacity.

COMPETITIVENESS VERSUS DEMOCRATIC DEVELOPMENT

At so many different points, the acceptance of competitiveness distorts public policy, limits opportunity, and truncates development. This can be vividly seen in respect to a broad range of public policy issues.

Community Adjustment and Regional Development Programs

Outside of vague commitments to retraining for adjustment, the competitive model ignores the economic impact of restructuring on communities – never mind the role of communities in directing the restructuring. Indeed, the very logic of the competitiveness model contradicts the goal of regional development ("It's not competitive to produce here"). In the competitive model, it is entrepreneurs, companies, and the market that shape the economy, not people, communities, or productive activity. As the Premier's Council put it: "Regional programs are important, but their objectives need to be understood separately from economic development objectives."

Our alternative perspective argues that regional programs devoid of economic development objectives end up as another spur to forced labour mobility ("Nice place to live but there's no place to work"). It holds, instead, that both social and economic objectives should influence the geography of development. Our perspective, with its focus on democratic control, social infrastructure, and development of productive capacities, recognizes the role of communities in economic life. It recommends the creation of local development boards that would have the power to force companies contemplating closures to justify their actions and to participate in forming alternative plans. It argues for access to a national pool of funds for expanding socially useful employment (production, service, environmental) and for the conscious planning of responses to future uncertainties (e.g., the impact of broad developments on the dependencies of one-industry communities).

Education and Training Strategies

The competitive model laments the decline of our education system, but its solution is to subordinate education to the business needs of companies. It is critical of broadly defined educational goals and of the role of the school as a forum for social discourse.

The alternative perspective sees education as integrally bound up in the development of individual capacity and the exercise of citizenship. In this view education is about values, the development of independent thinking, and preparation for democratic participation.

The difference between the two perspectives extends to training. The competitive model defines training needs either in terms of bottlenecks that require major training for a few or in terms of cultural training that facilitates the integration of the work force into the competitive agenda.

The alternative sees training as a right, a tool for equity, and a vehicle for giving workers more confidence and potential *control* over technology and the workplace (rather than just "adapting") and for increasing workers' options both within and outside their current workplace.

Social Policy Questions

The issue of affordable child care can be and is being squeezed into the competitiveness framework. Those of the competitive persuasion address this weakness in our social infrastructure with catch-phrases: they talk of "investing in human capital" and "removing barriers to participation." Such policy pronouncements, however, have amounted to little more than lip service to this need. Adequate child care has been subordinated to budget constraints, and the emphasis is placed on first creating "real" wealth that does not burden the private sector.

The alternative perspective identifies quality child care as fundamental to the overall development of the capacities of our children and recognizes it as a vehicle for removing one of the main barriers to women developing their own productive capacities. Since women carry this family responsibility in addition to working or trying to find time for training, addressing gender inequality in the labour market must be a priority issue.

The Environment

The competitive model has been insensitive to environmental issues, but corporations are now responding to public pressure by trying to incorporate these concerns. It is possible to present environmental arguments in terms of the long-term interests of capitalism and even to suggest that environmental issues offer market niches to some threshold companies. But it strains credibility to believe that the competitive model, which measures productivity only in terms of profits and development, will solve the deepening environmental crisis.

The alternative challenges the narrow calculus of productivity and business's continual effort to externalize as social costs the price of private irresponsibility. Such an approach begins to refine what we mean by "productive" and raises the question, productive for whom?

Services

The competitive model reinforces a polarized service sector: at the base, the low-paying "McJobs" in the hospitality and food services, which serve to both subsidize living standards and restrain general wages; and at the top, the high-paying "services to business," which serve as both a market for and an input to the traded sector. At both ends of the spectrum, the role of services is to contribute to the competitiveness of the traded sector.

In the alternative model, the goal would be to acknowledge the social value-added contribution of services through the expansion of high-skill, well-paying services (e.g., child care), to decrease discrepancies in pay within the economy, and to increase the economic value-added contribution services make to the development of our productive capacity.

In particular cases, the democratic development of our productive capacity may lead to policy conclusions similar to those reached by others on the left who support competitiveness. In other cases, our orientation may incidentally make us more competitive because it will make us more productive. It might even surpass what a capitalist strategy could have achieved because domestic capital is either too short-sighted or too insensitive to invest in strengthening local productive capacities. But this is not the crucial test of our strategy. If the goal is competitiveness, we do not defend our strategy on these grounds.

The most basic point of our argument is that accepting competitiveness is demobilizing; it robs workers of their independent values and weakens our ability as socialists to do battle. The competitive model ultimately asks how the *corporate sector* can be strengthened. Our perspective asserts that it is the very strength of that sector that limits our freedom and belittles the meaning of "community." Our project is to prepare for *our* future by strengthening our democratic, solidaristic, and productive capacities. This necessarily means taking on and taking away the illegitimate strength of the corporate elite.

CONFRONTING THE UNITED STATES

The big question is whether we can develop the space within the international economy to carry out our strategy. We can speculate on how we might build alternative economic ties. This could include, for example, developing bilateral or managed trade with other countries; replacing the General Agreement on Tariffs and Trade with a new UN-sponsored institution sensitive to domestic control over investment; and/or building new forms of solidarity with the developing world. But the real issue that continues to dominate Canada's external commercial future is its relationship to the United States.

It has always been clear that a break with the US economy, which is based on private ownership of the main financial and industrial institutions, would run into stiff opposition not only from Canada's elites but also, and especially, from the ruling circles in the United States. Since such a break is basic to fulfilling their goals, socialists have always accepted this inevitable danger. An awareness that a serious attempt to build a socialist Canada would mean an eventual confrontation with the United States preceded the signing of the Canada-US Free Trade Agreement; this latest development has now focused the question of independence from the United States on whether the agreement can in practical terms be abrogated.

Those on the left advocating the pragmatic need to accept competitiveness may still deplore the agreement. But they have in fact accepted it as the "new reality" or have, by endorsing competitiveness, become sadly ineffective critics. Our perspective, on the other hand, positions us quite differently.

First, we are not demobilized by what the alternative might be. In fighting to extend democracy and expand Canada's productive capacities, we will have to undertake daily actions that will inevitably aggravate tensions with the United States over the agreement. Second, in these confrontations, we can show that both Canadian and American business (through their support of and constant reference to the agreement) act as barriers to improving Canadian productive capacity. The fight against the free trade agreement and against dependency on the United States will, therefore, be a fight for sovereignty and democratic rights.

CONCLUSION

An orientation to the democratic development of Canada's productive capacities does not yet provide us with a blueprint for a workable alternative to a capitalist economy. What it does do, is give us an independent ideology that can sustain an alternative view of the world and direct us to a series of activities – large and small – that can affect the daily lives of Canadians and help us build our collective strength for future battles.

The questions for the left should not be about the least damaging way to become competitive, but about how to move towards a society that extends democracy into all spheres of life, particularly the economic, and that develops our country's individual and collective potentials. The issue should no longer be whether we should move in this direction, but what exactly we should focus on, what new kinds of institutions we should try to develop, and how far and how fast we can and must go.

PART TWO

Strategic Choices for Labour

4 Labour Movements and the Welfare State: Alternatives in the 1990s

GOSTA ESPING-ANDERSEN

INTRODUCTION

In capitalist economies, there is an inevitable tension between social policy and the labour market. Often, this tension is characterized in terms of a zero-sum trade-off between welfare and efficiency. We can identify three broad historical responses to this tension. First, in the liberal tradition, the market was thought to be welfare producing in the absence of state interference; social policies would essentially hinder the realization of the common good and should therefore remain absolutely residual. Second, in the conservative tradition (as it found expression in, say, Germany and Austria), the market was feared as a destructive influence on the social order; social policy was seen as a positive tool that could be used to preserve hierarchy and discipline in the labour market. Bismarck's conception of the ideal capitalist economy was absolutist (a monarchical welfare state) and militaristic ("Soldaten der Arbeit"). Social democracy can be said to represent a third response. Initially formulated by the "Stockholm School" economists, such as Gunnar Myrdal, the principle was that economic efficiency presupposes an active policy for equality and strong welfare guarantees.

There are basically three postwar welfare state models, each mirroring the principles of these three approaches.[1] In the *liberal* model, exemplified in nations such as the United States, Canada, and Australia, the welfare state was defined in minimalist terms. It emphasized targeting benefits only to those demonstrably incapable of finding employment. The goal of the system was to nurture market autonomy in terms of wage setting, private sector insurance, voluntarism, and bargained welfare. Public welfare programs tended in the main to be meagre and restrictive, typically relying on means-testing, and offered few social rights that might impair the work incentive. This kind of residual or minimal welfare state is typically associated with a large private sector welfare market.

The second, *conservative*, model found expression in the south-central European nations, in which a combination of authoritarian nation-building coalitions and Christian forces granted social rights early on. Bismarckian paternalism never came to play its hoped-for role, but other related principles did. Status hierarchies and privilege were deliberately preserved via corporatist differentiation of programs; rights became closely linked to employment and, in this way, helped strengthen "efficiency"; applying the Catholic principle of subsidiarity, governments refrained from expanding social services (which in this model belong in the domain of the family) and female labour force participation has thus remained quite low. Comprehensive and obligatory social insurance effectively has blocked the emergence of a large private welfare sector.

The third model is the *social democratic* one. It is most developed in Scandinavia and is doubly unique. On the one hand, its ideal is the promotion of a universalistic social citizenship in which all share equally the right to a basic standard of welfare; on the other hand, its accent is on "productivism" in the sense of maximizing the productive capacity of the population via social policies (such as education, training, and active manpower policies). This model deliberately pursues status equalization and is opposed to the private delivery of social services.

Each model in its own way expresses a particular synthesis between welfare and efficiency. Nonetheless, in each case the postwar welfare state was systematically designed so as to interfere minimally with the "automatic" clearing mechanisms of labour markets; strict entitlement rules were meant to discourage abuse, and modest benefit levels and/or long (often employment-linked) contribution records were meant to assure maximum labour supply and performance. No welfare state in the postwar era permitted the social wage to act as a genuine alternative to market income. Indeed, policy-makers deliberately constructed a wall between the welfare state and labour markets; this found its expression, for example, in the administrative separation of ministries of social affairs and ministries of labour.

One of the revolutions in our time is the crumbling of this wall. Today, labour market performance has become directly dependent on social policy. The different character of the various kinds of welfare states will, however, have vastly different effects on current as well as future changes in the labour market. In the following section, we examine how the various welfare state types affect the ongoing transformation of capitalist economies in terms of the formal economy, the informal economy, and the non-work economy.

THE FORMAL ECONOMY

The impact of social policy on labour market management has been especially dramatic with respect to social services and female employment. Comparatively speaking, there are great international differences in the growth of the new social service economy (health, education, and welfare services). Scandinavia is the undisputed vanguard; Continental Europe, the laggard. Social services account for 35 percent of total employment in Sweden; for 26 percent in the US; and for only 21 percent in Germany. These differences can be explained by the nature of the different welfare state regimes, especially by their relative transfer/collective services bias. Where welfare states have been heavily weighted in favour of transfers, as is the case in Germany and the other Continental European nations, the state's fiscal capacity to expand social services will be limited. Yet, when we consider the strong Catholic social influence in these countries' welfare state design, we would think it unlikely that they would have furnished massive social service employment growth in any case, since this would weaken the role of the family.

In the United States, almost half the social and health services are to be found in the private economy. Certainly, private sector social services are nourished by government tax expenditures, and their employment dividend must thus be regarded as implicitly a "welfare state" effect. Still, private sector social services generate a different employment mix. Because of the proliferation of programs, private welfare schemes demand more expenditure per capita on their administration than do publicly funded schemes; hence, we find a much larger number of managers, administrators, and billing clerks employed in US hospitals than in their state-funded Canadian counterparts. It is said, for instance, that an average American hospital employs at least thirty billing employees, and that administrative costs absorb 22 percent of total US health expenditures.[2]

Social services are an important source of female employment growth, partly because women workers depend on their existence and partly because they are a "natural" female employment area. In Sweden, the social services account for 85 percent of *total* employment growth and 75 percent of *female* employment growth in the past two decades. With Sweden's rigorous solidarity wage policy, it is highly unlikely that female employment growth would have been so strong had there not been the welfare state as employment generator. The lower and generally stagnant participation rates of women in countries like Germany, Italy, or Holland can best be attributed to the absence of child-care services and to overall welfare state employment stagnation. In the United States, women have benefited from social service growth as well, although the female bias is less pronounced than in Scandinavia.

The welfare state's policies with respect to paid absenteeism are of critical importance to women in general and women with children in particular. The extension of paid-leave opportunities constitutes one of the key elements in the realignment between labour market and social policy. The ability to be absent with pay during pregnancy, child birth, and children's illness is an obvious precondition for uninterrupted labour force participation. In Sweden, where paid-leave opportunities are, by far, the most advanced, more than 80 percent of women with infant children remain in the labour force. Yet, on any given day, their absenteeism rate is higher than 30 percent.

A paradox emerges when we consider that while paid absenteeism was promoted to minimize female labour market disadvantages, it may actually strengthen gender segregation. With the high risks and costs associated with absenteeism, it is to be expected that private sector employers will be less willing to hire women (particularly because of wage equalization). In turn, women with a high absenteeism probability are more likely to prefer public sector jobs.

These welfare state effects have immediate labour market consequences. In Sweden, the importance of gender can be seen in the way women are overwhelmingly concentrated in the public sector. This has had an important impact on the framework of collective bargaining and on the magnitude of industrial strife. The government's need to hold back wage growth has meant that tensions have mounted between public and private sector white-collar unions to the point where this has become one of the chief axes of labour market conflict. Unions representing private sector workers are increasingly unwilling to participate in solidaristic kinds of comprehensive wage settlements to the degree that occurred during the 1980s, when Sweden's system of collective bargaining was rocked by a wave of strikes.

In countries like Germany, the lack of adequate inroads for female employment is likely to generate serious tensions between labour "insiders" and "outsiders," a largely youth and female work force.

In the United States, a massive demand for female workers exists, but unlike in Sweden, it is concentrated in the private sector. In the US, the growth of women's employment has occurred on the basis of high gender-based wage differentials. It is not surprising that the debate on equal pay has come to such prominence in the United States over the past decade.

THE INFORMAL ECONOMY

Given the absence of hard data, our discussion here can be no more than speculative. There is, however, little doubt that the informal economy is fuelled to a surprising extent by the welfare state. On one side, the informal economy represents for employers an alternative to high labour costs associated with strong unions and a universal welfare state. On the other, it offers an entry point for welfare state clients, such as early retirees, the unemployed, and the disabled, as well as for groups excluded from the formal economy (often youth, women, and immigrants). In some cases, much of the informal economy owes its vitality to an indirect form of wage subsidization paid to those no longer in the labour market. In Italy, it is estimated that maybe half the early retirees and half the workers in the Cassa Integrazione (the long-termed unemployed) simultaneously work in the formal and informal economy. For the unemployed and those with pensions or other benefits, work in the informal economy remains marginally beneficial even with the low pay and the absence of social benefits. Clearly, this kind of "welfare state-subsidized" labour force imposes a cost on welfare state finances and affects the formation of wages and the operation of the industrial relations system more generally.

It is very likely that the informal economy has expanded where social service job growth is weak. Where female labour supply is in excess of demand in the official economy, women will seek out the informal economy. This is illustrated by the Italian case, where the unofficial economy employs about 2.2 million women workers, very often concentrated in precarious, home-based, putting-out types of production. Hence, where welfare states directly or indirectly fuel informal economy employment, they will tend to nourish an invisible but highly flexible labour force.

THE NON-WORK ECONOMY

There has been great variation in the way nations manage the twin effects of de-industrialization and structural change. Briefly, the

Scandinavian approach relied heavily on a retraining/re-employment strategy in which the welfare state played a dominant role in organizing the labour market. These countries not only averted mass unemployment and mass early retirements, they also managed to increase overall labour force participation; the non-work economy actually shrank. The European Economic Community (EEC) countries, in turn, opted for the opposite strategy and sought to reduce labour supply, especially by means of early retirement schemes.

The consequences have been dramatic, especially in the EEC countries, where participation rates of older (male) workers declined to less than 50 percent. In countries like the Netherlands, Austria, and even Germany, the effect of these retirement schemes has gone hand in hand with the slowdown in social service employment growth as well as the increased use of disincentives for women to remain in the labour force. The lack of real employment opportunities, combined with social policies to keep new entrants out of the labour market, has produced serious obstacles for youth and women and generally high levels of long-term unemployment. Where this scenario prevails, we see the contours of a new insider-outsider structure. It resembles van Parijs's world in which the growing ranks of labour force outsiders find their entry barred. This is a world in which jobs tend to become assets in their own right and, therefore, the object of bitter distributional struggles.[3]

Trade unions and industrial relations systems are likely to be deeply affected by such trends. First, as has clearly evolved in Germany, the trade unions prefer early retirement/work reduction as a solution to this problem. Be it via social pacts or merely implicit deals, the unions see no other option. Whether they really believe in the solution or not, the unions can at least hope that early retirement and/or the reduction in working time will give youth and/or women more of a chance to find work despite the declining number of new jobs being created.

More broadly, where labour markets evolve into a closed insider system, the trade unions can hardly avoid following suit. Structurally, unions are meant to represent the employed. As the divide between the employed and the surplus population deepens, unions are more likely to be imprisoned in an insider strategy. They become caught in the crossfire between the employed, who are protesting the mounting fiscal burden of pensions and welfare expenditures, and the outsiders, who are protesting the rigidity of the labour market while demanding improved social benefits. In turn, this crossfire may intensify. Since the productivity dividend of a slimmed-down insider economy will permit unions to negotiate what Freeman and Medoff call monopoly union wages, growing insecurity about the future of state pension plans will also motivate unions to bargain for private plans for their members.[4]

THREE EVOLVING SCENARIOS

There seem to be three basic future-growth scenarios that sum up current thinking. While they differ in detail, what they have in common is that they build on current trends. For the sake of simplicity, they can be described as the jobless growth model, the individual firm-based model of microcorporatism, and the new service economy model.

The Jobless Growth Model

The first scenario is one that we have already touched upon, namely the prospect of a technology-driven growth with a low-employment multiplier. This model is largely associated with highly competitive, technologically advanced, export-led economies, such as West Germany's. In it, industry retains its international position via restructuring both by increasing capital-intensive production technologies and by putting a strong emphasis on research. Simultaneously, labour retains high wages and the basic framework of job rights. The system will shed its erstwhile "Fordist," typically unskilled mass workers (absorbed by early retirement) and concentrate on a functionally flexible, more highly qualified work force. Traditional labour-intensive production will be exported abroad, and the macroeconomy will thus be characterized by high value-added products that can continue to support high labour costs. If trade unionism remains strong, the combination of high labour costs and low wage differentials will augment the problems of jobless growth, since this will arrest the possibility of compensatory employment in the private services and probably in the informal/hidden economy as well.

There are two basic social policy problems in this model. The first is fiscal-demographic, since the combination of an ageing population and a small work force will create huge burdens on the social security system. As the welfare state's clienteles mushroom, the system provokes a zero-sum trade-off between benefit reductions and higher taxes or contributions. Where social security benefits stagnate or decline (and where welfare state fiscal strains suggest an uncertain future), the chances are that private sector welfare plans will grow, particularly among the more privileged employee groups. Thus arises the second problem, which can be seen as a vicious circle. As the momentum for private occupational welfare grows, the welfare state will lose its relative importance among the employed middle classes; they will reduce their political support for the public welfare state and, instead, use their political clout to promote favourable tax treatment of private plans.

Hence, in the jobless growth model, the "Americanization" of the welfare system may be the unavoidable result. The more vulnerable members of the outsider "surplus population," such as the unskilled early retirees, the long-term unemployed, and single-parent families, are likely to emerge as high-risk poverty groups.

The Intra-firm Welfare State

Positive flexibility is often held up as a new mode of management, work, and enterprise organization.[5] It may go hand in hand with the "German" "post-Fordist" scenario depicted above or with the Emilia-Romagna model of small flexible enterprises. The model will operate on the basis of a core work force of, typically, skill-upgraded and secure workers, but it may also include a segment of peripheral, numerically flexible workers. In any case, for the core, the likely trend is towards "microcorporatism," in which the firm is the chief nexus of collective (or maybe even individual) bargaining. Industry- or nation-wide agreements will gradually fade as local deals are tailored to match a firm's performance and conform to the specifics of the internal labour force. The outcome is, almost certainly, greater labour force differentiation and, possibly, increased labour market segmentation as the pay and benefits of workers become more closely tied to their individual productivity and skills at the firm or enterprise level.

The microcorporatism model is emerging equally powerfully in the framework of the large transnational or multinational corporations. Firms such as IBM, whose operations span a diversity of nations, are developing their own internal welfare state apparatus independently of nation-specific legislation. IBM, for example, has its own internal labour adjudication system.

The upshot of either trajectory (and both are evolving together) is that a growing section of the labour force may be divorcing itself from dependence on the traditional, nationally confined welfare state *cum* industrial relations system. In the case of the multinational corporation, the drift is certainly associated with the rising internationalization of the professional/managerial class for which the conventional welfare state would appear inaccessible and irrelevant. It is also to be expected that microcorporatism with firm-based welfare will reinforce the trend to segmented labour markets and a more limited welfare state. If a growing proportion of the labour force bargains for its needs and interests within the firm, the conventional trade union *cum* welfare state apparatus will find its sphere reduced. Besides dualism, the twin forces of microcorporatism and "welfare firmism" will surely augment inequalities and welfare differentials. In the case of the United States, for example, it has been shown that ESOPs (employee stock ownership plans) are becoming one of the new fringe benefits of the 1990s; however, such growth disproportionately benefits the new technical cadres in the high-tech vanguard industries.

In extreme cases, the entire logic of industrial relations, as we traditionally know it, may be overtaken by events. The boundaries between managers, technicians, professionals, and workers have become fluid as more and more jobs in the technology-intensive sectors involve specialized *individual* know-how. Trade unions are more capable of bargaining the price of hours than the price of brainpower.

THE NEW SERVICE ECONOMY

There are two observable trends evolving in the service economy. Both pose severe problems for the future of social policy. In countries where low-level service jobs explode, such as in the United States, they do so precisely because of low wages. Even for a full-time worker, wages are often an inadequate guarantee against poverty. In this situation, we are facing the creation of a new service sector proletariat (cleaners, waiters, etc.) whose size will be considerable (10 percent of the US labour force according to my estimates). In some of the Scandinavian countries, high wage costs prohibit the emergence of such jobs in the private sector. However, unskilled service jobs have been growing inside the welfare state (hospital attendants and home helpers, for example). In their case, however, wage levels will be fairly high.

An understanding of the new postindustrial proletariat is based very much on its life-cycle profile. If, as in Sweden, most of the female work force is almost entirely concentrated in welfare state employment, the feminization of work will likely become the social problem of the nineties. In any case, the risk throughout the economy is that the new service proletariat will find itself becoming institutionalized. It is here that the life-cycle profile is decisive. If these jobs are largely filled with first-time labour market entrants (youth, older women, or immigrants) who subsequently move out of this particular job ghetto, the welfare implications are entirely different than if the jobs are manned by persons whose entire labour market career will be spent in marginal work.

In the American "extreme" case, there is some evidence that the first interpretation may be true; that is, the service sector proletariat is very much a youth/immigrant labour market. But if it consolidates itself into a ghetto and, consequently, if the postindustrial economy produces greater segmentation or dualism than presently exists in the labour market, the existing social policy apparatus will be highly inadequate.

First, service proletarian jobs are insecure and typically temporary. They usually offer no or little training or career advancement and often pay virtually poverty wages. In this sector, trade unions are the exception, and the traditional social protection arrangements do not cover the part-time casual world of work. And if the probability of escape to more secure employment situations is low, the average worker will likely face a poverty carousel: moving between low-paid jobs and various forms of social assistance, all depending on the business cycle and other forces beyond individual control.

EMERGING POLICIES

The dramatic reconstitution of our economies that has been under way for the past decade has compelled massive structural change in labour markets and industrial relations. Among the most important trends, we find the following:

- a new burst of occupational and social differentiation, particularly centred around the new professional jobs;
- new forms of segmentation and dualism giving rise to, respectively, a new service proletariat and a surplus population of labour market outsiders; and
- microcorporatism at the national and international level.

In this context, new social policy developments are under way, some of which have already been touched upon. First, several factors have conspired to promote a new burst in private sector welfare. The rise of the new international managerial/professional class will promote corporate and/or supranational welfare schemes; the demographic and labour supply–induced spread of private social security schemes is creating fears that future public pensions will be jeopardized. In many of the new postindustrial occupations and sectors, trade unionism is weak or absent, or perhaps is experiencing a return to the logic of craft unionism. Where this occurs, the tradition of collectively bargained wages and benefits will erode. Hence, in addition to a surge in private welfare, we may expect greater individualization and sectionalism, and thus inequality.

Second, the existing welfare state apparatus is inadequate to the task of managing any of the three basic postindustrial class scenarios. In the emerging insider-outsider model, the swelling outsider surplus population is maintained by welfare benefits, but at a huge cost that is less and less acceptable to the insiders. In countries like the United States, where employment expansion produces a large postindustrial proletariat at the bottom end of the new class structure, escape from poverty means that the welfare state is compelled to supplement wages with a social wage. And where – as in Sweden – job growth is fuelled by the expansion of welfare state services, the result is an impending fiscal crisis unless public sector wages can be held back. The solutions to these scenarios are evolving along three lines. One is a supply-side response, whose current main emphasis is on active labour market training programs. This approach assumes employment growth and that the problem is mainly a mismatch of skills and vacancies. The second flows from a more pessimistic assumption about employment growth, emphasizing either working-time reduction or a guaranteed minimum citizen's income (or, perhaps, a combination of the two). And the third approach entails the encouragement of greater wage flexibility and income differentiation; in this case, however, the consequence will likely be the rise of a full-time employed poverty group in need of social wage supplements. In other words, if our postindustrial economy is not to be organized around social Darwinian principles, it is inevitable that the trend towards a social policy–managed labour market will strengthen. Indeed, the walls that have been crumbling may fall down entirely.

NOTES

1 For a much more detailed treatment of different welfare state regimes and their historical origins, see Gosta Esping-Andersen, *Three Worlds of Welfare Capitalism* (Princeton: Princeton University Press; Oxford: Polity Press, 1990).

2 Organization for Economic Co-operation and Development (OECD), *Measuring Health Care* (Paris, 1985).

3 For a discussion of this phenomenon, see P. van Parijs, "A Revolution in Class Theory," *Politics and Society* 4 (1987).

4 The union monopoly wage model is developed in R. Freeman and J. Medoff, *What Do Unions Do?* (New York: Basic Books, 1984).

5 As opposed to negative, or "numerical," flexibility, which mainly refers to a peripheral labour force of temporary, casual employment, with few or no job rights and flexible wages. For a discussion, see R. Boyer, *The Search for Labour Market Flexibility* (Oxford: Oxford University Press, 1989).

5 Fragmented Flexibility: Labour and the Social Dividend Solution

GUY STANDING

INTRODUCTION

The 1980s was a period of growing inequality almost everywhere. This was certainly true of Canada, as well as the United States and much of Europe.[1] Although various international comparative projects on trends in poverty and inequality are in progress, the available income and earnings data almost certainly understate the extent to which actual income inequality has grown. They also understate the extent to which income *insecurity* among the lower-income groups has intensified. In the 1980s, so-called supply-side changes in economic and social policy eroded income security among many vulnerable groups in society, while more privileged strata gained in non-monetary as well as monetary ways.

The following presents a perspective on labour market trends and options, highlighting the process of socio-economic fragmentation that has been associated with the growth of various forms of labour "flexibility." It relates to an ongoing international research program in the International Labour Organization (ILO), to which passing reference will be made. The main objective here is to pose in sharp relief two scenarios – contrasting what is likely if the supply-side agenda set out in the 1980s were to continue through the 1990s with an alternative that places the principles of progressive redistribution back onto the social agenda.

LABOUR FORCE FRAGMENTATION

As a result of the growth of more flexible labour practices and employment relations in the 1980s, the norm of workers in regular, full-time wage or salaried employment was considerably eroded, to the extent that one can identify seven distinctive strata deviating in some way from the dwindling group in such regular employment. The seven strata can be defined by reference to the erosion or the relative strengthening of different aspects of labour security, which are discussed in detail elsewhere.

At the very peak is a tiny category of rapacious individuals, whose heady mix of "animal spirits" seems to mean that they live on the margins of sanity, crazed by the pursuit of their nth million dollars. But below such Brechtian monsters is what might be described as a *detached elite* stratum, consisting of wealthy sober groups detached from national regulatory frameworks. Essentially, they are "capitalist employees," earning much of their income through profit-sharing, the acquisition of subsidized shares, and a growing range of fringe benefits, some of which have a full value well in excess of any taxable monetized value. Thus, senior executives increasingly rely on "performance-related" bonuses; in 1989, these bonuses accounted for 20 percent of management salaries in Britain, beyond which were numerous perks that had been growing relative to other sources of income.[2] In the United States, senior executives receive on average over half their total income in non-salary form.

Those in this elite have income security and other forms of labour security to the extent that they want it. In terms of inequality, much of their power lies in the concealed way they accumulate their income and wealth. It is hardly comforting that their lifestyle is fraught with stress, which ultimately threatens any individual's hold on positions of status and control.

Below this elite is a stratum that might be called *proficians*. This hybrid term is probably appropriate for the category of nominally independent "consultants" and self-employed specialists. The rapid expansion in their numbers in the past decade has been a spectacular feature of the pursuit of "flexible specialization" about which so much has been written. Key characteristics of this stratum are their relative youth, their frenetic work style, and their self-satisfaction. In general, they have little labour security, but they remind us of Tawney's tadpoles – most of them have relatively short lives but some live to become smug croaking frogs. Those who reach this level thrive because they have taken advantage of an enterprise's pursuit of flexibility and its desire to cut overhead costs. Whether the growth of this stratum will continue into the 1990s is hard to predict. There might be a tendency for their "market power" to decline when such enterprises find that it is more advantageous to reintegrate those specialist-knowledge functions "in-house" rather than rely on outside consultants. However, it is more likely that the external flexibility granted to firms and the contractual liberty granted to the proficians will work in their favour to preserve their semi-autonomy.

A key aspect of the elite and profician strata is that they do not depend on the welfare state and other regulatory institutions, having access to privatized benefits, while neither contributing to nor gaining entitlement to national benefits. Their elitist detachment leads them to give political support to the transformation of the welfare state from what Richard Titmus called the "institutional redistributive model" to a selective "residual model." They are unlikely to be too worried about the implications for other groups in the labour market unless unrest threatens their own well-being.

These first two labour strata represent the upper echelons of "popular capitalism."[3] Below them are what would be called *state bureaucrats*, senior functionaries who serve the interests of the economic elite and who retain the high degree of labour security that they obtained in the expansive times of the 1960s and early 1970s. In some countries, they have lost some of their security and have been affected by the erosion of protective labour regulations.

A fourth category might be called the *capitalist worker* stratum. It consists of those fortunate wage workers who have access to successful profit-sharing schemes or who have accumulated sufficient levels of savings to set themselves up in some small full-time or part-time business. The group may be only a tiny fraction numerically, but it is ideologically rather important. To the extent that its members have gained income security, they have less need for employment or labour market security. Accordingly, they are likely to be unconcerned about measures to erode protective regulations. They could be expected to be critical of collective-bargaining institutions geared to labour representation security based on solidaristic principles. They could also be expected to oppose redistributive mechanisms to promote increased income security or other initiatives to provide security for those at the lower end of the wage ladder.

Fifth down the labour process ladder is the old *proletarian* stratum, made up mainly of unionized, male workers in regular wage employment. This was the Beveridge and Bismarckian norm for the national insurance social security system. For well-known reasons, workers in this stratum have been declining in number and their labour security has been eroded in various ways. They have become a major source of the growth of the bottom stratum outlined below. In general, they have tended to lose in terms of all aspects of labour security, that is, income, job, work, labour market, and, most crucially of all, labour representation security. A key aspect of their declining bargaining strength and loss of social cohesion has come from the erosion of job security, which has been much less noticed than their loss of labour security. That has stemmed in part from the introduction of new technologies and the concessions that have been made when bargaining with management. Wages are now tied far more to job or task assignments, and when workers and their unions are forced to concede the right to job retitling and rebundling to management, wage flexibility is increased. This is what has been occurring. Thus, for example, data from the regular CBI (Confederation of British Industries) employer surveys in the United Kingdom indicate that in the 1980s between a quarter and a third of all pay settlements included concessions on working arrangements.[4] This implies a reduction not only in job security but in income security as well.

For similar reasons, the fifth stratum has also lost employment security. It too has been threatened by two-tier or multiple-tier employment contract and wage structures, which may be transitional phenomena en route to a rather flexible decentralized system of industrial relations. Such workers have also been affected by the pressure to increase working-time flexibility. This could be beneficial for both employers and workers, but unless such flexible working time is regulated by collective bargaining, as is still the rule in Italy and the Federal Republic of Germany, the abolition of restrictions on night and weekend work, for example, will let employers define the terms and conditions of labour market flexibility unilaterally. In sum, one can envisage that a growing proportion of this stratum will possess a rather precarious position; they are likely to be moved across job categories without the same degree of labour security they and their predecessors fought so hard to achieve. As their labour insecurity grows, they can be expected to swell the ranks of the sixth stratum.

This sixth category might best be called the *flexiworker* stratum. In many countries, it has grown enormously in recent years due to the erosion of protective and collective forms of labour regulations. It encompasses many forms of "non-regular" wage labour, and one might be tempted to think that the members of this rather large and heterogeneous category have little in common. However, what these groups share is an absence of any of the normal forms of labour security, including labour market security and, most notably, labour representation security. Whereas, like the proletarian stratum, they are expected to be functionally flexible, flexiworkers are also "labour status" flexible, likely to shift between wage and non-wage forms of employment, sometimes combining activities, sometimes not. As a result, official labour force classifications are often unreliable. New terms have emerged that are little more than euphemisms for precariousness. Some firms have called groups of these workers "permanent temporaries," "self-employed employees," or "in-house out-workers." Some firms keep workers on temporary contracts for many years; some employment agencies put workers on permanent contracts as temporaries, guaranteeing them a retainer and employment status but not any particular job or level of income. These workers' untenable position in today's work world often has grim effects that highlight their insecurity. Recently there was a wretched court case in the United Kingdom involving fishermen who had been working for a firm for twenty years or more. The court decided that they were not entitled to mandatory redundancy benefits because they had not satisfied the condition of being regularly employed for at least two years. As their work in the period immediately preceding their redundancy had become irregular, they had lost their entitlement. The sad fact was that the fishermen had become flexiworkers without knowing it.

Flexiworkers need not be "unskilled" in a technical sense. For instance, teleworking (telecomputing, or remote work involving computer skills) has been an expanding factor in the growth of flexiworkers.[5] However, such workers are unlikely to have employment security or labour representation security, being typically isolated from the work process, ignored in promotions, easily dismissed, and unlikely to identify with existing industrial or craft unions. Telecomputing has also become a mechanism for geographical decentralization, nationally and internationally. Some firms have set up regional centres in which out-workers can assemble to work part-time. A case in point is the New York Life Insurance Company. It was having difficulty in retaining trained staff in its US offices and decided to set up an office in Ireland to process insurance claim forms from its American-based operations. Once the data had been entered, they were telephoned back to New York. Companies have even used remote working decentralization to shift jobs to high-unemployment areas without having to shift the whole of their operations away from strategically placed central locations. The UK's National Economic Development Council has recently launched information-based technology work centres in five inner cities for precisely that purpose. In short, by such methods, capital can remain concentrated, while labour becomes more fragmented and decentralized.

Typically, flexiworkers are in and out of jobs, but rarely remain in particular niches long enough to earn occupational welfare benefits, entitlements to social security, or even privatized insurance coverage, let alone develop the confidence to join or form unions.

Some other aspects of the growth in the number of flexiworkers are too well known to bear repetition. But one trend worth stressing is that large parts of the employment function itself may be in the process of being contracted out to intermediary institutions, such as labour agencies or "employee-leasing" companies, the latter term being favoured in the United States. It will take many forms, including the provision of "turn-key" work teams. One confidently anticipates a lucrative profession mushrooming in the 1990s – employment contract lawyers. They will bargain for many types of workers, just like agents for footballers or actors, not only for salaries and benefit packages but over such matters as employee loan arrangements between companies (a growing practice in Japanese firms), zero-hours contracts, maximum/minimum working-time contracts, on-call contracts, annual-hours contracts, and the like.

Symbolic of moves towards employee subcontracting was the recent abolition of Britain's national dock labour scheme. The dockers had obtained some income and employment security through a registration system that had helped maintain minimum wages and regulated training and skill standards. For over fifty years this symbol of decasualization had been preserved; now the prospect of labour auctions, wage undercutting, and market clearing is back. That is only one of many such moves. Temporary employment agencies have been on the increase for secretaries, contract cleaners, building workers, hotel kitchen staff, security services, maintenance workers, electronics workers, production workers, and numerous others. Some labour-only employment agencies have become multinational enterprises and, in some cases, monopsonist-monopolists with strong rent-acquisition possibilities. Already there is the International Confederation of Temporary Work Firms, which recently reported that the number of workers in the European Community (EC) on temporary contracts grew by between 15 and 20 percent a year in the 1980s, a rate expected to increase with the EC's single market after 1992. Apparently, the growth has been greatest in the Netherlands, France, Germany, the UK, and Belgium. The European Commission's concern for "social dumping" is leading to the consideration of new regulations, but the European Court of Justice's decision in March 1990 authorizing Spanish and Portuguese firms to transport their own temporaries to work for them in other parts of Europe seems to open the door to further expansion on their part.

One can paint these developments as benign or malign. The modern libertarian would contend that competition will force the agencies to provide incentives for workers to stay with them. There may indeed be some stabilization of employment in those agencies that provide workers allocated to firm *x* or *y* with pensions, sick pay, paid leave, and the rest. However, this will still entail low levels of job security in that workers will be shifted at the will of the agencies *and* the firms to whom they are contracted. This is *subordinated flexibility*, which is a threat to occupation by its incessant insecurity and casualization at the point of production. Skills that will be fostered include mobility; those that will be underdeveloped will include a broad understanding of specific production processes.

In recent years there has been a proliferation of forms of employment contracts, many of which are characterized by employment insecurity – the trademark of flexiworkers. Some contracts cover specific groups of workers; others reflect prevailing production or management strategies. In ILO enterprise-level labour flexibility surveys, we have been probing how to disaggregate labour statuses. The experience has highlighted the inadequacy of the dualistic vocabulary in this area. The term "temporary," for instance, covers a wide spectrum of usefully distinctive contractual relations. This is not the place to go into the distinctions or their implications, but just listing the main forms of contract highlights the fragmentation process:

1 Casual, without oral or written contract, typically day work
2 Temporary, fixed term, oral agreement, non-retention – for either (a) stop-gap work or (b) job work
3 Temporary, fixed term, oral, on a continuing basis – for either 2a or 2b
4 Temporary, fixed term, written contract, as for 2a or 2b
5 Temporary, age-limited, e.g., for youths aged 16–19 or for pre-retirement workers
6 Apprenticeship contracts, with or without assurance of subsequent employment
7 Trainee, probationary, specified or unspecified duration
8 Adaptation contracts, for post-training practical purposes
9 Temporary contracts for first-time job seekers, as in the FDR
10 Job-sharing contracts
11 Employment-orientation contracts, particularly for youth
12 Solidarity contracts, involving shared cuts in wages and working time in recessions

13 Variable-time contracts, where the length of the working day or week is adjusted to meet the firm's requirements
14 Part-time contracts, also involving features of other forms of contract
15 Regular, full-time contracts

This list is scarcely exhaustive, and it excludes forms of dependent "self-employment." Flexiworkers fit into all of the first fourteen categories; while most of these have always existed, it is their growth that is striking. The scope for employment insecurity and income insecurity in this "contractual fragmentation" is considerable, even though the diversity provides potential flexibility for firms and workers that could be advantageous for either or both. Labour representation security will be minimal because such workers have no social space within which they might bond cohesively. Moreover, such flexiworkers typically lack entitlement to occupational welfare or insurance-based state welfare. Some groups may have access to certain benefits, other groups to other benefits. But the dominant picture is one of exclusion or inadequacy of entitlement. Ironically, of course, they have a greater need for such benefits simply because they lack labour security in most of the respects outlined earlier. This means they are always under threat of sinking into the seventh stratum.

This stratum, which seems to have grown enormously in some countries in the 1980s, has attracted various epithets, the most popular and controversial being "underclass" or "lumpenproletariat." The former term seems to have stuck, despite criticisms. The underclass has been treated as a conservative instrument by writers such as Charles Murray, presented as a segment of the population who lack a work ethic and are dependent on welfare to the point where they need to be rehabilitated. But liberals too have sentimentalized the growth of this segment, often failing to criticize the productive, technological, and labour structures that generate lumpen components. In any case, one might best describe it as a *detached* stratum, since the defining characteristic is a loss of attachment to regular economic activity, often involving long-term or chronic recurrent unemployment and an equally chronic need for state transfers from outside the national insurance system. The loss of labour security by those in the old proleterian stratum and the absence of labour security among flexiworkers, particularly in entitlement to social security, mean that the potential source of growth of the detached stratum has boomed in the 1980s.

To a certain extent, it is from this group that the state can draw low-paid labour to help create wage and employment flexibility in other strata. But perhaps the stratum's main social impact lies in its being a major inducement for workers to become subordinately flexible – fear of joining the underclass makes the next-to-the-worst-option more bearable.

"Detachment," "social exclusion," and "marginalization" have become popular terms in recent debates on labour market developments. The Fordist system may have broken down, but if so, this is not only because mass production based on regular wage labour has shrunk, but because the regulatory framework has become dysfunctional, given that more of the population of advanced industrialized countries have become detached from productive society, that is, detached as workers. Consumer capitalism depends on workers consuming mass-produced products; increasingly, most people's identities are tied to consumption and their status as consumers, not to production and their status as workers. This applies to most of the labour fragments, none of which can be easily organized to pursue a coherent strategy of labour security, since they have no collective identity. It has almost reached the stage where one cannot envisage collective *class* action anymore, only sectional action – for instance, on ethnic, age, or gender issues.

Detachment is complex. Many people are formally detached from productive society, as in the case of the long-term unemployed and many of those in "labour market schemes." Others are behaviourally detached even though employed; many flexiworkers, for example, have little employment security and thus little access to non-wage components of "working-class" income, such as earnings-related benefits that, as in Germany, were built up as incentives to continuity of employment. Historically, the social insurance welfare system has had a regulatory function, with earnings-related mechanisms expected, first, to increase productivity through incentive and worker commitment effects, and second, to raise the firms' expected return on investment in training. But if the labour process is not generating the sort of employment required for such regulations to function to raise efficiency, then one can anticipate attempts to revise the system in order to secure a more effective regulatory framework.

Labour process fragmentation erodes the integrative capacity of both Beveridge and Bismarckian social security systems, which were conceived primarily to foster productivity while ensuring income security for the working population and their dependents. In many respects, these systems have become a means of weakening labour process security, since that depends crucially on the existence of common interests. They have also been a means of undermining labour market security, since labour market security depends on workers having effective freedom in the labour market, which has been corroded by "poverty traps," "unemployment traps," work-test rules, and so on. The more complex the system, the more one can expect the regulatory objectives to be dominant. Moreover, as argued elsewhere, with labour flexibility and fragmentation, social security's contributory base tends to shrink and benefit entitlement tends to become narrower and more fragile. Yet many of those advocating more flexibility in labour and product markets contend that welfare encourages and strengthens behavioural dependency. It is in that spirit that governments have shifted towards more "targeting," greater use of means tests, tighter conditionality for benefits, tighter behavioural monitoring, and the promotion of "welfare pluralism." In many countries one sees a strong trend towards some variant of "workfare," defined as the payment of benefits conditional on predetermined employment-related activity. In the United States, so often the pattern setter, the number on workfare increased by over 60 percent in one year. We are in danger of creeping to workfare.

Another related trend is the changing role of "training." This trend stems from the perceived need to raise productivity. The basic supply-side view is that in order to raise skills, wage differentials need to widen and be more individualized. But along with more flexible payment systems, ostensibly designed to promote productivity, has been a trend to what might be called "trainingitis," which derives from the erosion of skill in the traditional sense of that term.[6] The more occupations are split into different jobs, the more labour statuses are flexible; the larger the lower labour strata grow, the more significant will be the role of job and labour market training. In various European countries, the state's role in this area has grown enormously. One script on offer is that a growing proportion of the population will have work "careers" consisting of flexible combinations of short-term jobs preceded and succeeded by training and retraining, a pattern that could lead to a whirlwind of jobs interspersed with training. There is talk of an "active society" for the 1990s based on benign presentations of this twilight zone of intermittent training and productive activity. But workers obliged to shift from pillar to post in a fashion determined by some regulatory body are scarcely likely to lead the way to the *acta vita*.

In sum, if the libertarian, supply-side path to labour flexibility persists, something like the following scenario seems most likely:

- a contractualization of the labour process, with pro-individualistic regulations constraining collective action;
- welfare pluralism, with the state as fall-back, "safety net" provider, with privatized benefits for the upper strata, and with voluntary

private services to fill the gaps left by an incomplete insurance system (a model presented as "the caring society" in the Netherlands);[7]

- privatization of social as well as economic policy;
- workfare replacing means-tested and universal transfer payments for the employable;
- more policing of welfare "scroungers";
- a greater police presence in civil society to control the losers in an aggressively competitive economic environment; and
- a neo-corporatist state based on an overt employer-government alliance in place of tripartism, with trade unions shrinking or shackled by legislation and their own fragility in flexible labour markets.

Some might think that this scenario takes present-day trends to an extreme; nevertheless, the strength of these trends suggests that parts of this scenario have already been adopted by governments. What then is the alternative?

TOWARDS CO-OPERATIVE FLEXIBILITY

The nucleus of such an alternative does exist. This scenario would build on the positive features of the corporatist traditions kept alive in the Nordic region in the 1980s. An essential element of any viable alternative must be the avoidance of labour fragmentation and income insecurity. Yet the danger is that critics of the dominant trend towards subordinated flexibility will continue to give primacy to labour market security and employment security. Although both are valuable and should be seen as instrumental in the promotion of other rights, neither is what could be called a "meta-right," that is, an ultimate social objective. Treating them as such ultimately undermines their political legitimacy.

The error of the old "labourist" model surely lies in a faulty syllogism: there is a right to work; all rights imply duties; therefore, there is a duty to labour. One could give countless examples of unfortunate deductions from this line of reasoning. For instance, a recent international meeting of trade unionists concluded that the answer to the inadequacy of social security provisions associated with the growth of more flexible forms of employment was more full time jobs.[8] But perhaps full-time wage labour is neither desired by the majority nor desirable on efficiency or equity grounds. If full-time wage employment is treated as a meta-right, then one must favour market-clearing wages, whatever they may be, and a compromise on various other forms of labour security, notably labour representation and work security.

Full employment is always possible. However, it is neither an effective means of overcoming labour fragmentation nor, any longer, a reliable means of reversing growing inequalities and the erosion of labour process security. Recognition of this is needed if policy reform is to relate to current realities without drifting into some atavistic cul de sac, such as the mass creation of "public sector jobs." Fortunately, in some European economies, alternative strategies are taking shape. We may be in an era of social experimentation in the course of which partial reforms will be pieced together to create the basis for a much more flexible lifestyle by the end of the twentieth century. The vision must surely be a social structure in which labour representation security and income security are guarded and enhanced as meta-rights.

Such reforms are taking various complementary directions. The sooner they spread, the sooner it will be possible to articulate a different kind of social and labour structure. Here it might be useful merely to outline the types of reform that may be shaping an alternative path to labour flexibility.

First and foremost, unless organizations can be revived to represent the collective voice of the vulnerable segments of society, notably those in the sixth and seventh strata, the necessary impetus to sustainable non-subordinated flexibility will not emerge. That is why the regrouping of unions and their evolving structures and strategies are crucial, particularly the possibility that "community unions" will take the place of industrial or craft unions. A variant of this has been called "associational unionism," the theme being that the union would represent workers who are not constantly in the same trade or industry. If workers are "postcapitalist" in the sense of not being in stable wage labour, they will be uncommitted to industrial unionism (just as flexiworkers can scarcely be expected to be committed to craft unionism), in addition to being hard to organize or retain as union members. However, it is unlikely that community unionism will flourish if the organization merely represents an agency for job placement, advisory services, and personal loans, and serves as a source of social security for its members, even though all these functions are desirable. If that is all unions become, the state or private commercial firms will be able to pit these individualistic entities against one another. Only if they are constantly concerned with the primary problem of the era – redistribution – will they develop a pivotal role. There are signs that moves to redefine communal solidarity are strengthening and that economic democracy, as well as political and industrial democracy, will be high on the agenda in the 1990s. Without economic democracy, one can see no alternative to the type of subordinated flexibility sketched earlier.

Perhaps more advanced in practice are those kinds of experimental policies aimed at promoting flexible lifestyles. Such policies actually build on the fragmenting tendencies in the labour process, but many of them are double-edged in that they can either be converted into instruments that would intensify subordinated flexibility or be integrated with other policies that together promote a more co-operative, egalitarian flexibility.

If there are more part-time employment slots, and if there is a need to respond more speedily to economic restructuring as a result of more rapid and pervasive technological innovation, then it makes little sense to buck the trend. It makes much more sense to facilitate flexible work patterns on terms desired by workers. Hence, there is reason to believe we are entering an era of social experimentation. Haltingly, one sees the outlines of what could be a *social dividend* route to flexibility. It is so named because it is based on redistributing the economic surplus in ways other than by wage income and welfare. This approach would also give the right to work precedence over the right to employment (one must bear in mind that a right to do something can only exist if there is a matching right not to do it).

Something like a social dividend approach is gaining ground in the various experimental policies and institutional developments taking place in some parts of Europe. One thinks of "sabbatical year" and "time bank" debates in Sweden and Finland, solidarity contracts in Belgium, partial retirement schemes, career-break and parental leave arrangements, the revenue minimum *d'insertion* in France, wage-earner funds, renewed interest in profit-sharing, the renewed growth of co-operatives in Italy and elsewhere (including the Soviet Union, in a big way), industrial districts in Baden-Wuerrtemberg and in Italy, and so on.[9] Experimentation is the order of the moment. Thus, old ideas about time banks have been repackaged as less radical reforms. And in Finland, for instance, a government committee has proposed the phased introduction of sabbatical years for all workers, giving them the right to periodic breaks from their main labour force activity. Partial retirement schemes and the removal of arbitrary retirement-age notions are widely regarded as cautious steps in the direction of lifetime flexibility, especially in the context of the ageing of European societies. Although such schemes can be and have been easily turned into sources of inequity and discrimination, they can be developed for quite different ends if the appropriate institutional context exists.

There is also more constructive discussion of unconditional income transfers, or citizenship income grants, than previously. Such transfers would uncouple labour market status and behaviour from income security and facilitate flexible combinations of productive and reproductive activities, thus helping to legitimize the black economy and encourage the growth of the "informal" economy. As long as governments lack the courage or the vision to promote unconditional, universal, and individual rights to income security, the potential for "flexible specialization" will be restricted.

Basic security from deprivation as a citizenship right will be a necessary condition, but it will not be the only one. Essential to an environment of co-operative flexibility will be labour representation security, which will prevent the vulnerable in the lower labour strata from being detached and will combat the oppressive potential implicit in contract law replacing collective regulation of labour relations. Necessary as well will be institutions and regulations to provide safeguards against the structural inequalities that market mechanisms by themselves are bound to produce and intensify. That is why work security and payment system security (including minimum-wage protection) will remain essential components of any regulatory framework.

Ultimately, however, the institutional structure for developing labour process security will be far more significant than any number of regulations. New forms of unions, new forms of collective agencies, new voices, and new meanings of solidarity will need to emerge.

CONCLUSION

The search for a viable mix of social and labour policies in the agonizing events in Eastern Europe and the Soviet Union has given discussions of frameworks for the 1990s a new poignancy. A bogeyman has been removed, and hopefully, debates about the direction of social policy may become decidedly more progressive as a consequence. In the European Community, fears about social dumping, raised by the rhetoric concerning 1992, will have to be addressed more urgently. And in Canada and the United States, similar debates will continue, particularly bearing in mind the huge low-wage Mexican labour force to their south. The market-oriented orthodoxy is promoting subordinated flexibility everywhere, but in the wings is an emerging paradigm of flexibility based on co-operation and security. For this alternative to succeed, it is essential that the means for recovering and extending labour representation security are strengthened. Craft unions are almost anachronistic in societies where trades or crafts are ephemeral. Industrial unions are enfeebled by the multinational, multi-industrial nature of modern conglomerates. There must be moves downstream so that unions represent the aspirations and needs of all the groups in our fifth, sixth, and seventh labour strata. Unions can only emerge as restructuring organizations if fear and insecurity factors are diminished; this will only happen if the social security system is shifted in the direction of decoupling the labour market from the provision of income security.

If one sees the existing welfare system as increasingly becoming a regulatory device rather than a network for effectively and equitably combatting poverty, marginalization, and social exclusion, then critics of the trends towards subordinated flexibility should want to revise the system radically. Surely this is one of the two keys to co-operative, secure flexibility, the other being economic democracy in some form.

At present, the fragmentation of society is such that the existing welfare institutions are far more likely to deepen social divisions than to reduce the marginalization of flexiworkers and detached groups. A simple majority can almost always be mobilized politically to limit the rights and the security of vulnerable minorities. Enabling large numbers to make the transition out of the bottom three strata is scarcely feasible unless the institutional basis of income provision and work organization is revised.

Deliberately, this paper has not speculated on the socio-demographic fragmentation that could be expected to accompany different types of labour fragmentation. Surely, however, women have predominated in the flexiworker stratum in most countries, just as middle-aged and older men have been the principal losers in the erosion of labour security among the old proletarian stratum. In some societies, workfare-type options are likely to be concentrated on women and ethnic minorities; in others on youth and immigrants. In most societies, the new forms of labour fragmentation are likely to intensify inter-household inequality because of the high probability of joint entry into specific labour strata by husbands and wives, or partners. But these are speculations that need to be addressed in the light of more detailed analyses of labour fragmentation.

In sum, an alternative approach to the supply-side libertarian route will have to be based on the promotion of the meta-rights of labour representation and income security, which are the necessary conditions for positive liberty.[10] If democracy is to become a reality in the 1990s, rather than a rapidly debased term, it is surely necessary for institutions to promote political democracy, industrial democracy (through co-determination to ensure work security, occupational security, protective regulations), and economic democracy (through institutional mechanisms that redistribute economic surplus via citizenship income dividends). This strategy would effectively reverse the traditional social democratic and socialist agenda. Rather than nationalize the means of production, social democrats would accept the privatization of management and ownership functions and redistribute (socialize) the surplus. The form of this alternative democratic framework is still far from clear, but the contours are beginning to take shape.

NOTES

1 Economic Council of Canada, *Good Jobs, Bad Jobs: Employment in the Service Economy* (Ottawa: Supply and Services Canada, 1990).

2 CBI, "Pay, Performance and Inflation" (Memorandum to the National Economic Development Council, London, 18 October 1989), 5.

3 It is something like a combination of these two strata that Peter Townsend seems to have in mind as his overclass. See P. Townsend, "Underclass and Overclass: The Widening Gulf between Social Classes in Britain in the 1980s" (Plenary address to the annual Conference of the British Sociological Association, Plymouth, March 1989), in G. Payne and M. Cross, eds., *Sociology in Action* (Basingstoke: Macmillan, 1990).

4 CBI, "Pay, Performance and Inflation," 6, 13.

5 The CBI forecast in 1988 was that by 1995, 4 million workers (about 17 percent) would be working from home.

6 This is analyzed in more detail in a closely related paper: G. Standing, "Alternative Routes to Labour Flexibility" (Paper presented to Conference on Pathways to Industrial and Regional Development in the 1990s, UCLA, Los Angeles, 14–18 March 1990).

7 C. de Neubourg, *Unemployment and Labour Market Flexibility: The Netherlands* (Geneva: ILO, 1990).

8 Organization for Economic Co-operation and Development (OECD), "The Future of Social Protection" (Report on a meeting of trade union experts held under the OECD Labour Management Programme, Paris, October 1989), 7.

9 R. Leija, T. Santamaki-Vuore, and G. Standing, *Unemployment and Labour Market Flexibility: Finland* (Geneva: ILO, 1990), chap. 6.

10 If, following Isaiah Berlin, one defines liberty negatively as the absence of coercion, then the welfare state has tilted in the direction of reducing liberty. Traditionally, the welfare state has been defended as promoting positive liberty, since it provides the basis for individual choice in conditions of security. In labour market terms, at least, positive liberty has not been promoted very effectively in recent years.

6 Full Employment – Still a Viable Goal?

ARMINE YALNIZYAN

REFLECTIONS ON FULL EMPLOYMENT

Crossing the threshold of the 1990s, we find ourselves moving into a recession that is likely to be deeper and to last longer than the recession of 1982–83, at least with regard to the labour market. This recession will be deeper because the continued heamorrhage of jobs from an already weakened industrial sector is now accompanied by a new vulnerability in the service sector, related in large part to the shrinkage of the manufacturing economy. It will last longer because the emerging trading bloc between Canada, Mexico, and the United States will reinforce and draw out the nature of the crisis through the slow continental realignment of resources.

The heightened volatility and unpredictability of the labour market is the enduring legacy of the recession of 1982–83. While there was great prosperity and opportunity for some in the boom years of the 1980s, hundreds of thousands of people faced job loss, obsolescence of their working skills, and erosion of their earning power in the face of economic recovery. Even in that time of plenty, earning a living became an increasingly precarious enterprise.

The "full employment" enjoyed so briefly in so few places in Canada in 1989 has already begun to look irretrievable. As elsewhere throughout the industrialized nations, there are thoughtful arguments being made in Canada from every point on the political spectrum concluding that, given the current conjuncture in global economics, it is now beyond the capacity of government to provide full employment for its citizens and that the central pillar of social and economic policy must now rest on income security. Damage control is the order of the day.

Is the attainment of a full employment rate of unemployment a good indication of a "healthy" labour market? What is meant and what is assumed by the term "full employment"? Should modern labour market policy abandon the pursuit of full employment?

These questions are first explored by looking at the experience of Toronto since the last recession, sketching out key structural changes in the labour market in order to reveal the picture behind the success story of low unemployment rates.[1] The state's response to a dramatically changing job market is the subject of the next section. This leads to a discussion about the inadequacies of traditional full employment analysis as a useful tool for critiquing present policies, followed by a different perspective on full employment. The paper ends with a set of questions and a list of ideas in which to frame a discussion about this period of rapid and profound transformation of our social and economic life.

RESTRUCTURING THE LABOUR MARKET

Ontario is the economic heartland of the country, accounting for four out of every ten jobs in Canada. The process of economic recovery from the recession of 1982–83 has further reinforced regional disparity, a hallmark of Canadian life. By 1989 regional unemployment rates ranged from 3 percent to more than 19 percent across the country, compared to a range of 4 percent to 17 percent in 1981. Since the recession, almost half of the new jobs created in Canada were located in Ontario, more than 20 percent in the Toronto region alone.*

* Though focused on Toronto, the analysis here is not specific only to a large urban, diversified economy. Polarization of wage income, blurring of the lines between the working poor and the welfare poor, dramatic increases in part-time work, etc., have been widely experienced throughout Ontario and Canada. What sets Toronto apart, however, are the engines of its economic growth during this period. The mechanisms for attaining high rates of job creation are necessarily more difficult in regions dominated by small urban, rural, or resource-based economies with a restricted range of economic activity. In such areas, unleashing market forces – the "strategy" that produced lower unemployment rates in Toronto – has led to the demise, rather than the strengthening, of communities. In the discussion that follows, full employment is examined from a perspective that is pertinent to all these economies.

Table 6.1
Employment Levels, 1983–89 (in thousands)

	1983	*1989*	*Change in* Number	*Change in* % Change	*% of Canada*
Metro Toronto	1,034.0	1,329.6	295.6	28.6	16.9
Toronto CMA	1,573.6	1,950.8	377.2	24.0	21.5
Ontario	4,096.0	4,949.0	853.0	20.8	48.7
Canada	10,734.0	12,486.0	1,752.0	16.3	100.0

Source: Statistics Canada, *The Labour Force*, Catalogue no. 71-001.

Given the degree to which economic growth has been centred in Southern Ontario, it is of some interest to identify the major trends that characterize the recovery in Toronto, the largest and apparently the most resilient labour market of our nation. (See Table 6.1.) This empirical backdrop shows how the combined effects of the economic recession and recovery have resulted in three central features of the changing labour market, regardless of low unemployment rates: (1) an increasingly polarized job market with fewer points of access or bridges to good jobs; (2) increased insecurity (and lowered expectations) in the labour market both for the employed and the unemployed; and (3) intergenerational injustice in work opportunities for both older workers and young entrants to the job market.

Engines of Growth

Total employment in Metro Toronto expanded by a soaring 29 percent between 1983 and 1989. The most rapid job growth, in relative terms, during this recovery period took place in the construction industries. This development was wedded to the rapid expansion of the finance, insurance, and real estate industries. Rapid real estate growth was fuelled by an influx of foreign capital (largely from Hong Kong), demographic pressures of a baby-boom generation coming into the first-time home-buying market, and increased inequality of income distribution, which permitted greater speculative activities for those with greater disposable income. The recent deregulation of the banks also contributed to the growth of employment opportunities in the financial/insurance sector as firms broadened their spheres of economic activity.

The greatest number of jobs generated during the recovery were in community, business, and personal services. This sector, representing 35 percent of all jobs in Metro, has generated more than one-third of the new jobs added to Metro's labour market since 1983. The strongest growth took place in women's employment in this sector. Leading writers such as André Gorz identify this transformation as the commodification of domestic labour. These changes are documented in tables 6.2 to 6.5 in the Appendix to this chapter.

Part-Time Employment

Between 1983 and 1989 the number of part-time jobs in Toronto increased by a staggering 99 percent. The number of full-time jobs increased by 15 percent. Of the 257,000 net new jobs added to Toronto's labour market between 1983 and 1989, 42 percent were part-time opportunities. Part-time jobs now make up 16 percent of Metro's labour market, up from 10 percent in 1983. (See Table 6.3 in the Appendix.)[2]

Two out of three part-time jobs do not last a full year, and of those that do, only 15 percent are unionized.[3] Part-time work is increasingly used to permit more flexible staffing arrangements around seasonal production needs, peak-hour volumes, crisis situations, and vacations. Unions have made few inroads in this sphere, and without them to protect workers' access to benefits, employers can use part-time staffing to reduce labour costs.

Most sectors of the economy at least doubled their use of part-time workers since the recession. The largest absolute increase was in the office sector, where nearly 30,000 part-time jobs were added in the last seven years. A more disturbing trend is the rapid post-recessionary expansion of part-time manufacturing jobs. While these industries have traditionally relied almost exclusively on full-time workers (and use of overtime hours), the number of manufacturing jobs that were permanently classed as part-time in Metro almost tripled between 1983 and 1989.

Changing Patterns of Unemployment

Although the official unemployment rates for Toronto had fallen to "full employment" levels by 1988 (3.7 percent), other interpretations of unemployment patterns show that considerable change has occurred since 1981.

For example, the average period of joblessness for young people in Toronto has dropped to historically low levels (5.7 weeks in 1989 compared to 9 weeks in 1976). At the same time, the average worker over forty-five years old will remain unemployed for 18 weeks (compared to 14 weeks in 1976). The Metro Labour Education Centre provides adjustment assistance to displaced industrial workers through their unions. About half of these people are older workers with fifteen or more years' work experience in Canada. The majority speak English as a second language. The centre has documented that the average duration of unemployment for its clients in 1988 was 10 months.

Another emerging trend is the use of very short-term layoffs to respond to temporary downturns in production. Employers are adapting production schedules by cutting back hours, cutting out one week in four for a few months in a row, or eliminating one or two days a week on a non-routine basis. Significantly, most workers caught in this process do not qualify for unemployment insurance (UI) because of the minimum two-week waiting period before benefits are paid.

Since November 1989, this type of unemployment has become more commonplace across a wide range of manufacturing and retail industries in the greater Toronto area. It can be partially attributed to increasing demands by retailers for shorter turnaround times between orders and deliveries. Furthermore, as the market continues to soften, retailers are less prepared to take risks in committing themselves to standing orders with producers.

Without a certain volume of reliable standing orders, an employer is less able to keep production flowing. Previously, a slowdown in the economy might mean a reduction in the work force, but the remaining workers could expect to be employed throughout the week. Employers could spread out the work on both current stock and semi-secure orders for later in the season. The just-in-time system of inventory management demands that the production process operate at maximum capacity while an order is being filled, creating erratic production schedules. The size of the required work force thus varies substantially from one part of the week to the next, resulting in a just-in-time labour model of employment.

It is difficult to assess how many people are being affected by these developments because short-term layoffs are folded into Statistics Canada reports under the category of "unemployed four weeks or less." Nevertheless, it can be verified, however conservative the estimate, that this technique is being increasingly used. Section 37 of the Unemployment Insurance Act, referred to as the work-sharing option, permits employers engaged in non-seasonal economic activities to avoid a plant closure by laying off their work force for one to three days per week for up to twenty-six weeks while they try to recapture the firm's financial health. Workers receive unemployment insurance benefits for those days not worked. In January 1989, 78 firms in Ontario used the work-sharing option. In March 1990, 375 firms were using it. By November 1990, 877 agreements covering 24,115 employees had been approved in Ontario. Provincial program administrators indicated that 400 applications had been received in the first three weeks of November 1990.

Rate of Job Loss

It should first be noted that there is no accurate and comprehensive source for measuring the rate of dislocation of workers during this period of profound economic restructuring. Most measures capture only the net outcome of job loss and job creation. Virtually all available data that attempt to document job loss provide only gross underestimates of the phenomenon because of the triggers for reporting the information.

With that caveat in mind, it is estimated that between 1981 and 1987 approximately 10,000 manufacturing jobs were lost in the city of Toronto due to major closures.[4] Between November 1988 and December 1989, at least 7,588 unionized jobs were lost in Toronto, with the vast majority in manufacturing industries; it was announced that another 4,260 would be cut in the following months. Thus, in a one-year period, *before* the acknowledged start of the recession, almost 12,000 unionized industrial jobs were lost in Toronto.[5]

Erosion of Wage Structure

Metro Toronto wage data show a continued trend away from salaried jobs and towards wage jobs and contractual/seasonal jobs across all sectors of the economy. This supports the findings of the Economic Council of Canada's recent report *Good Jobs, Bad Jobs,* which documents the expansion of "nonstandard" forms of employment. For example, the report shows that over 10 percent of job growth in Canada has been "own account" self-employment, which includes work by the self-employed who do not themselves have employees. In 1986 just over half of the self-employed earned less than $10,000 compared with 27 percent of paid workers.[6]

Wage jobs in the finance sector, the most rapidly growing area of employment opportunity in Metro, are paid 45 percent of the amount paid for wage jobs in manufacturing. In 1989 this translated to less than $250 a week for an average wage worker in the finance sector as compared to almost $550 a week for a wage worker in manufacturing. The difference was due to a combination of lower average weekly hours and lower average hourly wages.

The wage *floor* has also been eroded. In Ontario the real purchasing power of the minimum wage declined by between 20 and 30 percent (depending on where in the province you lived) between 1975 and 1985. In 1975 the minimum wage was 47 percent of the average industrial wage. By 1985 it was worth 38 percent of the average industrial wage.[7]

In 1975 a single person without dependents earning the minimum wage at a full-time, full-year job was slightly above the poverty line (106 percent). In 1985 that minimum-wage job translated into an income at approximately 80 percent of the poverty line. For a single parent living in Toronto with one dependent child, the minimum wage provided an income at 62 percent of the poverty line in 1985.

The Social Planning Council's *Guides for Family Budgeting* (1987) estimates that the gross yearly income needed to cover basic costs of living in Toronto in 1986 was $20,938 for a single mother with one dependent. A full-time, full-year job earning $10.50 an hour would be required. A person with no dependents would need to earn $7.50 an hour to maintain this minimum adequate standard.[8]

Polarization of the Job Market

Between 1981 and 1986, 92 percent of the new jobs created in Ontario earned less than $6.77 an hour. Of ten wage categories, the one that grew most quickly over this time period was the lowest paid, where people earned less than $5.25. (The minimum wage in Ontario was $5.00 in 1989.) At the same time, there was an expansion of jobs earning $11.88 to $13.52 – upper-middle range – and an erosion of jobs earning middle-income wages.[9]

Similar trends have changed the shape of wage distribution in every region of the country and intensified the segmentation of the labour market. The dual economy we now operate in is characterized by two strong poles of growth: a low-skill, low-wage segment with limited benefits and marked by high turnover, and a segment featuring highly skilled, well-paid work with good fringe benefits and substantially greater job security.

These changes were less influenced by the rise in part-time employment or the de-industrialization of the economy than by a changing wage structure *within* every industry and occupational sector. The most dramatic change was a downward shift in the distribution of wages paid to young workers (those under the age of 35 but especially workers aged 15 to 24). Relative (and real) earnings among 15- to 19-year-olds in full-time, full-year jobs were 15 percent lower in 1986 than in 1981 and 27 percent lower than in 1977.[10] The new generation of workers is bearing a disproportionate burden of the costs of economic restructuring, both in terms of the purchasing power of their current earnings and in terms of the bleak prospects for their future working lives.

The Poverty Connection

Economic restructuring can, through the types of jobs being created and lost, affect rates of welfare dependence in at least three ways: the rate of turnover in the labour market; the distribution of wages in the labour market; and the purchasing power of wages, particularly the minimum wage, which represents society's "consumption floor."

There is normally a close relationship between reliance on social assistance and unemployment rates: as unemployment goes down, more people can turn to employment opportunities and are less reliant on the social safety net to get by. In 1984 this historical relationship broke down. Unemployment rates started to decline, but the caseload of "employable" welfare recipients remained high.

In Toronto there are now more food banks (180) than McDonald's outlets. In every month of 1989, 80,000 to 84,000 people used food banks in the country's hotbed of economic activity. By November 1990 over 100,000 were using them. About 3 to 4 percent of these users are transients. It is estimated that at least 17 percent (about one in six users) are minimum-wage workers.

It is of some note that the only group to post an increased incidence of falling below the poverty line at the peak of the economic recovery (1986–88) was young families. Today 34.3 percent of all Canadian families with heads twenty-four years old and younger live below the poverty line.[11]

The Big Picture

Two predominant trends have emerged during this process of restructuring in the labour market:

Increased Insecurity. Employment opportunities have become less of a force for social equalization during and since the recession. The increased polarization and insecurity of jobs, measured by a wide variety of parameters, has created a more precarious climate for workers. Taken in combination with the continuous explicit and implicit references made to the global (read low-wage) work force, such developments have constituted a major assault on how people define their expectations and rights both in the job market and in the workplace.

Intergenerational Injustice. The forces that have played themselves out in the labour market over the last decade have devalued two groups of workers: the older worker, displaced after many years of experience, and young workers, whose opportunities seem to be constrained occupationally and economically. The options being presented to the younger generation constrain their choices regarding, in turn, family formation and, regionally, the communities in which they will be able to survive. If the tiers in the labour market become entrenched on an age basis, the possibilities for intergenerational conflict will increase because as younger workers attempt to move up the remaining career ladders, they will be blocked by the babyboom generation, and as the population ages, growing numbers of people will rely on transfer payments.

THE STATE RESPONSE

The following section offers only a brief sketch of the major initiatives recently taken by the three levels of government in response to changing social and economic conditions. It does not refer to cutbacks in expenditures for established program funding or to unemployment insurance benefits, both significant "responses" of the federal government that will impact on the labour market.

The Federal Government

The Canadian Jobs Strategy (CJS) was initiated in 1985 and integrated training and job creation programs into one funding/policy envelope. Its emphasis is on short-term (less than six months) entry-level skills development.

In 1987 the "four-cornered agreement" between federal and provincial ministries was signed to enhance the employability of social assistance recipients (SARs). The aim of the agreement is to increase the number of spaces for SARs in CJS and/or provincial training programs and improve their ability to access these options by maintaining some direct and indirect income support during training.

The Labour Force Development Strategy, coupled with Bill C-21 (legislation which restructured the Unemployment Insurance Act), was introduced in 1989. The objective was to provide more "active" labour market adjustment mechanisms through the unemployment insurance fund. These include increased purchases of training, wage subsidies for employers providing entry-level skills training, mobility assistance, capitalization of benefits to promote self-employment, and start-up financing to initiate sectoral training networks among industries.

The Provincial Government

The Ministry of Skills Development (MSD) was created in 1985, bringing together different skills development programs for youth, apprentices, and workers (primarily in small- to medium-sized businesses). The Ontario Training Strategy was put forward in 1986 and administered by the MSD. By 1989 the bureaucratic and policy role of the ministry was in question. At the time of writing, it is unclear whether the ministry will be disbanded and the programs returned to their original ministries.

The ministry's report *Transitions*, tabled in 1988, provided a comprehensive blueprint for welfare reform. Beyond the recommendation to raise welfare rates, two key sets of recommendations emerged: (1) voluntary "opportunity planning" for social assistance recipients in order to help them determine a feasible path to economic independence, often centring on more training/upgrading, and (2) income supplementation (STEP) for the working poor as well as for those who are making the transition from social assistance to the labour market via very poorly paid work. Introduced in October 1989, the STEP program has grown from 2,840 cases to over 7,000 in less than a year.

The Municipal Government

In 1990, the Toronto municipal government established a Workers' Information and Action Centre at city hall to provide information and education on workers' rights in the workplace and act as an advocate on behalf of unorganized, primarily immigrant, workers around issues of employment standards and occupational health as well as other emerging issues.

The municipal government is examining the possibility of offering municipal subsidies (in the form of tax abatements, low-interest loans, and outright grants) to industries the city is anxious to attract or retain. Referred to as bonusing, this practice is widespread throughout the United States. However, section 112 of Ontario's Municipal Act prohibits municipalities from giving grants or loans, tax abatements, or land at below market value. The city is seeking amendments to the act. Even with these amendments, the outcome is unclear, as there is, as yet, no definition of unfair subsidy in the Canada-US Free Trade Agreement.

What's the Message?

Training is being offered as the catch-all labour market panacea for our economy's ills. Most expenditure in training is at the lowest end of the skill spectrum. This is unlikely to change for two reasons: (1) the increased pressure to move social assistance recipients off welfare rolls, and (2) Ontario's track record of job creation in the labour market. Evaluations of these programs suggest that participants are generally no better off than non-participants when it comes to competing for jobs, nor do their jobs pay higher wages. "Training" has simply become the politically acceptable term for wage subsidies in short-term job creation programs.

Industrial strategy is cast in the light of international competitive forces and the need to maintain Ontario's position in the global forum. This tends to limit the discussion to higher value-added/export-oriented industries, despite the acknowledgment that such a strategy will only affect a small margin of firms and people. The sectoral training strategy that appears to be emerging from this formulation will similarly be most effective at the margins. Some observers have characterized this approach as "train the best, forget the rest."

THE POVERTY OF FULL EMPLOYMENT ANALYSIS AND AN ALTERNATIVE

A commitment to full employment – paid work for all who seek it – was the cornerstone of economic and social policy in the post–Second World War period throughout the industrialized world. This commitment was at least in part a political response to the pressures of working-class movements demanding full employment as the means of ensuring the rights of labour. Arising from the experiences of the Great Depression, these demands for decent jobs at decent wages were founded on the principles that work is dignity and labour is not a commodity.

For decades the benchmark of success in pursuing this policy, translated into measurable terms, was unemployment rates of 3 or 4 percent, estimated to be the amount of voluntary turnover in a labour market as people seek new jobs. But after years of living with double-digit unemployment in most regions of the country, the notion of devising policies to return us to these levels of unemployment seems atavistic.

Over the last fifteen years the explicit pursuit of full employment (defined by *any* trigger level of unemployment, such as 6 or 8 percent) has slipped off the menu of acceptable macroeconomic levers for shaping our national economy. In its place the federal government has single-mindedly focused on market solutions to our economic and social problems, invoking the nineteenth-century theology of the market as the most "neutral" social force. The result has been some easing of chronically high unemployment after seven years of economic recovery, but only in the most advantaged of regions.

Full employment has become a numbers game, referring only to *reductions* in unemployment rates and increases in jobs generated, not what the overall unemployment rate is, where the jobs are being created, whether they are full-time or part-time, how long they will last, or whether they will pay enough for people to live on. This reductionist nightmare of full employment presents us with the caricature of Mulroney promising, and briefly delivering, "jobs, jobs, jobs."

Full employment rates of unemployment were not an overt policy goal, but rather a geographically specific and short-lived windfall of market forces at play. With governments not pursuing such a policy, the rhetoric of full employment has facilitated the integration of workfare programs into the policy agenda in recent years. And now, in the context of the globalization of the economy and the fight to remain competitive with low-wage economies, the logical extension of pursuing the modern version of full employment "policy" would be to sanction further downward pressures on wages. In the face of this reality, both the right and the left have argued that full employment is no longer attainable and that the key right of citizenship in highly industrialized and interdependent economies is income security.

Is it time to abandon full employment as policy lever? I would argue emphatically that we should not, that policies aimed at minimizing unemployment are an insufficient but necessary condition for a more just society, a society that offers people the opportunity to participate directly in the making of their own world. Clearly, however, the concept of full employment must address the limitations of the modern labour market in a relevant manner, and in language that creates the space for a progressive vision of society, especially for the younger generation.

One possibility lies in reframing the notion of full employment, not in macroeconomic terms, but in terms of the individual's working life cycle. This would take account of the social dimension of full employment by including both paid and non-paid work. In this light, education and training, family formation and maintenance (including child raising and care of the elderly), and volunteer activities in the community all contribute to the individual and common good as much as does paid work.

Such a conceptualization of full employment places *time* front and centre in the debate. It calls for a revitalized campaign to reduce (paid) working hours by increasing demands for job sharing, flexitime, career breaks, sabbaticals, time bank formulations (annual hours contracts), longer vacations, early retirement, and so forth. It requires creative options in collective agreements and strong improvements in employment standards to provide more flexibility and protection.

The great challenge in the face of today's global economic pressures is to hold on to the goal of maintaining income while reducing hours. En route to maximizing the individual's autonomy and control over his or her working life cycle, there is no centrepiece in the strategy to reduce working hours, such as a legislated shorter working week. But the "cafeteria" approach to reducing working hours for all workers is only possible if there exists a range of mechanisms that kick in at different phases of workers' lives: for example, unemployment insurance, extended parental benefits, training allowances (greatly enhanced), child tax credits, pensions, etc. So, ironically, this version of full employment is predicated on income security.

The life-cycle approach to full employment would be problematic if it stopped here because it would appear to place so many of our eggs in the income security basket. The danger is that interpreting income security as the necessary infrastructure for achieving full employment would subtly work in the favour of business's rather than workers' interests. In most industrialized nations, the dialogue around income security has become synonymous with a (basic) guaranteed annual income, a sure-fire recipe for marginalizing citizens and dooming them to poverty. Unless the political momentum is strong, it would be easy to lose control of the mechanisms that would be put into place and we could end up with measures that facilitate "flexibility" (i.e., movement in and out of the labour market) and open up greater possibilities for legitimating the proliferation of jobs that are paid below-poverty wages. It is no coincidence that the corporate agenda has adopted and is promoting the income security approach.

To prevent income security policies from undermining the creation of decent jobs at decent wages, three main strategies must be pursued: (1) industrial strategies that put a premium on self-sufficiency and domestic demand; (2) regional development strategies based on cost recovery rather than profit; and (3) solidaristic wage strategies that bring up the wage floor and start to close the gap between the highest- and lowest-paid workers in the economy. (This latter does not refer to state-defined wage policy but rather to a voluntary change in the labour movement's approach to wage bargaining.)

To these it is necessary to add a more controversial fourth strategy: a compulsory citizen's service. Similar to the notion of compulsory military service in other nations, this would see young people, after completing secondary school or dropping out, work a full calendar year in such areas as child care, elder care, shelters for the homeless or abused, hospitals, food banks, the environment, waste management, the construction of affordable housing, energy alternatives, etc. Adults could be given unpaid leave for three or six months to voluntarily put in their citizen's service. All who work in the service of their community during this time would receive 60 percent of the industrial wage (i.e., the minimum wage). Such work would give everybody a much more direct experience of how things could be made better in their own community and would provide much-needed labour for indispensable but underfunded non-profit services. It would give all young people a similar sort of working experience at the start of their working life. The *quid pro quo* of the citizen's service is the citizen's right. In return for time given in service to one's society, the unpaid work done over the course of one's working life is acknowledged and at least partially financially supported.

However, without control over the resources with which to mount this social project, the government would find it impossible to undertake this entire program of action. To permit the pursuit of home-grown industrial and regional development strategies, we need to restructure the finance capital market by introducing pools of countervailing capital. The primary objective of the corporate agenda is to eliminate barriers to capital movement. The free trade agreements now in place and being negotiated, as well as the emergence of giant transnationals that dominate world markets, are creating a climate in which it is becoming harder to defeat that objective.

Regaining some degree of control over finance capital must become a primary objective of governments and the popular sector.

Increased control over pension funds is but one obvious choice for promoting public investment, an experiment that has proved highly successful in Quebec with the Caisses de dépôts et placements.

TOWARDS A FRAMEWORK

What follows offers a starting point for discussing a framework that would, ultimately, permit the emergence of a coherent alternative program of action.

Recasting Full Employment

- What are the best ways to incorporate paid and non-paid work?
- How do we recapture the broad social dimension of full employment? (A good start would be to create socially useful jobs to deal with the pent-up demand for public goods, such as affordable housing, day care, etc.)
- Is the formulation consistent with sustainable economic development?

We will have to reduce our current consumption levels if this last point is taken seriously. The parallel dialogue is about creating a "healthier" standard of living, including more time for non-economic activities involving less stress. How can we fold non-economic measures of well-being into discussions on how to maintain our standard of living without undercutting the importance of the economic concerns? Is the notion of full employment throughout one's working life a useful one?

The Role of Income Security

- Does the logic of this period of economic restructuring, especially with respect to job creation patterns, inevitably lead us to focus on income security?
- What is the relative trade-off in putting emphasis on full employment versus income security?
- How likely are we to attain and maintain a comprehensive and adequate level of income security in the context of a continental trading bloc that includes Mexico?

Our choice of mechanisms, and their range, is crucial in this discussion. For example, minimum-wage legislation is clearly a more comprehensive and socially powerful mechanism than income supplementation. But given our recent track record on job creation (92 percent of jobs created in Ontario between 1981 and 1986 earned below $6.77 an hour), will raising minimum wages to a living level create a substantial loss of employment? Would it matter if we lost most of those jobs?

Choices for Economic Development

- Through what terms of reference, and at what scale, can we realistically discuss economic self-reliance and the development of our national economy?
- What is the role of non-tariff barriers in developing regional and national industrial strategies (content legislation? tax incentives? tax expenditures? rebirth of the crown corporation?)? What types of manufacturing matter?
- How can we harness existing pools of social equity (such as pension funds) and create new ones?
- Can we both encourage decentralization and channel it into a more coherent social expression?

Protectionism is no longer an option for building our economy; neither is haemorrhaging our jobs to locations further and further south. In articulating an industrial strategy, we must look not only to those firms in the economy that are indeed poised to compete on an international scale but also to those sectors of the economy that are of importance to us on a local and regional scale. This means that industrial strategy should encompass ways of creating "socially useful" goods and *services* (e.g., affordable housing, day care, energy-saving devices, shelters and counselling for abused women, environmental testing equipment, etc.). It also means we should be thinking seriously about what kind of manufacturing activities we are not willing to lose, nationally or regionally.

Conjuncture of the National and Global Contexts

- What levers do we already have that can be used in a fight for either full employment or income security measures in Canada? In other words, where does our bargaining strength come from?
- Who is "we"?

In the new global economy, people's attachment to nation-states is being transformed into other forms of patriotism, some based on fear of economic reprisals from other places (most notably West Germany and Japan), some based on the intolerance of others' agendas. There is a real concern about what others can do to our standard of living. An ideological war is being waged to get people to accept the notion that we can only survive the economic onslaught as North Americans, not as Canadians. Are we moving towards acceptance of a North American government? Can the traditional popular sector groups – labour, women's groups, environmental groups, church groups – provide a realistic counterweight to this development or even precede it, thus defining the process?

SUMMARY AND CONCLUSIONS

Recasting the full employment option as the most viable project in revitalizing the national economy poses three tactical problems: (1) creating the *time* to provide a life-cycle work model of full employment; (2) ensuring the *money* is there to do this through income security mechanisms and solidaristic wage bargaining; and (3) developing industrial and regional development strategies that put an emphasis on *self-sufficiency*.

Acknowledging that a full working life includes many time-consuming non-paid activities means we have to create more "legitimate" time off for the paid labour force. This translates into a panoply of improvements in employment standards such as the following: statutory paid educational leave, longer parental leave,[12] family (sickness/care) leave, a shorter work week, and/or longer vacation leave. These would be available to all workers, not just full-time workers. The fact that a shorter work week is not the centrepiece of this agenda simply reinforces the goal of incorporating non-paid work into the definition of full employment. Maximizing our control over our ability to move in and out of the labour market to do the "work" of our lives is the objective.

The great challenge in today's global economy is to retain and regain control over what we produce and for whom. Industrial strategy must focus on consumer-oriented regional development, stressing as much as possible self-sufficiency in a regional economy. This flies in the face of an internationally structured marketplace for goods, but the fact remains we still consume food, water, shelter, and energy and most of these essentials are produced within our own national economy. While there is an important role for an export-oriented component to industrial strategy, the spin-off effects of focusing on domestic demand would be much greater. Content legislation and other forms of non-tariff protection could provide the necessary stimulus for more manufacture of both durable and non-durable goods, while increasing the minimum wage broadens the market for such goods. The likely result would be a made-in-Canada, demand-led recovery.

Is it inevitable that full employment is out of reach in parts of Canada? It seems a strange question, given that full employment policies, even in their most crude form, have not been pursued in this country for at least the last ten years. Before we leap to the conclusion that the best we can offer any worker in an increasingly unstable labour market is some degree of income security, most commonly defined as a form of guaranteed income (read guaranteed poverty), let's look at where we could create stability and control in the production process and the financial markets. We do not have to accept that more people will be marginalized by developments in the labour market. We do not have to accept that fewer people will have control over what they do with their lives. Redefining the ways we think about and the ways we could attain full employment is a first step in this direction.

APPENDIX

Table 6.2
Full-Time Jobs in Metropolitan Toronto, 1981–89

	1981	*1983*	*1986*	*1989*	*Percentage Change over* *1981–89*	*1983–89*	*1986–89*
Office	437,544	434,414	481,692	560,484	28.1	29.0	16.4
Sector %	41.3	43.9	45.4	49.2			
Full time %	N.A.	94.9	93.5	91.3			
Manufacturing & warehousing	284,264	236,516	252,890	235,730	−17.1	−0.3	−6.8
Sector %	26.8	23.9	23.9	20.7			
Full time %	N.A.	98.3	96.6	95.1			
Institutional	112,414	111,571	116,958	121,967	8.5	9.3	4.3
Sector %	10.6	11.3	11.0	10.7			
Full time %	N.A.	85.8	79.6	76.4			
Retail	105,160	98,184	92,255	95,903	−8.8	−2.3	4.0
Sector %	9.9	9.9	8.7	8.4			
Full time %	N.A.	73.5	66.6	61.9			
Service	105,302	95,984	98,576	102,959	−2.2	7.3	4.4
Sector %	9.9	9.7	9.3	9.0			
Full time %	N.A.	81.5	74.3	70.5			
Other	15,972	12,841	17,760	21,550	34.9	67.8	21.3
Sector %	1.5	1.3	1.7	1.9			
Full time %	N.A.	66.7	63.8	63.8			
Total	1,060,656	989,510	1,060,131	1,138,593	7.3	15.1	7.4
Sector %	100.0	100.0	100.0	100.0			
Full time%	N.A.	90.0	86.7	84.0			

Source: Employment, Land Use and Assessment Data Bank, Metropolitan Toronto Planning Department, Research Division, P 3.13.

Note: Full-time employment is defined as 20 or more hours per week in this survey. "Sector %" is the share the industry sector contributes to all full-time jobs. "Full time %" is the share of full-time jobs in the industry sector's total employment.

Table 6.3
Part-Time Jobs in Metropolitan Toronto, 1983–89

				Percentage Change over	
	1983	*1986*	*1989*	*1983–89*	*1986–89*
Office	23,318	33,463	53,488	129.4	59.8
Sector %	21.3	20.6	24.6		
Part time %	5.1	6.5	8.7		
Manufacturing & warehousing	4,056	8,952	12,083	197.9	35.0
Sector %	3.7	5.5	5.6		
Part time %	1.7	3.4	4.9		
Institutional	18,523	29,933	37,661	103.3	25.8
Sector %	16.9	18.4	17.3		
Part time %	14.2	20.4	23.6		
Retail	35,397	46,191	58,932	66.5	27.6
Sector %	32.3	28.4	27.1		
Part time %	26.5	33.4	38.1		
Service	21,784	33,956	43,016	97.5	26.7
Sector %	19.9	20.9	19.8		
Part time %	18.5	25.7	29.5		
Other	6,410	10,065	12,209	90.5	21.3
Sector %	5.9	6.2	5.6		
Part time %	33.3	36.2	36.2		
Total	109,488	162,560	217,389	98.6	33.7
Sector %	100.0	100.0	100.0		
Part time %	10.0	13.3	16.0		

Source: Employment, Land Use and Assessment Data Bank, P 3.13, Metropolitan Toronto Planning Department, Research Division.

Note: Data on part-time employment were not collected before 1983. Part-time employment is defined as less than 20 hours per week in this survey. "Sector %" is the share the industry sector contributes to all part-time jobs. "Part time %" is the share of part-time jobs in the industry sector's total employment.

Table 6.4
Total Jobs in Metropolitan Toronto, 1983–89

	1983	*1986*	*1989*	*Percentage Change over* *1983–89*	*1986–89*
Office	457,732	515,155	613,972	34.1	19.2
Sector %	41.6	42.1	45.3		
Manufacturing & warehousing	240,572	261,842	247,813	3.0	–5.4
Sector %	21.9	21.4	18.3		
Institutional	130,094	146,891	159,628	22.7	8.7
Sector %	11.8	12.0	11.8		
Retail	133,581	138,446	154,835	15.9	11.8
Sector %	12.2	11.3	11.4		
Service	117,768	132,532	145,975	24.0	10.1
Sector %	10.7	10.8	10.8		
Other	19,251	27,825	33,759	75.4	21.3
Sector %	1.8	2.3	2.5		
Total	1,098,998	1,222,691	1,355,982	23.4	10.9
Sector %	100.0	100.0	100.0		

Source: Employment, Land Use and Assessment Data Bank, P. 3.13, Metropolitan Toronto Planning Department, Research Division.
Note: Total jobs refer to all full-time and part-time employment in Metro. Data on part-time jobs offered in Metro were not collected before 1983. "Sector %" is the share the industry sector contributes to the total number of (full- and part-time) jobs in the Metro area.

Table 6.5
Duration of Unemployment, Annual Averages: Toronto CMA, 1976–88
(in thousands)

	1976	1981	1983	1985	1987	1988	*Percentage Change over* 1976–88	1981–88	1983–88
Both sexes									
Less than 5 weeks	27	34	38	42	33	31	14.3	−9.4	−19.2
5–13 weeks	26	26	43	34	25	20	−22.9	−22.1	−53.4
More than 13 weeks	20	20	72	44	27	17	−15.6	−16.0	−76.3
Average duration (in weeks)	11.6	11.2	19.6	15.4	14.0	11.4	−1.5	1.6	−41.9
Males									
Less than 5 weeks	15	16	19	20	17	15	2.9	−8.5	−23.0
5–13 weeks	15	14	23	17	13	10	−31.9	−26.3	−56.2
More than 13 weeks	11	11	43	26	13	9	−16.5	−20.4	−79.2
Average duration (in weeks)	11.7	12.0	21.2	16.9	13.7	12.3	4.9	2.3	−41.9
Females									
Less than 5 weeks	13	18	19	22	15	16	27.5	−10.2	−15.2
5–13 weeks	11	12	20	17	12	10	−11.1	−17.5	−49.9
More than 13 weeks	9	9	28	18	14	8	−14.7	−10.6	−71.8
Average duration (in weeks)	11.4	10.4	17.7	13.8	14.2	10.4	−8.6	0.2	−41.1
15–24 years old									
Less than 5 weeks	12	18	18	20	15	14	14.3	−22.4	−24.2
5–13 weeks	46	13	18	12	8	6	−86.8	−54.3	−66.4
More than 13 weeks	6	8	21	10	5	NA	−13.0*	−37.0*	−75.7*
Average duration (in weeks)	9.0	8.8	15.0	10.3	7.8	5.7	−36.7	−35.0	−61.9
25–44 years old									
Less than 5 weeks	11	11	15	15	13	13	19.8	13.5	−11.9
5–13 weeks	11	9	18	15	11	10	−7.8	12.4	−43.7
More than 13 weeks	10	8	33	21	13	9	−10.2	7.5	−72.3
Average duration (in weeks)	13.1	11.4	21.2	17.1	15.8	12.0	−8.0	5.3	−43.3
Over 45 years old									
Less than 5 weeks	5	5	5	5	4	5	1.0	−5.1	−2.4
5–13 weeks	6	6	7	7	6	5	−12.3	−10.7	−30.6
More than 13 weeks	5	5	19	13	10	6	25.9	15.4	−67.8
Average duration (in weeks)	14.3	17.6	25.1	20.5	19.5	18.0	25.9	2.4	−28.3

Source: Statistics Canada, Catalogue no. 71-001.

* Changes in long-term unemployment for youths are calculated up to 1987 because of incomplete 1988 data.

NOTES

1 The first section of this paper is largely drawn from Armine Yalnizyan, *A Statistical Profile of Toronto's Labour Market, 1976–1987* (Toronto: Social Planning Council of Metropolitan Toronto, May 1988). The data used here have been updated to 1989.

2 Metro's survey defines part-time employment as "less than 20 hours per week" and therefore underestimates the use of part-time employment. Statistics Canada defines part-time employment as "less than 30 hours per week" but does not provide data below the provincial level.

3 Commission of Inquiry into Part-time Work, *Part-time work in Canada* (Ottawa, 1983), 66, 72.

4 Based on Metro Planning Department Employment surveys. Ontario Ministry of Labour (MOL) figures for the same time period indicate 2,500 jobs were lost in the city of Toronto. This is based on the ministry's closure notification requirement that notification must be given when over fifty employees are involved. Intra-Ontario relocations are excluded from the MOL requirement. Similarly, Ministry of Labour figures for 1989 show approximately 10,000 jobs lost in Ontario, about the same as the job loss for Metro Toronto over the same period as documented by the Metro Labour Education Centre.

5 This data, from the Metro Labour Education Centre, reflects only a fraction of displaced workers in organized workplaces who, through their union, come to the centre for assistance with labour market adjustment issues.

6 Economic Council of Canada, *Good Jobs, Bad Jobs: Employment in the Service Economy* (Ottawa: Supply and Services Canada, 1990), 12.

7 The NDP government of Ontario has recently announced plans to increase the minimum wage to 60 percent of the average industrial wage – about $7.40 in 1990 – over the next five years.

8 These figures represent a standard of living that is about 25 percent above Statistics Canada's low-income cutoffs. This income would cover all basic costs but provide no luxuries. In 1987 the average yearly earnings of Toronto's wage workers in the finance sector (the sector of highest job growth) was $12,312; in the service sector, $14,014; and in the manufacturing sector, $23,666.

9 John Myles, Gannett Picot, and Ted Wannell, "The Changing Distribution of Jobs, 1981–1986," *The Labour Force Survey*, Statistics Canada, Catalogue no. 71-001 (October 1988), 85–138.

10 Ibid.

11 Statistics Canada, *Income Distribution by Size in Canada*, Catalogue no. 13-207 (1988), Table A.

12 The NDP government of Ontario has announced 18 weeks *unpaid* parental leave for parents of newborn or adopted children on top of the 17 weeks unpaid pregnancy leave already available. The new UI rules provide partial income replacement (60 percent of wages) for up to 25 weeks, up from 15 weeks. At the risk of sounding wildly utopian, I would argue that some form of paid leave should be made available for parents to take care of children under the age of two-and-a-half (i.e., generally speaking, the age at which a child can begin to communicate).

PART THREE

Restructuring Labour Markets

7 The Feminization of the Labour Market: Prospects for the 1990s

MARCY COHEN

THE TREND TOWARDS POLARIZATION IN CLERICAL WORK

Over the last thirty years clerical work has replaced factory work as the largest single occupational category in the Canadian economy. By 1981 close to one out every five jobs was clerical. It has become, in effect, the predominant "working-class" occupation in a service-based economy dependent almost entirely on a female labour force. Today one out of every three women who work outside the home is employed in a clerical occupation, and almost 80 percent of all clerical workers are female.

In the late 1970s media attention focused on predictions that computerization would result in a dramatic reduction in clerical jobs and that female unemployment, which has persisted well above male levels since the late 1960s, would increase further unless women were moved into non-traditional jobs in the goods-producing sector. However, concerns over an impending crisis in clerical employment were soon overshadowed by the events of the 1980s – the severe economic recession, the restructuring of manufacturing industries that followed, and the resulting job loss in male-dominated blue-collar occupations. Because the changes in clerical employment did not result in similar headlines about "office closures" or massive layoffs, the restructuring of clerical employment has gone virtually unnoticed. In fact, there has been a very dramatic decline in the growth of clerical work – from 59.5 percent in the 1971–81 period

Table 7.1
Employment Growth by Occupation, Canada, 1971–89

	1971–81 (%)	*1981–89* (%)
Overall employment growth	39.1	13.5
Growth in clerical	59.5	7.4
Growth in managerial	118.7	76.0

Sources: Statistics Canada, *The Labour Force Survey*, Catalogue no. 71-001 (1989 and 1981 annual averages); Statistics Canada, *Occupational Trends 1961–1986*, Catalogue no. 93-151 (1988).

to 7.4 percent from 1981 to 1989 (Table 7.1). Clerical work went from being one of the fastest-growing occupations to become one of the slowest-growing occupations in the 1980s. As a consequence, only 14.7 percent of women entering the labour market found work in the clerical area in the 1980s compared to over 40 percent who found jobs in clerical work in the 1970s. In contrast, almost one-third of the new jobs for women in the 1980s were in managerial and administrative work compared to 8 percent in the 1970s (Table 7.2).

The shift from clerical to managerial employment and the trend towards slowed growth in clerical work are consistent with the findings of current case study research.[1] In general, these studies have identified three trends in the reorganization of office employment with computerization: an integration of managerial/professional jobs with senior-level clerical functions; the elimination of many traditional clerical occupations; and the expansion of more routinized computer-related clerical jobs, such as data entry operator. The consequence of these changes has been to create a smaller, more polarized clerical work force with two distinct labour markets for clerical workers and few routes for mobility from routine to senior-level jobs. Increasingly, senior-level clerical jobs are being transformed into para-professional positions that require some college-based training in data processing, business practices, and general problem-solving. This point is confirmed in a major study in the United States on the impact of computer-communication technology on women's employment:

> ... the new technology is not resulting in broad-scale deskilling of jobs. Rather, the reverse is true ... There is a tendency for management to re-examine hiring standards in the face of this changing work content in order to add to its ranks only those with the educational and social qualifications

Table 7.2
Occupational Distribution of Female Employment, Canada, 1971–89

Occupation	*Occupation as Percentage Growth Experienced Female Labour Force* 1971–81 (%)	1981–89 (%)	*Average Annual Income 1988 ($)*
All occupations	100.0	100.0	15,054
Man./Admin.	7.6	32.5	24,843
Nat. sciences	2.1	2.0	23,819
Social sciences	3.7	4.4	23,418
Medicine/Health	8.5	10.6	21,428
Teaching	4.2	6.4	25,861
Clerical	40.3	14.7	16,315
Product fab.: assembly/repair	4.0	.9	14,196
Processing	2.4	–.5	14,627
Sales	11.6	8.9	12,746
Service	15.9	11.7	9,749

Sources: Statistics Canada, *The Labour Force Survey*, Catalogue no. 71-001 (1989 and 1981 annual averages); Statistics Canada, *Occupational Trends 1961–1986*, Catalogue no. 93-151 (1988); Statistics Canada, *Earnings of Men and Women*, Catalogue no. 13-217 (1988). The average annual salaries are for all full-time and part-time employees and are based on 1986 constant dollars.

deemed necessary to effectively perform the new tasks at hand. In many instances, these new hiring standards are interpreted as requiring at least a junior college degree.[2]

However, it is important not to draw the wrong conclusion from this trend towards the professionalization of clerical work and assume that computers have at long last given women the opportunity to free themselves from the bondage of routine, low-paying, and boring clerical tasks. Given that there are a limited number of senior positions and given that employers are hiring college graduates to fill these positions, the professionalization of clerical work has pushed older, often less-educated women and women with family responsibilities further down the occupational ladder. In case study research conducted by myself and Margaret White, we found that it was generally the better-educated younger single women who were able to take advantage of an employer's offer to pay the tuition costs of night school. Older women with family responsibilities had neither the time nor the confidence to undertake further schooling. These women were increasingly ghettoized in data entry and what remained of the routine manual work in the office – jobs that were in danger of being eliminated in the next phase of office automation.[3]

Another very important dimension of polarization in clerical employment has been the shift from full- to part-time work and the consequent decline of the traditional "9 to 5" work pattern in clerical work. In Canada between 1981 and 1989, part-time clerical employment among women rose by almost 25 percent compared to an increase of 6.6 percent for full-time employment.[4] The shift to a part-time clerical work force can be related to restructuring strategies designed to increase what employers refer to as "labour market flexibility." For instance, a recent survey of employers in the Vancouver area revealed that the most important reason employers gave for using part-time clerical workers was not the lower costs but rather the potential to increase "organizational flexibility and at the same time avoid future layoffs of full-time employees."[5] Before this survey was conducted, it was unclear whether the majority of part-time/casual clerical jobs would be located in large or small enterprises. Since 92 percent of the employment growth in Canada between 1978 and 1985 was in firms with less than twenty employees, there was some reason to believe that the increase in part-time clerical employment would be located in the small-business sector.[6] However, the survey evidence pointed in a very different direction. Firms with over 100 employees in the Vancouver area were more than twice as likely to use part-time/casual employees as were firms with less than 100 employees. This suggests that part-time/casual clerical workers are not being employed as the new recruits in the rapidly expanding small-business sector. Rather, they are being used in larger firms to create a two-tiered employment structure based on a core/periphery model.

There is also mounting evidence that the public sector in Canada, as elsewhere in the Western world, is actually taking the lead in this shift to a more contingent clerical work force. In another example from the survey of employers in the Vancouver area, public sector organizations reported a higher proportion of part-time and casual clerical employees than private sector firms did; they were also more likely than private sector firms to have increased their use of these workers from 1983 to 1987.[7] Although there are no statistics available on the overall decline in full-time public sector clerical employment, information available through individual unions confirms this trend. Specifically with respect to the federal and Ontario governments, full-time clerical employment in these two jurisdictions declined by 8.3 percent from 1981 to 1989 compared to an overall increase in full-time clerical employment in the Canadian economy

Table 7.3
Changes in Full-Time Clerical Employment, OPSEU and PSAC, 1981–89

	OPSEU	*PSAC*	*Clerical*
1981	16,955	66,995	1,599,000
1989	14,864	62,137	1,655,000
Difference 1989–81	(2,091)	(4,818)	56,000
Percentage diff.	(12.3)	(7.2)	3.5

Sources: Research Department, OPSEU, 1989; Research Department, Human Resources, Government of Ontario, 1990; Annual reports of the Public Service Commission, 1981 and 1989; and Statistics Canada, *The Labour Force Survey*, Catalogue no. 71-001, 1989 and 1981 annual averages.

of 3.5 percent over the same time period (Table 7.3). Given that overall employment grew more rapidly in Ontario than in any other province, the *absolute decline* in full-time clerical work in Ontario is particularly significant. Over the same period, both the federal and Ontario governments shifted to using more temporary agency clerical workers. Moreover, the combination of computer and telecommunications technology made it possible for these employers to transmit information electronically over long distance and consequently to privatize many more clerical functions. There is growing case study research evidence to show that this trend is becoming increasingly prevalent and that when public sector positions are privatized, there is an erosion in economic status. Wages drop, the work is more likely to be temporary and/or part-time, and there are fewer, if any, benefits for workers in these positions.

The reduction in full-time public sector clerical work and the increase in part-time, temporary agency, and privatized work have very serious implications for women. Traditionally, public sector unions have taken the lead on a whole range of women's issues and have set the standards in terms of equal-pay settlements, paid maternity leave, and benefits for part-time workers. As a result, clerical workers in this sector have been paid better and have had more employment opportunities than clerical workers in other sectors of the Canadian economy. This holds particularly true for women in single-industry towns where employment in the public sector is the only alternative to low-paying jobs in the competitive small-business sector.

Despite the very remarkable changes that have been occurring in the structure of clerical employment over the last ten years, there has been very limited discussion of these changes in the union move-

Table 7.4
Employment by Sex by Industries in Which Canada Is at a Comparative Disadvantage, 1986

Industry	*Males*	*Females*	*Total*	*Percent Female*
Knitting mills	5,560	11,400	16,960	67.2
Clothing	28,085	94,000	122,085	77.0
Leather	5,230	9,210	14,440	63.8
Textiles	38,805	30,945	69,750	44.4
Printing and publishing	88,280	64,580	152,860	42.2

Employment by Sex by Industries in Which Canada Is at a Comparative Advantage, 1986

Industry	*Males*	*Females*	*Total*	*Percent Female*
Wood	122,165	15,450	137,615	11.2
Paper and allied products	111,500	19,885	131,385	15.1
Primary metals	110,310	11,025	121,335	9.1
Petroleum and coal products	19,395	5,385	24,780	21.7
Transportation equipment	184,150	37,185	221,335	16.8

Source: Economic Council of Canada, *Employment Policies for Trade-Sensitive Industries* (Ottawa: Supply and Services Canada, 1988), 19.

ment and/or business community. The consequences of the restructuring of clerical work have not been taken up as a political issue in the same way as the consequences of the restructuring of manufacturing employment have been. In fact, the burden of adjusting to change remains almost entirely the responsibility of the individual women who must cope as best they can with lack of job security, limited access to training and education, and/or the inability to find alternative employment opportunities.

THE RESTRUCTURING OF THE GARMENT AND TEXTILE INDUSTRIES

Like their male counterparts, women in manufacturing industries have experienced an absolute decline in employment in the 1980s.[8] However, because women are located in those industries that are most vulnerable to international competition, there is growing evidence that women in manufacturing will be particularly hurt by the free trade agreement with United States and the upcoming agreement with Mexico. A recent study by the Economic Council of Can-

Table 7.5
Changes in Employment in the Clothing, Knitting, Textile, and Leather Industries, 1971–86

	Total Employment	*Female Employment*	*Percentage of Total Employment Female*
1971	210,490	119,685	56.9
1981	260,080	165,570	63.7
1986	235,640	152,465	64.7
Increase 1981–71	49,590	45,885	92.5
Percentage increase 1981–71	23.6	38.3	–
Decline 1986–81	(24,440)	(13,505)	(44.7)
Percentage decline 1986–81	(9.4)	(7.9)	–

Source: Statistics Canada, *Industry Trends, 1951–1986*, Catalogue no. 93-152, census data (1988).

ada confirms this view.[9] The study points to the fact that women are disproportionately represented in those goods-producing industries that are most at risk, and are underrepresented in those industries in which Canada has a comparative advantage (Table 7.4). Four of the five industries most at risk – textiles, clothing, knitting mills, and leather goods – together represent the second-largest sector of manufacturing employment in Canada and are by far the largest employers of women in manufacturing. By 1986, 65 percent of the work force in these four industries were female (Table 7.5).

In Canada, as in other advanced capitalist countries, the restructuring of the textile and clothing industries began in the early 1960s when clothing production began to shift to low-wage countries in the Third World. In response to the increased competition from cheap imports, Canadian manufacturers have either closed down, moved all or part of their operations to the Third World, or sought out new and cheaper sources of labour in Canada. In the 1970s, Canadian employers increasingly hired women and new immigrants to work in their factories. From 1971 to 1981, of the approximately 49,600 net new jobs in these four industries, 45,900, or 92.5 percent, went to women, many of whom were new immigrants (Table 7.5). Whereas in 1951 only 12 percent of the work force were immigrant women, by 1981 immigrant women represented 36 percent of the work force in the garment trades.[10]

With the onset of the recession in the early 1980s, the pressure of international competition intensified. There was for the first time

Table 7.6
Comparison Unemployment Rate Based on Hours and the "Official" Rate, Male and Female

	1981		*1988*	
	Hours-Based Rate	*Official Rate*	*Hours-Based Rate*	*Official Rate*
Women	10.8	8.3	11.6	8.3
Men	7.8	7.0	8.5	7.4

Source: David Gower, *Perspectives on Labour and Income,* Catalogue no. 75-00E (Spring 1990), Table 1.

an actual decline in employment in these four industries – between 1981 and 1986, 24,440 jobs were lost (Table 7.5). As well as moving operations overseas, employers anxious to find cheaper sources of labour began contracting out work to immigrant subcontractors, who often operated illegal establishments reminiscent of the sweatshops at the turn of the century. In addition, work was subcontracted to individual women living in rural communities and/or working in their own homes who had few alternative sources of income and who were willing to work on a piece rate, often earning less than the minimum wage. It is estimated that in 1981 "in Quebec alone there were 20,000 garment homeworkers, more than the total number of unionized workers in the industry."[11] Not surprisingly, over the 1980s wages in these industries deteriorated as well, dropping from 66.5 percent of the average industrial wage in 1979 to 58.6 percent in 1988.[12]

Although conditions improved slightly during the "boom" years of the mid- to late 1980s, in 1990 the negative effects of the free trade agreement combined with the current recessionary conditions in the Canadian economy resulted in a deterioration in employment conditions in manufacturing industries. From October 1989 to October 1990, 134,000 manufacturing jobs in Canada were lost and the "official" unemployment rate for manufacturing workers jumped from 6.6 percent to 9.5 percent.[13] What is particularly significant is that the unemployment rate for women in manufacturing increased far more dramatically than the unemployment rate for men, substantiating earlier predictions that women would be disproportionately hurt under the terms of the free trade agreement.[14]

Although the government has acknowledged the need for adjustment programs in response to plant shutdowns, these programs

Table 7.7
Real Changes in Male/Female Average Wages, 1979–88

	All Workers	*Male*	*Female*
1979 ($)	21,371	26,691	13,671
1988 ($)	21,200	26,236	15,054
Difference ($)	(171)	(455)	1,383
Percentage change	(0.8)	(1.7)	10.1

Source: Statistics Canada, *Earnings of Men and Women 1988*, Catalogue no. 13-217.
Note: In 1988 constant dollars, median wage includes both full- and part-time work.

have little relevance for women in the garment and textile industries. Most of these programs are voluntary and therefore dependent on the good will of employers. As well, many are only available in English, and are based on a standardized curriculum geared towards white, blue-collar male workers and not immigrant women. Research surveys on the women who lost jobs in the garment industry in the early 1980s indicate that these women tended to be older than the average female labour force participant, to have higher levels of illiteracy (one study found that 42 percent of the women had less than a grade nine education), and to have very limited English skills.[15] It is difficult to imagine how women who lose their jobs as a result of the current recession and the free trade agreement will avoid poverty. The only alternative sources of income available to many of these women – homeworking, part-time and/or minimum-wage jobs in the service sector, unemployment insurance, and welfare – all but ensure a standard of living at or below the poverty line.

OVERALL CHANGES IN WOMEN'S EMPLOYMENT OPPORTUNITIES

If only aggregate statistics are considered, it would appear that the position of women in the labour market improved in the 1980s.[16] The official unemployment rate was the same in 1989 at it was in 1981; real earnings went up on average by more than 10 percent; and there was a shift in employment from traditional female occupations to managerial/professional work (tables 7.6, 7.7, and 7.2). In fact, over 60 percent of all new jobs for women in the 1980s were in what are generally considered the higher-skilled and better-paying managerial/professional occupations, with the most dramatic growth having occurred in the managerial/administrative category.[17]

Table 7.8
Earnings Gap for Women Working in Managerial and Clerical/Sales/Service Occupations, 1981–87*

	1981 *($)*	*1987* *($)*	*Percentage Increase*
Managerial/clerical	6,091	7,537	23.7
Managerial/service	10,226	13,297	29.1
Managerial/sales	7,760	7,482	−3.6

Source: Statistics Canada, *Women in Canada*, Catalogue no. 89-503E, 2d ed. (1990).
* These comparisons are for full-time workers only and the earnings are in 1987 constant dollars.

However, a more careful reading of the labour force statistics suggests that the gains made by women are very uneven. While some women have been integrated into the mainstream of economic activity, others have been increasingly marginalized. To take one example, if comparisons are made only for full-time women workers from 1981 to 1987, the earnings gap between women working in managerial/administrative occupations and those employed in clerical and service jobs increased by 24 percent and 29 percent respectively (Table 7.8). In fact, while salaries for women working in managerial and administrative jobs increased by 5.8 percent during this period, women working in service jobs (the lowest-paid female employees, apart from female agricultural workers) experienced a decline in real earnings of 10 percent (Table 7.9).

The increasing inequality among women becomes even more visible when the relative increase in full-time work is compared with that of part-time/temporary work across occupations. Whereas 44 percent of the job growth for women in clerical, sales, service, and processing occupations in the 1980s was part-time, part-time work only accounted for 17 percent of growth in managerial and professional work (Table 7.10). In fact, in the first half of the decade, there was an absolute decline in full-time employment in clerical, sales, and processing occupations: *all* the job growth in these occupations was part-time.[18] In 1988 women who worked less than full-time, full-year, earned on average less than $8,000 a year, indicating clearly that the lack of access to full-time, full-year employment all but ensures an income level below the poverty line (Table 7.11).

As a consequence, for women who do not have the experience or educational background to qualify for managerial and professional work, the likelihood of being marginalized in part-time work that

Table 7.9
Change in Male and Female Earnings by Occupation, 1981–87

	Women's Earnings as a % of Male Earnings 1981	*Women's Earnings as a % of Male Earnings 1987*	*% Change Female Earnings 1987–81*	*% Change Male Earnings 1987–81*
Man./Admin	57.9	64.1	+5.8	−4.4
Natural sc.	68.0	69.7	+1.9	−0.7
Soc. science	69.8	62.1	−0.8	+11.5
Teaching	76.5	78.1	−0.2	−2.3
Med./Health	50.8	53.5	+7.6	−2.3
Clerical	66.7	68.9	+0.1	−3.1
Sales	59.6	62.6	+10.0	+4.8
Service	57.4	52.9	−10.1	−2.5
Processing	54.6	62.9	+15.1	−0.1
Product fab.	56.8	57.8	+1.0	−0.7

Source: Statistics Canada. *Women in Canada*, Catalogue no. 89-503E.
Note: These comparisons are for full-time workers only and the earning are in 1987 constant dollars.

pays poverty wages or of being unemployed increased dramatically in the 1980s. Although it is true that women with limited education have always experienced higher levels of unemployment than women with university degrees, the increase in unemployment in the 1980s has been remarkably polarized. From 1981 to 1988, unemployment rates for women with less than a grade nine education have increased eighteen times as much as unemployment rates for women with a post-secondary certificate, diploma, or university degree (Table 7.12). As the authors of a recent report on women and poverty note, "low levels of education are particularly important in explaining why only 12 percent of poor women under 65 were employed on a full-time, year-round basis in 1987, while 36 percent had less regular jobs and 52 percent stayed home."[19]

These statistics on the unequal distribution of unemployment by educational attainment reflect the shift in employment growth from traditional, lower-skilled female occupations in clerical, sales, services, and processing jobs to managerial and professional work. Several government studies argue that these trends are likely to continue into the next century. According to projections from Canada Employment and Immigration, 64 percent of new jobs to the

Table 7.10
Growth in Part-Time Employment by Occupation, 1981–89

	Percentage of Part-Time New Jobs
All occupations	26.2
Managerial/Prof.	16.8
Clerical	48.7
Sales	37.9
Service	42.7
Processing	40.0

Source: Statistics Canada, 1989 and 1981 annual averages, Catalogue no. 71-001. These figures are only for part-time workers (workers who work less than 30 hours a month) and do not include women who work part year.

year 2000 will require some post-secondary education compared to only 44 percent of jobs in 1986.[20]

These figures suggest that the relationship between educational stratification and economic restructuring should be an increasingly important focus of feminist analysis and policy development.

THE IMPACT OF GOVERNMENT POLICIES

Government strategies have contributed to the erosion in the economic well-being of low-wage and part-time workers over the decade. Rather than increasing the minimum wage and/or improving benefits and pay rates for part-time workers, provincial and federal governments in Canada have developed strategies that have the effect of lessening the bargaining power of minimum-wage and part-time workers.

Wage subsidy, income supplementation, and job orientation programs have been introduced to encourage women at home and women on social assistance to seek work in the marginal economy. The federal government's Canadian Job Strategy program is a case in point. This program has focused primarily on providing short-term job orientation programs, rather than longer-term skills training. In fact, over a three-year period, from 1987 to 1989, federal government spending on skills training declined by 40 percent, while the purchase of courses such as basic life skills, job orientation, and language training more than doubled.[21] The training programs available for women encourage single-parent mothers on welfare and women at home to return to the work force by providing them with three months of on-the-job experience and three months of in-school preparation. These programs lead women to believe that as

Table 7.11
Average Female Earnings, Full-Time, Part-Time, Part-Year, 1988

	Full Year	*Part Year*
Mostly full time	$21,918	$8,137
Mostly part time	$11,615	$4,320

Source: Statistics Canada, *Earnings of Men and Women,* 1988 annual averages, Catalogue no. 13-217. The average salary for women *not* working full time, full year, 1988, was $7,991.

new and/or returning labour market entrants they simply need to enrol in job orientation programs and that they can then move up the occupational hierarchy on the basis of years of experience and seniority. What these programs actually do is increase the female labour supply available for work in low-wage, part-time, and casual employment in the rapidly expanding service sector. As a result, there is less pressure on governments to raise the minimum wage or to improve pay and benefit provisions for part-time and casual workers. While these training programs may serve the interests of low-wage employers, they do little to help women make the transition from entry-level positions to more highly skilled and generally better-paying jobs in administrative, professional, and/or scientific occupations, which increasingly require post-secondary educational qualifications.

Similarly, several provincial welfare departments have initiated a variety of income supplementation programs in recent years in order to give single parents the incentive to work in low-wage, casual, and/or part-time jobs. For example, in British Columbia and Ontario, regulations regarding income exemptions and medical benefits were recently changed to remove some of the barriers in the welfare system that prevented single-parent mothers from seeking work in low-wage occupations. Similar reforms in Quebec have been particularly comprehensive. The Parental Wage Assistance Program (PWA), introduced in 1989, increased the differential between the incomes of low-wage earners and the benefits of welfare recipients by providing low-wage earners with a direct grant and a tax deduction for child care. As Eric Shragge points out, this policy

> lends legitimacy to the payment of wages that allow a standard of living that is well below the poverty line. The government can keep the minimum wage low by arguing that it is supplementing the income of those with children. This measure thus acts to reduce costs to employers. In addition, in an era

Table 7.12
Unemployment Rates for Women by Educational Level

	1981 (%)	*1988* (%)	*Change 1988–81* (%)
Less than grade nine	9.9	11.7	+1.8
High school	9.4	9.7	+0.3
Some post-secondary	7.6	8.0	+0.4
Post-secondary diploma or certificate	5.7	5.8	+0.1
University degree	4.7	4.8	+0.1

Source: Statistics Canada, *Women in Canada,* Catalogue no. 89-503E, Table 19.

of free trade and international economic competition, the economic climate of Quebec is enhanced and it may be more attractive to new capital if wages can be kept low.[22]

THE INCREASED IMPORTANCE OF SKILLS TRAINING

The emphasis on policies that increase the supply of low-wage, low-skilled labour runs counter to the mounting evidence that an increased supply of skilled workers, together with investment in education and training, is essential if Canada is to maintain productivity levels in the face ever-increasing international competition. Since 1989, the debate on skills training has intensified with the publication of several major policy documents. They argue that globalization, technological change, and the shift to the service sector represent fundamentally new structural challenges with respect to labour force development. The reports are unanimous in their opinion that greater analytical, problem-solving, and communication skills will be required by Canadian workers.[23] However, they contain little discussion of where and how women fit into this new picture.

At present Ontario's Premier's Council report is seen by many business, labour, and government leaders as offering the most promising model for skills training and labour market adjustment with its proposal for a joint union and management board and sectoral committees, and its emphasis on generic skills training. However, the authors of the report focused quite specifically on the immediate need for workplace training to increase productivity in the manufacturing industries that have only recently been integrated into the North American market. Absent is any discussion of employment-equity provisions in terms of access and representation. The rec-

Table 7.13
Changing Patterns in Employment Growth, Male and Female, 1961, 1971, 1981, and 1989

	1961–71 (%)	*1971–81 (%)*	*1981–89 (%)*
All occupations	24.6	39.9	13.5
Managerial/Professional	34.7	33.9	69.9

Source: Statistics Canada, 1989 and 1981 annual averages, Catalogue no. 71-001; Statistics Canada, *Occupational Trends 1961–1986*, Catalogue no. 93-151, 1988; and Statistics Canada, *Earnings of Men and Women*, Catalogue no. 13-217, 1988.

ommendations in the report specifically rule out the possibility of incorporating existing government training programs targeted at the "disadvantaged" despite the fact that, at present, these programs in Ontario are aimed primarily at integrating youth and low-income women into low-paid service sector jobs.[24] In effect, the mechanisms established through the Premier's Council replicate the polarization in the labour market within the training system. They create a new and improved system of training for core workers in manufacturing industries but fall short of challenging the existing job-preparation programs targeted at youth and low-income women.

Related to this is the failure of the report to come to terms with the dramatic shift from clerical and production work to managerial and professional employment that has become the characteristic feature of the labour market in the 1980s. In Canada, 70 percent of total employment growth from 1981 to 1989 was in managerial and professional work – a very dramatic change from the two previous decades when managerial and professional employment accounted for approximately one-third of all employment growth (Table 7.13). According to Canada Employment and Immigration's own statistics, close to 50 percent of new jobs between 1986 and the year 2000 will require seventeen or more years of education.[25]

In terms of the labour supply, the majority of new labour market entrants in the 1990s, as in the 1980s, will be women. Moreover, changing demographics – the decline in the youth population and the ageing of the work force – point to the need for an increasing emphasis on retraining adult women, as well as men, to fill these new higher-skilled positions. As a consequence of these changes, it is now more widely accepted in business and government circles that employment equity is an economic necessity and not just a desirable social goal. However, there is no employment-equity legislation in

Table 7.14
Changes in Women's Employment by Occupation, 1981–89

	1981 (%)	*1989* (%)
Clerical	34.3	30.5
Sales	10.1	9.9
Service	18.3	17.0
Man/Prof.	24.7	31.6

Source: Statistics Canada, *Labour Force Survey*, annual averages, 1981 and 1989.

Canada to date that integrates employment-equity principles with the provision of education and/or on-the-job training. Nor is there a linkage between employment equity and initiatives for democratizing the workplace that could include, for example, demands for more participatory forms of work organization or the recognition of experience in lieu of formal qualifications.

Research studies show that women have been consistently disadvantaged in terms of gaining access to on-the-job training.[26] For example, the results of a study conducted by the Ontario Ministry of Skills Development indicated that workers in clerical occupations received less on-the-job training than did managerial, professional, and blue-collar workers. Other research shows that the training that is offered to clerical workers is often available only in the evenings or on weekends, leaving women with family responsibilities at a distinct disadvantage.

The demographic changes and the shortage of skilled labour in the 1990s may provide an opening for a dialogue with business and government about the social support mechanisms and the educational programs that would be required to help adult women with child-care responsibilities gain access to higher-skilled employment opportunities. Mandatory requirements for child care in the workplace and in educational institutions, the provision of training during working hours, and paid educational leave provisions that are funded under a training tax and include an employment-equity clause are some of the possible legislative initiatives that would lead in this direction. In addition, government-funded training programs that recognize experience in lieu of formal qualifications and assist women in moving from service and clerical work to para-professional and technical occupations would ensure both a more equitable as well as a more efficient use of public training dollars.

CONCLUSION

More progressive training and education policies that work in women's interests cannot by themselves reverse the trend towards polarization in the labour market. Although proactive labour market policies are an increasingly important aspect of our industrial strategy, other social and economic initiatives are needed to ensure an adequate supply of high-quality jobs. However, the realization of this broader policy framework is more remote than ever given the integration of Canada in the North American economy. The so-called imperatives of global competition and technological change that gave rise to the Premier's Council report set very clear limitations on the scope of decision-making in terms of labour market policy; export-led growth, the abandonment of full employment policies, and pressure to lower costs appear as given in the equation. The only area in which the government seems able and willing to set policy is in relation to skills training and adjustment programs. The proposals for improving the training and educational opportunities for low-income women that are presented in this paper are intended to push the limits of what can be achieved in this context. In this respect, they must be understood as only one aspect of a longer-term struggle that challenges the underlying logic of market-driven economic development.

NOTES

1 Paul Adler, "Rethinking Skill Requirements of the New Boston Technologies" (Working paper, Harvard Business School, October 1983); Eileen Appelbaum, "Technology and Work Organization in the Insurance Industry," *I.L.R. Report* 23, no. 1 (1985); and Marcy Cohen and Margaret White, "The Impact of Computerization on the Clerical Work Process: Some Bargaining Implications" (Unpublished paper, Distance Education, Women's Studies, Simon Fraser University, Burnaby, BC, 1988).

2 Eli Ginsberg, Thierry J. Noyelles, and M. Stanback, *Technology and Employment: Concepts and Clarifications* (London: Westview Press, 1986).

3 Marcy Cohen and Margaret White, "Impact of Computerization."

4 Statistics Canada, *The Labour Force Survey*, Catalogue no. 71-001 (1989, 1981).

5 Cohen and White, "Impact of Computerization," 22.

6 Pat Thompson, *Job Vacancies in the Independent Business Sector: Part II –*

Provincial Analysis: British Columbia (Toronto: Canadian Federation of Independent Business, 1987), 2.

7 Cohen and White, "Impact of Computerization," 22. The five years that are referred to in the study were from 1983 to 1987.

8 Canadian Labour Market Productivity Centre, "Labour Market Developments," *Quarterly Labour Market Productivity Review*, Spring/Summer 1990, 14.

9 Economic Council of Canada, *Adjustment Policies for Trade Sensitive Industries* (Ottawa, 1988), 19.

10 Ann Porter, "International Restructuring in the Clothing Industry: The Implications for Women in Canada" (Unpublished paper, March 1989), 30–5.

11 Ibid., 46.

12 Statistics Canada, *Employment Earnings and Hours*, Catalogue no. 72-002 (1983–86, 1988).

13 Statistics Canada, *The Labour Force Survey*, Catalogue no. 71-001 (October 1989, October 1990).

14 From October 1989 to October 1990, the unemployment rate for women in manufacturing increased from 8.9 to 12.9 percent, while the unemployment rate for men increased from 5.6 percent to 8.1 percent.

15 Ann Porter, "International Restructuring," 54.

16 In order to examine the labour market changes over an entire business cycle, the statistics reference in this sector covers the period just prior to the last recession in 1981 to the last year of the current expansion in 1989.

17 Although women are still underrepresented in managerial and professional work, the proportion of women employed in these occupations increased from 24.7 percent of employed women in 1981 to 31.6 percent in 1989. At the same time there has been a decline in the proportion of women employed in the traditional clerical, sales, and service occupations – in 1981, 62.7 percent of all women in the paid work force were employed in these occupations compared to 57.0 percent in 1989 (Table 7.14).

18 Cohen and White, "Impact of Computerization," Table 4, 46.

19 National Council on Welfare, *Women and Poverty Revisited* (Ottawa: Minister of Supply and Services, 1990), 21.

20 Advisory Council on Adjustment, *Adjusting to Win* (Ottawa: Minister of Supply and Services, March 1989), 24.

21 Canadian Labour Market Productivity Centre, "Update of Funds in Federal Expenditure on Training and Enrolment in Federal Training Programs," *Quarterly Labour Market Productivity Review*, Fall 1990, 16.

22 Eric Shragge, "Welfare Reform: Quebec Style or Poor Law Reform Act, 1988?" *Canadian Review of Social Policy* 22 (1988): 17–18.

23 Economic Council of Canada, *Good Jobs, Bad Jobs: Employment in the Service Economy* (Ottawa: Supply and Services Canada, 1990); Advisory Council on Adjustment, *Adjusting to Win*; Canada Employment and Immigration, *Success in the Works* (1989); and Ontario Premier's Council, *People and Skills in the New Global Economy* (1990).

24 Ontario Federation of Labour, "A Comment and Review on the Report of the Premier's Council on Education, Training and Adjustment," July 1990, 19.

25 Advisory Council on Adjustment, *Adjusting to Win*, 24.

26 Ontario Ministry of Skills Development, *Training Women in the Workplace* (12 June 1987); Employment and Immigration Canada, *The Canadian Job Strategy: A Review* (July 1988); and M. Corcoran and G. Duncan, "Work History, Labour Force Attachment and Earnings Differences between Races and Sexes," *Journal of Human Resources* 14, no. 1 (1979).

8 The Disappearing Middle

GORDON BETCHERMAN

INTRODUCTION

A variety of developments, including economic globalization, technological innovation, and a changing work-force composition, are reshaping the labour market in all industrialized nations. Indeed, a recent study of emerging employment trends undertaken by the Economic Council of Canada (ECC) found that the labour market in this country has been transformed in fundamental ways in recent years.[1] Those changes are likely to have major consequences for Canadian workers and their unions and employers. They will also have important consequences for a wide range of public policies affecting education, training, labour adjustment, employment standards, and social assistance.

Overall, the council's research painted a picture of a "new" labour market where jobs are being created in different ways, employment relationships are being revamped, new skills are in demand, and compensation patterns are changing. One of the most evident characteristics of this labour market is the concentratration of employment creation in the service sector. Over the 1970s and 1980s, about nine out of every ten new jobs have been in the service industries. While goods industries were still the dominant employer in this country as recently as the 1950s, now over 70 percent of Canadians work in services.

In some ways, the changing nature of employment is directly due to the growth of services. For example, we have found that services are an overwhelmingly urban phenomenon. To a disproportionate degree, service industries – particularly the most "dynamic" ones like financial and business services – create jobs in our largest cities. The increasing employment difficulties experienced by Canadian workers outside these centres, then, reflect the predominance of service jobs now and the locational patterns of service industries.

Other trends we have observed, however, are pervasive in the sense that they are taking place throughout the economy, that is, in the goods sector as well as the service sector. One example is the proliferation of nonstandard employment forms. While the conventional notion of a "job" is a full-time, relatively permanent attachment between an employer and a worker, it turns out that virtually one-half of the employment created in the 1980s was nonstandard in the sense that it departed from this traditional relationship. Together, the nonstandard forms, which include part-time, short-term, temporary, and temporary-help agency employment, as well as "own-account" self-employment, now describe the work arrangement for roughly 30 percent of employed Canadians. While there are a number of factors – including the increasing participation of women and young people in the labour market – behind the proliferation of these employment forms, it is clear that the growth of nonstandard work reflects a basic change in the types of jobs that employers are generating.

THE DECLINING MIDDLE

One of the major findings of the Economic Council's research, and undoubtedly the one that has attracted the most attention, concerns the evidence we found of a "declining middle" in the distribution of earnings in Canada over the past two decades. In recent years, income polarization has become a major issue, first among academics and more recently among policy-makers and the public. This is particularly the case in the United States, where there is now general agreement that the proportion of the work force in employment with middle-level earnings has decreased, at least since the mid-1970s, and that the relative numbers of workers in high- and low-paying jobs have increased correspondingly. Many studies have also found that this shrinking-middle pattern also characterizes the trend in the distribution of total income (i.e., including income from investments and transfers, as well as employment) in the United States.[2]

The attention given to the polarization of American incomes reflects the potentially wide-ranging consequences of such a development. Indeed, there are likely to be economic, social, and political implications of a declining middle if it turns out to be more than a transitory phenomenon. Polarization means more people with low incomes and, therefore, more poverty and greater pressures on the transfer system; this is particularly troublesome in the present context (both in the US and Canada) of large budgetary deficits and growing public debt. Furthermore, for those in the "bad job," or low-income, sector, the possibility of mobility and greater income security through employment diminishes in a polarized labour market. Ultimately, economic segmentation such as this runs the risk of becoming social and political segmentation, where preservation of the status quo motivates the "haves" and alienation from the mainstream describes the "have-nots."

Canadian researchers turned to the issue of polarization later than their American counterparts. In the last few years, however, analysis in this area has been gaining momentum. Overall, there has been less consensus in the Canadian research than in the work done in the United States. Some studies, particularly the earlier ones, have been inconclusive, showing either modest polarization or stability in the distribution.[3] Some of the more recent analyses in this country, however, do find evidence of a declining middle in earnings.[4]

The Economic Council's study of Canadian income distribution trends was carried out in conjunction with Statistics Canada. Our research was based on data from the Survey of Consumer Finances for 1967, 1973, 1981, and 1986. The major conclusion from that analysis is that the earnings distribution of the Canadian work force became increasingly polarized over the two-decade period we considered. Figure 8.1 shows the evolution of the declining middle since 1967. In each of the years shown, we have calculated the median earnings level and identified a "middle-income" band stretching from 25 percent above this median to 25 percent below. We then allocated workers into the high-, middle-, and lower-earner groups, depending on their employment income. In 1967, the middle group represented about 27 percent of the work force; by 1986, only 21.5 percent were in this category.

While Figure 8.1 presents the result of one measure of distributional change, the declining-middle result is a robust one in the sense that the same conclusion was reached by using a range of quite different measures. We also found that the polarization in the earnings of individuals applies to families as well: the middle-earner group, defined as above, declined from 34.4 percent of all families in 1967 to 29.6 percent in 1986. It should be noted, however, that the distribution of total income for families appears to have been

Figure 8.1
The Declining Middle, 1967–86

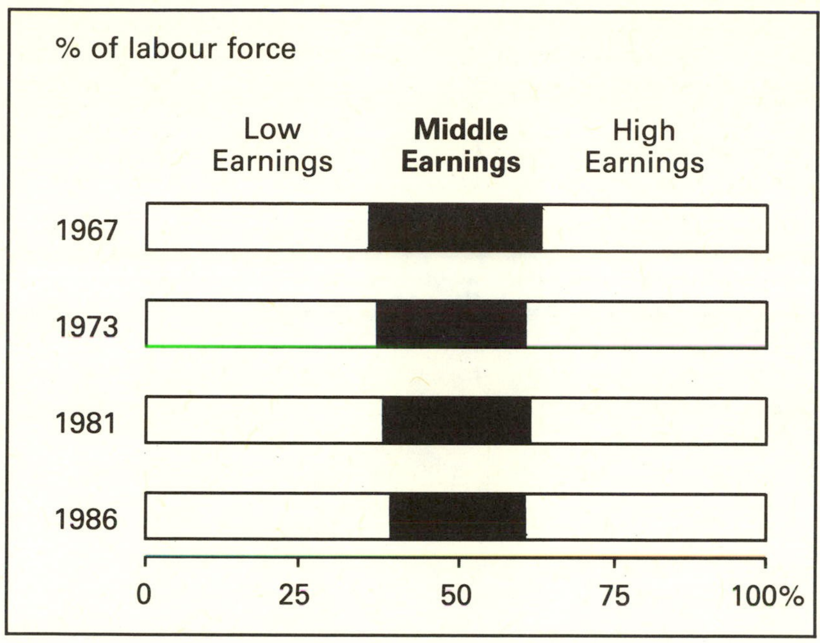

Source: Economic Council of Canada, *Good Jobs, Bad Jobs: Employment in the Service Economy* (Ottawa: Supply and Services Canada, 1990).

more stable; after some shrinking of the middle group between 1967 and 1973, there has been little change since. Apparently, non-employment income – specifically transfers – has been offsetting some of the increasing disparity in earnings.

The important question emerging from this declining-middle story is whether the observed polarization is merely a phenomenon of the two-decade period that the analysis covered or whether it is part of a more permanent, longer-run trend. Looking backwards first, we examined Survey of Consumer Finances data that were available between 1951 and 1967. Although the nature of the database in these early years permits only limited analysis, it does appear that the distribution of employment income was relatively stable, at least through the 1950s to the mid-1960s.

Conjectures about future trends depend on what caused the polarization during the period when it was observed. Unfortunately, arriving at an empirically based emplanation turns out to be a difficult task, largely because of the numerous and complex problems associated with identifying, disentangling, and measuring the various potential underlying forces.

WHAT HAS CAUSED THE DECLINING MIDDLE?

Conventional explanations for the declining middle typically can be grouped into three categories: cyclical, supply side, and demand side. The cyclical hypothesis argues that earnings distributions are heavily influenced by business-cycle conditions: that is, growth in solid, middle-income jobs is strongest during good times; as labour market conditions worsen and unemployment rises, however, the wage bargaining power of labour declines and much of the job creation that does occur is therefore in low-wage employment, with only those in the strongest position able to maintain their earning power.

While there is clearly a cyclical element to income distribution patterns, this explanation is, at best, only a partial one for the earnings polarization that has taken place in recent decades. A number of American studies that have controlled for the business conditions factor have still found evidence of a declining middle.[5] In our research, the selection of the four years for analysis was based on identifying years that occupied relatively similar positions in the business cycle. This methodology, then, allowed us to make distributional comparisons over time on an essentially cycle-neutral basis.

If the cyclical explanation is no more than a partial one, then we are led to the proposition that the declining middle has been the result of changes that are more structural in nature. The various structural contentions have incorporated both supply and demand arguments. The supply-side hypothesis attributes the polarization to the shifting composition of the work force that has taken place over the past two decades. The essential argument here is that the increasing participation of women in the work force and the entry into the labour market of the large numbers of young people in the baby-boom generation have shifted the shape of the earnings distribution. These two groups tend to have relatively poor wages, and as a result, the contention is that the changing labour force make-up has skewed the distribution from the middle and towards the lower end.

It does turn out that the changing composition of the work force has had some effect on the distribution. To assess the impact of this factor, we carried out a series of "standardization" exercises in which we observed what would happen to the 1986 earnings distribution if the labour force was frozen at its 1967 make-up (in terms of age,

Table 8.1
Work Force Share of Individuals in the Middle-Earner Group, by Age and Sex, 1967 and 1986

	Share of the Labour Force in the Middle-Earner Group	
	1967 (%)	*1986 (%)*
Age		
Under 25 years	18.1	15.9
25–34 years	38.1	27.6
35–49 years	33.9	25.6
50+ years	28.6	23.5
Sex		
Males	35.9	24.8
Females	23.7	21.3
All workers	26.8	21.5

Source: Based on Survey of Consumer Finances.

sex, and proportion employed in nonstandard jobs). According to our analysis, whereas the middle group (as defined above) actually declined 5.3 percentage points between 1967 and 1986 (26.8 percent of the work force to 21.5 percent), the decrease would have been 3.5 percentage points – or about one-third less – if the make-up of the labour force had not changed over the two-decade period.

As this estimate suggests, then, women and young people coming into the labour market has been a factor, but not a major one. These compositional changes do not explain the great part of the decline in the middle. Nor do they explain why the earnings distribution *within* every labour force group – all age categories and both males and females – became more polarized between 1967 and 1986 (Table 8.1). In fact, as the table indicates, the polarization was actually most significant among the traditional worker groups, men and those in the prime-age categories.

The other structural hypothesis focuses on the demand side. It argues that the declining middle is the product of the transition of the industrial structure from the traditional goods-based profile to one dominated by service industries. The contention here is that the traditional structure had a heavy concentration of medium-wage jobs, while the emerging one is oriented towards the high and low end, with less in between.

This hypothesis has a lot of intuitive appeal and, at first blush, evidence to support it. Certainly, the structural transformation that it assumes has been striking in Canada over the period when the declining middle was observed. The sectoral transition and the concentration of new employment in services since the 1960s have already been noted. Moreover, as Figure 8.2 shows, the shift from goods to services has been a shift from a medium-wage sector to industries that have either relatively high or relatively low average wages. Figure 8.2 organizes the economy into four sectors, with each representing roughly one-quarter of total employment: the goods sector includes primary industries, manufacturing, and construction; non-market services comprise public administration, health, education, and social services; the dynamic services are transportation, communication, utilities, wholesale trade, financial services, and business services; and traditional services include retail trade, accommodation and food, and a range of personal services. The three service groups that have accounted for virtually all of the employment growth have average wages either well above the all-industry mean (non-market and dynamic services) or very much below (traditional services). On the other hand, the declining sector, goods, is close to the overall average.

The problem with pictures sketched out with aggregate data is that they often miss important things that are going on. And the most important thing taking place on the demand side has not been the shifting industrial structure but, rather, the growing polarization *within* industries. When we just look at the goods sector, or when we just look at the service sector, we see a declining middle of roughly similar magnitude between 1967 and 1986.

Overall, then, where do the traditional hypotheses lead us? The changing work-force composition has played some role, although not a major one, in the earnings polarization. Other than that, it appears that the conventional explanations – be they cyclical or structural – do not explain a great deal of the declining middle.

ALTERNATIVE HYPOTHESES

The data present a major problem for interpretive purposes. The conventional hypotheses have generally been the ones that are tested, in no small part, because the data are there to do so. Our analysis suggests, however, that they are not subtle enough to capture the most important observation emerging from the data – that is, the pervasiveness of the polarization within virtually any subpopulation we choose to isolate. It seems likely, then, that there are forces within

Figure 8.2
Wage Differences across Sectors, 1986

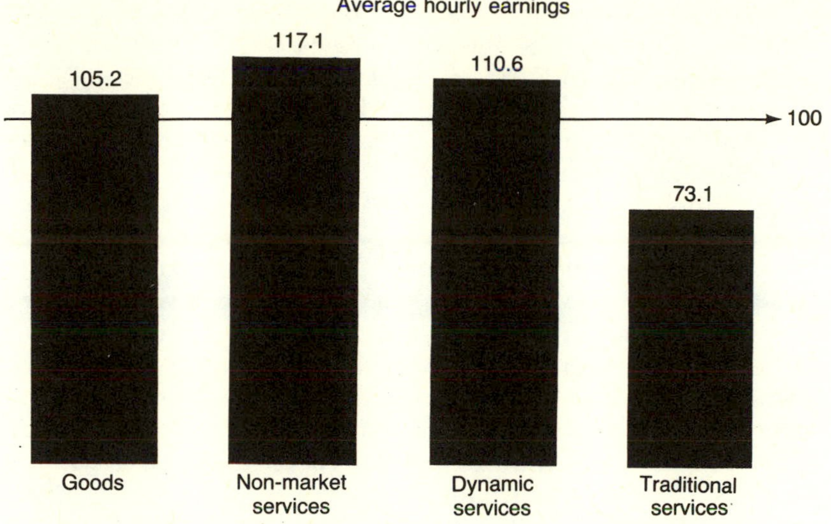

Source: Based on Labour Market Activity Survey.

industries and perhaps even within firms that are driving the declining middle.

What might some less conventional hypotheses be that could explain the polarization and its pervasiveness? While candidate explanations may not be as easily tested with available data as the more conventional blunt hypotheses, nevertheless it is clearly time to broaden the analysis, given the limitations of traditional approaches. None of the conventional explanations really considers the possibility that, within industries (and likely within firms), the employment structure may be in the process of being increasingly transformed into a "good-job/bad-job" duality. And that, for a variety of reasons, the bargaining power of workers in the good-job sector is being enhanced while it is diminishing for those in the bad-job sector. It seems plausible that these developments may be occurring because of economic globalization, technological change, and the diminished role of unions, particularly in the fast-growth service industries.

The potential role of globalization was considered by Robert Reich in a 1989 article, "As the World Turns."[6] Essentially, Reich argues that because of advances in technology and business organization, the US (read North American) economy has ceased to exist as a system of production independent from the rest of the world. As North American workers take part in an increasingly globalized labour market, they are subject to global supply-and-demand pressures. Individuals skilled in technology and information (the good-job sector) are in growing demand around the world, but their supply still comes from relatively few countries, including the US (and Canada); the result, then, is rising wages for those with these skills. On the other hand, North Americans who do not have these sorts of skills and who find themselves in more routine production or service jobs (the bad-job sector) directly or indirectly face a labour market where supply can increasingly originate anywhere, with the result that their wages are being bid downwards.

Indeed, a relevant issue about which we do not have much evidence concerns the effects of the new technologies on wages. One thesis, consistent with what Reich is arguing, is that we are creating a scenario of "technoexperts" and "technopeasants." My own research does offer some support for this hypothesis. On the basis of data from about 1,000 companies across Canada, I was able to observe how wage relationships in firms where computer-based technologies were being introduced differed from firms where no innovation was taking place.[7] According to this database, the differential between the wages of high-skill workers (i.e., in professional and technical occupations) and less-skilled workers (i.e., in office occupations) widened substantially over the 1980–85 period in firms that were introducing computer-based technological change at the time; on the other hand, the premium paid for the highly skilled employees remained essentially constant over these years in firms that did not innovate with new technologies.

Another factor meriting some consideration is the changing nature of wage determination and, in particular, the role of unions in this process. While the fact that wages tend to be higher under collective bargaining is well known, the union effect on the distribution of wages is less familiar. Traditionally, unions have been a strong centralizing force in terms of compensation; where wages are not bargained collectively, they tend to be more widely distributed towards the high and the low end.

While Canada has not experienced the unionization declines that have taken place in the United States, the pressure unions have been under in this country should not be ignored. In the private sector, Canadian unionization has been falling. Indeed, some of the most important industries in terms of employment growth have single-digit, or close to single-digit, union density rates. For example, just 13 percent of the work force in wholesale and retail trade were unionized in 1986; 9 percent in finance, insurance, and real estate; 7 percent in business services; 8 percent in personal services; and

9 percent in accommodation and food.[8] As well, collective-bargaining coverage appears to be lowest in industries where a lot of high technology has been introduced.[9] In the growth areas of the economy, then, there is reason to believe that the wage-determination process is less influenced by the centralizing force of unions than has been the case in the traditional sectors of the economy.

CONCLUSION

What does all of this mean for the likelihood of the continued erosion of the middle in the future? On the one hand, the ageing of the work force is bound to help at least a little bit; much of the low-wage employment generated in the 1980s was filled by young people, and as their relative numbers continue to fall, it can be expected that wages in these jobs will be bid up somewhat. On the other hand, if there is anything to my speculations, the closely related forces of globalization and technological change may well continue to be polarizing forces. While economic trends may not be acting in the direction of equality, that does not mean that nothing can be done to influence the earnings distribution. Indeed, changes both within and outside the Canadian workplace could be effective.

First, education and training are critical. As global competition accelerates, high-cost countries like Canada cannot compete on the basis of low wages. Therefore, if we are to maintain our standard of living, we must be at least as productive as other countries. Only by being highly productive will Canadian industry get as many of the "good jobs" that are available worldwide as possible. Obviously, what economists call human-capital development is essential, since education and training are directly tied to productivity growth, competitiveness, and, ultimately, incomes of Canadian workers. The importance of this issue means that, as a society, we must place a very high priority on our education system; there must be a far greater commitment to training in industry; and we must develop public policies that open rather than close doors for workers who want to upgrade their skills or retrain.

Education and training, though, are not panaceas. In addition, the income security of workers in nonstandard employment must be enhanced. Many of these jobs are tenuous, poorly compensated, and not well protected. Stronger policies are required to support people with nonstandard work arrangements. Traditionally, employment standards and benefits were designed with a stereotypic image of a worker as a male employed full-time in the goods sector.

Some progress has been made, but still there is an inadequate degree of protection for employees in part-time, short-term, or temporary positions. These workers – many of them females in the service sector – often have an ongoing attachment to the labour force but, for one reason or another, are not able to secure full-time or more permanent positions. Employer-sponsored benefits should be available for these employees on a pro-rated basis. And, in light of the proliferation of different employment forms, diversity should be recognized in the design of public benefit programs and employment standards.

Organized labour also has a role to play. Certainly, polarization is likely to be alleviated to the extent that unions are able to organize high-technology and service industries, and also the small-firm sector. Unions also have to develop strategies for influencing how technological and organizational changes are introduced into the workplace. To achieve the productivity gains that are necessary, innovations are required in Canadian industry. However, they need not be introduced in ways that polarize the work force. Different approaches to how technological and organizational changes are implemented can have very important differences in terms of their distributional impacts. Unions have to be more active in developing innovation strategies that contribute to the interest of all workers while supporting the economic objectives of productivity growth and competitiveness.

Finally, a strong Canadian economy is critical. Although structural factors underline the earnings polarization we have observed in this country, it is true that the wage distribution becomes more unequal in lean years. High rates of economic growth cannot help but contribute to less hardship for the Canadian work force.

NOTES

1 For a summary, see the Economic Council of Canada, *Good Jobs, Bad Jobs: Employment in the Service Economy* (Ottawa: Supply and Services Canada, 1990). The detailed research is reported in the Economic Council of Canada, *Employment in the Service Economy* (Ottawa: Supply and Services Canada, 1991).

2 For a review of the extensive US literature on earnings and income polarization, see Garry W. Loveman and Chris Tilly, "Good Jobs or Bad Jobs? Evaluating the American Job Creation Experience," *International Labour Review* 127, no. 5 (1988); and Charles M. Beach, "Dol-

lars and Dreams: A Reduced Middle Class?" *Journal of Human Resources* 24, no. 1 (1988).

3 For example, Norm Leckie, "The Declining Middle and Technological Change: Trends in the Distribution of Employment Income in Canada, 1971–84," Economic Council of Canada, Discussion Paper No. 342 (Ottawa, 1988); Michael C. Wolfson, "Stasis amid Change: Income Inequality in Canada, 1965–1983," *Review of Income and Wealth*, series 32, no. 4 (December 1986).

4 See Garnett Picot, John Myles, and Ted Wannell, "Good Jobs/Bad Jobs and the Declining Middle, 1967–1986," Statistics Canada, Analytical Studies Branch, Research Paper No. 26 (Ottawa, 1990); and Catherine J. McWatters and Charles M. Beach, "Factors behind the Changes in the Family Income Distribution and the Share of the Middle Class," *Relations industrielles* 45, no. 1 (1990).

5 See, for example, Gary Burtless, "Earnings Inequality over the Business and Demographic Cycles," in Gary Burtless, ed., *A Future of Lousy Jobs? The Changing Structure of U.S. Wages* (Washington, D.C.: Brookings Institution, 1990).

6 Robert Reich, "As the World Turns," *New Republic*, 1 May 1989.

7 The data source is the Working with Technology Survey. For a summary of the results, see Gordon Betcherman and Kathryn McMullen, *Working with Technology: A Survey of Automation in Canada*, Report prepared for the Economic Council of Canada (Ottawa: Supply and Services Canada, 1986).

8 Based on data from the Labour Market Activity Survey. See Gordon Betcherman, "Union Membership in a Service Economy," in Michel Grant, ed., *Industrial Relations Issues for the 1990s* (Proceedings of the Twenty-sixth Conference of the Canadian Industrial Relations Association, June 1989).

9 Economic Council of Canada, *Innovation and Jobs in Canada* (Ottawa: Supply and Services Canada, 1987).

9 Pay Equity: Closing the Gender Gap

PATRICIA McDERMOTT

INTRODUCTION

In 1951 the International Labour Organization (ILO) called for "equal pay for work of equal value." Yet forty years later a significant gender-based wage gap continues to persist in all industrialized nations. In Canada this male/female wage differential has hovered around the 35 percent mark for decades, one of the largest for an OECD country. There is no need to explain the importance to a social democratic agenda of closing this gap – it is fundamental. As women move swiftly towards constituting 50 percent of the labour market, the demand for wage justice will continue to mount.

In response to the ILO's postwar challenge to equalize wages, Canadian provinces each passed "equal pay for equal work" legislation requiring employers to pay the same wages to men and women if they were doing the same work. These so-called "equal pay" laws, the poor cousin to "equal value" legislation, are complaint driven and require workers or their unions to launch actions against employers. This approach has been relatively ineffective in terms of closing the wage gap primarily because of the complaint-based character of these provisions. Only a relatively small number of women in unions have felt secure enough to challenge their employers. The other serious problem with equal-pay legislation has been that men and women, for the most part, do different work. The strength of the ILO's convention was precisely that it encouraged "value" comparisons between those doing dissimilar work in a highly segmented labour market.

After Canada finally signed the ILO's convention in 1972, three Canadian jurisdictions passed equal-value legislation. While these provisions now allowed comparisons between predominantly male and female jobs, the complaint-based character of this legislation again meant that only organized women could realistically access this remedy. As a result, only a handful of cases have been brought forward, primarily by large public sector unions. Although these cases were quite successful for small groups of federal and provincial employees doing women's work, they did nothing to close the overall wage gap.

In the late 1980s a wave of "pay equity" legislation was introduced to once again tackle the wage gap.[1] Ontario has the dubious honour of being internationally recognized as "having gone the furthest in the world" in the pay-equity arena.[2] Unlike the pay-equity legislation introduced in other Canadian jurisdictions, Ontario's statute covers both the public and the private sectors. This extensive private sector coverage, however, did not come without a price. The complexity and lack of clarity of the act clearly demonstrates that the Liberal government was not truly committed to closing the wage gap but introduced pay equity primarily because it had been part of the 1985–87 Liberal-NDP accord.[3]

Ontario's Pay Equity Act requires that all employers with ten or more employees in the province undertake a pay-equity exercise to determine the extent to which they are engaging in discriminatory pay practices and that they remedy this problem via a wage-adjustment program. This process involves dividing the employees into predominantly female (60 percent or more) and predominantly male (70 percent or more) job classes. Employers must then establish the allegedly true value of these job classes by using a "gender neutral" job-evaluation technique. If it can be demonstrated that a female job class is undervalued when compared to a male job class, the female job class must be paid the same as the male job class.

This process sounds relatively straightforward, and indeed it can be if it is done solely by an employer without employee input. Pay-equity exercises, however, must be negotiated with each separate bargaining unit in an establishment. Given the fragmented nature of collective bargaining in Canada, this has meant that numerous pay-equity plans must be put in place in a single establishment. Thus, as has been the case in most other jurisdictions with pay equity in Canada and the United States, Ontario's model does not require that all the unions in one workplace jointly bargain the issue of how to assess and close their employer's gender-based wage gap.

Besides the difficulties arising from the fragmented nature of Ontario's pay-equity process, there are other major weaknesses in the act: the lack of a monitoring mechanism; the reliance on job evaluation as the key tool for establishing the value of work; and the "job-to-job" method of comparison. Remedial employment legislation, especially in the area of compensation practices, that does not have compliance monitoring built into it is literally asking to be ignored. Since employers are required to post pay-equity plans in the workplace, it would have been easy to have them file these plans with the government as well. This could help ensure that a pay-equity exercise has been meaningful, that it has not been simply a matter of stating that because of the presence of a job-evaluation system the female job classes already have pay equity.

In the past two to three years, thousands of pay-equity plans have been posted in workplaces across the province. The government has no idea what was in these plans. In non-union settings, employees have only ninety days to complain to the Pay Equity Commission about their plan. After that the plan is deemed to be approved.

JOB EVALUATION

The use of job evaluation as the method of comparing male and female jobs is inherently problematic. It is a pseudo-scientific technique that has long been criticized as a highly gender- and class-biased exercise used by employers to establish both job and compensation hierarchies. Employers do not typically conduct their own job evaluations but purchase the services of a management consulting firm. Unfortunately, the firms that have been undervaluing women's work for years are the same ones hired to conduct the pay-equity exercises.

An incredibly confusing aspect of pay equity in Ontario results from the fact that there can be as many different systems of job evaluation in one establishment as there are bargaining units. This is because each job-evaluation plan in considered unique. The use of multiple systems in one workplace creates frustrating and time-consuming problems. For example, a bargaining unit of the Service Employees International Union (SEIU) in a hospital might agree to the use of an XYZ job-evaluation system, while the Ontario Public Service Employees Union (OPSEU) unit uses the ABC system. How can the female job classes in SEIU that lack male comparators within their own unit be compared to male comparators in OPSEU that have been evaluated according to a completely different plan?

For decades most unions either have fought job evaluation or at the very least have treated such schemes as a management prerogative. Even the few unions that have participated in job-evaluation schemes would not likely agree that jobs at the bottom of a hierarchy are truly "less valuable" than those higher up. What unions are interested in is a system that can guarantee their members promotions and access, based on seniority, to higher-paid jobs. They want a crack at the more interesting "better" jobs, not necessarily the more "valuable" jobs.

In workplaces shaped by social democratic principles, job hierarchies would be viewed as artificial and divisive – as a justification for the all-important function of management. Indeed, job-evaluation exercises that result in supervisors being paid less than those being supervised (as occurred in the University of Toronto pay-equity implementation) are quickly "corrected" and the managers' wages increased. The wholesale introduction of job evaluation by employers across Ontario has been the price of pay equity. These exercises have resulted in red-circling (wage freezing) in some workplaces. Indeed, in establishments without a strong union, pay equity has been an invitation to red-circle. After all, the act holds out job evaluation as the approved method for assigning wages. Why should an employer ignore findings that demonstrate that some jobs are overpaid? Job evaluation has also meant the creation of more-inclusive job descriptions that entail the full range of duties an employee can be asked to do without a pay increase.

Although the Ontario act requires that job-evaluation exercises be gender neutral, the legislation gives no guidance about what gender neutrality is. The policy of the Liberal government was to let complainants come forward and litigate the issue, as is currently being done at the Pay Equity Tribunal. As of September 1991, more than four years after the act was passed, there has been only one decision that relates to what makes a pay-equity plan gender neutral, and this decision only provides some guidance as to what constitutes gender neutrality.[4] Even when more of these decisions are released, they will only be binding on the parties involved in the litigation. For example, the finding of gender bias in an XYZ evaluation plan in one unit does not mean that any employer using XYZ will automatically be considered in violation of the act. The matter would have to be taken to the tribunal – a surprising requirement, since gender bias is a methodological issue. One would think that once a plan is found to be biased, its use would be ruled out in all situations for the purposes of pay equity.

One of the major problems concerning pay equity in Ontario has been the virtual lack of easily accessible gender-neutral job-evaluation systems. These will essentially have to be designed from scratch. The process is expensive and time-consuming, and locating the expertise needed to develop such systems is difficult. Only a handful of experts in North America, most of them in the United States, have written about, and indeed have developed, the concept of gender neutrality.

The Liberals found it politically expedient to put the standard in the legislation, but the Ontario act fails to define what constitutes gender neutrality. Without such a definition, the act cannot be effective as an instrument of redress; it cannot transform the process of job evaluation into one even partly free of gender bias, at least not without lengthy and costly litigation.

JOB-TO-JOB COMPARISONS OR AN AVERAGE PAY LINE APPROACH?

The job-to-job comparison methodology of Ontario's pay-equity scheme is another weak feature of the process. Coupled with the false promise of gender neutrality, this methodology severely reduces wage adjustments under the act. It is an exercise in which each female job class must seek its own "male comparator" (and thus a claim to its pay), and where a female job class can be compared to more than one male class of "equal or comparable value," the female job class is entitled to only the *lowest* male wage.

The job-to-job approach, the entitlement to only the lowest male wage, and the necessity that each bargaining unit negotiate a separate plan have all combined to create a complex and fragmented approach perfectly designed for a government not serious about reducing the wage gap.

For over two decades, job-evaluation exercises in the United States have employed an average pay line methodology, a politically important tool even though it typically employs traditional job-evaluation and gender-predominant job classes. The approach involves the creation of a visible and comprehensible summary of the wage gap in each individual establishment. The mathematical tool is a simple linear regression line understood by most people as the "average of the averages." Once these revealing wage graphs are produced, the goal is to push the female wages up towards the average wage line by increasing the earnings of *every female job class* below

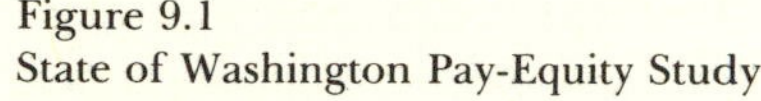

Figure 9.1
State of Washington Pay-Equity Study

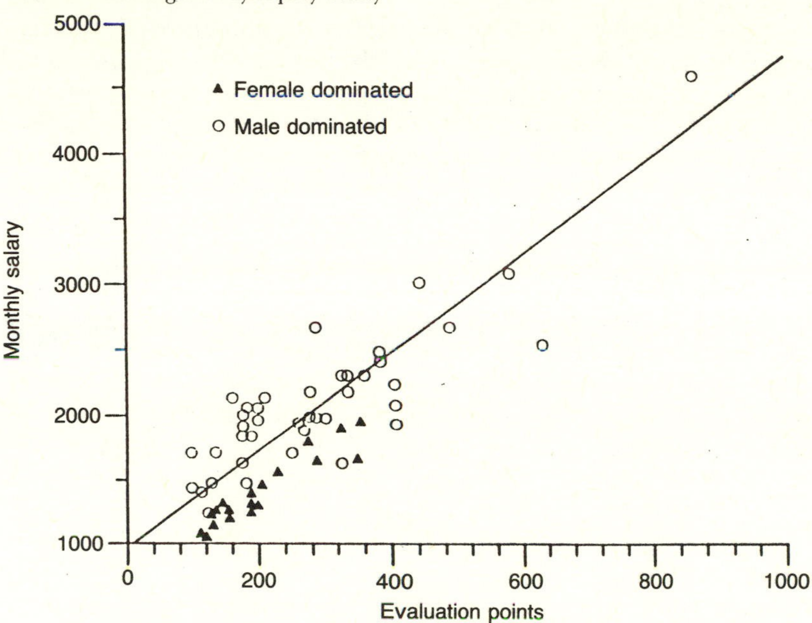

Source: Helen Remick, *Comparable Worth and Wage Discrimination* (Philadelphia: Temple University Press, 1984), 105.

the line. There is no need for each female job class to "find an appropriate male comparator" to be entitled to a wage increase.

While Ontarians must wrestle with a haphazard system, most people involved in US wage-equalization schemes understand the basic problem primarily because of these wage graphs. Although there has been a debate about whether the male wage line or the average wage line should be the standard, such technical issues have not blurred the basic goal of fair wages. Furthermore, the average wage line technique has the advantage of not matching a specific female job class with a specific male job class, a feature of the Ontario system that could lead to downward pressure on male wages pegged to a large female job class.

The most striking feature of a wage graph is the way the gender-based wage differential graphically appears: women cleaners make significantly less than male caretakers; female child care workers less than male gardeners; librarians less than engineers; nurses less than cooks; and clerical workers less than truck drivers. Figure 9.1 is an example of one graph used in the well-known pay-equity study undertaken by the State of Washington.

Another valuable aspect of a wage line approach is that one can avoid the laborious, disruptive, and expensive job-evaluation exercise. The degree of gender predominance is plotted along one axis, and the wages for male and female job classes along the other. This gender-predominance approach is extremely elegant and again comprehensible. In 1985 the Ontario Public Service Employees Union undertook a study of its approximately 55,000 public service membership and discovered that for each increase of 1 percent in the number of women in a job, the weekly wage decreased by $1.15, producing an annual differential of just under $6,000.[5]

Another important political point that must be made about the use of an average wage line is that the goal of the exercise is to close each employer's *entire gender-based wage gap*. This is a crucial difference between the pay line and the job-to-job approach. When the Ontario Liberal-NDP accord was holding hearings on pay equity in Ontario in 1986, the document under discussion was not, as one would expect, a draft of the actual legislation, but a Green Paper outlining the principles on which pay equity could be introduced. As it turned out, the similarity between the statutory proposals in the Green Paper and the terms of the Pay Equity Act passed in 1987 suggests that the hundreds of presentations made by labour and women's groups to the government's business-oriented "consultative panel" had little impact on the Liberals' formulation of the act.[6]

The Green Paper contained a discussion concerning what proportion of the wage gap a pay-equity policy could hope to close. This discussion set the stage for legislation that would make only a small dint in male/female wage differentials. The paper noted that "experts differ in determining what proportion of the wage gap could be closed by pay equity legislation, although most agree that it could exceed one quarter of the overall gap of 38 percentage points."[7] Although most "experts" may agree that pay equity could close at least 8 to 10 percent of the overall wage gap, for decades most equal-pay advocates have expected pay equity to completely close the wage gap individually calculated for an employer. This is how most of the thousands of US pay-equity implementations have been done, and this is what most of those pushing for pay-equity legislation in Ontario expect. Not only did the Green Paper's analysis of the closure of the wage gap set up a very limited goal, but it also provided a rationale for implementing the job-to-job approach rather than the obviously more equitable, if more costly, average pay line approach, which shifted the focus to each employer's individual wage gap.

American pay-equity experts who praise the gender-neutrality requirement in Ontario's pay-equity legislation have been quite surprised to learn that no regulations have been established for implementing this standard. They are even more surprised to encounter Ontario's strange job-to-job technique, which often produces minimal wage adjustments because a female job class is entitled just to the wages of the lowest-paid male comparator. Further, if there is no appropriate male comparator class, or no male job class at all, those in female job classes receive no pay-equity wage increase.

WHAT IS THE NDP DOING?

What is Ontario's NDP government going to do to rescue the current pay-equity legislation? After all, this is the party that put pay equity at the top of the agenda during the Liberal-NDP accord. The NDP was the most outspoken critic of this act when it was going through the legislative process.[8] On 19 June 1987, the day the Pay Equity Act was passed in the Ontario legislature, NDP member Evelyn Gigantes stated that the statute was seriously flawed and would come back to haunt the Liberals. Ironically, it is the NDP this law threatens to haunt. As pay-equity plans are posted in workplaces around the province throughout the early 1990s, it is becoming clear that there are few significant wage increases for those doing women's work. The "success stories" covered in the media (e.g., a receptionist received a $6,000-a-year wage adjustment) are rare exceptions rather than the rule.

In early 1991 the Ministry of Labour released a discussion paper outlining guidelines for the proposed amendments to Ontario's pay-equity legislation.[9] These amendments were disappointing, to say the least, and demonstrated that the NDP has been unable or unwilling to come to grips with the seriously flawed, overly complex, and ineffective act passed by the Liberals. The NDP government should have begun by reiterating Gigantes's original assessment of the legislation – the act is a mess. It should then have announced its intention to bring in significant amendments.

This is not the route that has been taken. The Ministry of Labour's information paper, entitled "Extending Pay Equity by Proportional Value and Proxy Comparison," details new provisions directed primarily at female job classes that did not find a male comparator during the job-to-job process and were thus unable to make a claim for a wage increase. It is crucial to note that both the proportional value and proxy methods are a direct extension of the initiatives taken by the former Liberal government. Earlier in 1990 the Liberal Ministry of Labour held consultations about these two techniques to see what the "stakeholders" thought of them. Thus, the proposed

NDP amendments signal not a new direction for pay equity at all, but the continuation of a policy of extending the coverage of a clearly weak act.

The tone of the ministry's discussion paper was reminiscent of the Liberals in that it did not include draft language but, like the Green Paper, only "principles" that the amendments were to follow. It stated that the proportional value approach had already gone through a series of "extensive consultations" that had confirmed "broad support among both labour and management." The paper suggested, however, that the government was open for further discussion about the proxy comparison, which was to be introduced only into the public sector. The principles that were to guide the amendments made it clear that little change was in store. Existing pay-equity plans using the job-to-job method will not be reconsidered, except where a male comparator could not be found for a female job class.

When there is disagreement between the union and the employer about whether to use proportional value or job-to-job comparison while developing a new plan, the amendments would require that the job-to-job method be used first. The document also states that the solutions proposed in the amendments should be "as simple as possible" and cause "minimum disruption" to existing plans. Perhaps the most revealing aspect of the amendments is that they would not "prescribe any particular method" of proportional value, but allow the continuation of the "self-managed" mode that has been so typical of Ontario pay-equity implementation.

In other words, the amendments would permit an already arbitrary and idiosyncratic process to become even more convoluted by introducing yet another layer of possibilities that hold little promise of truly tackling the wage gap in an effective and forthright manner. The very fact that the changes to the act will likely encourage the use of the job-to-job technique first, followed by an undefined process called proportional value, suggests that the data to be used in constructing a proportional value exercise will be those of the "lowest possible comparators." The use of these data will keep the wage adjustments at a minimum. Those female job classes that do not find a male comparator in their establishment will not get a higher standard of equity than those that receive wage adjustments under the job-to-job technique.

The document outlining the proposed amendments does, in fact, hint that the proportional value technique bears some resemblance to wage line methods. It notes that "one of the *most common* proportional value methods, *the wage line*, is a *widely accepted* compensation practice and has been adopted, in some form, by *most* jurisdictions which have pay equity laws [emphasis added]."[10] This brief reference to a wage line is baffling, since a true pay line technique would not be compatible with a job-to-job approach, especially one that offers only the lowest comparator's wage. Once some female job classes have received wage adjustments under the job-to-job system, which male comparator wages are to be used to construct a wage line? The wages of all of the lowest male comparators in the establishment? An average of both female and male wages? Answers to all of these technical questions are critical to ensuring that even the low standard of wage adjustments delivered by the job-to-job approach is achieved for those under the proportional value technique.

WHAT COULD AND SHOULD BE DONE?

The first and most obvious amendment that is needed to save the pay-equity legislation is *the requirement that plans be filed with the government.* The Pay Equity Commission, then, could monitor the filed plans and inform the employer, where appropriate, that it must now engage in a proportional value exercise. Most importantly, the government could study the wage data set out in the plans and assess the effectiveness of the act. If, for example, a large insurance company has developed a plan with few or not significant wage adjustments, it could be called in for a "pay-equity review." If a retail chain has sent in a plan with all of the part-time workers excluded from the pay-equity exercise, it could be made to include these workers. If the government was in possession of all the plans filed in the province, it could calculate how many times each commercial job-evaluation plan was being used. In short, the simple amendment of requiring that plans be filed would mean that the government could determine what is going on in the pay-equity arena and then develop informed strategies for change. The filing of plans also has the obvious benefit of putting pressure on employers to undertake a pay-equity exercise (clearly many have not yet done so) and to engage in a meaningful exercise when they do.

The second much-needed amendment would involve *a move to a comprehensive average wage line approach.* The policy of entitlement to only the lowest male comparator wage should be abandoned. If some pay-equity plans are to be opened up anyway, why not open them all? Why not have everyone do an average pay line exercise, and insist that the employers move towards closing their own wage gap?

This may sound like a tall order, but if a proper pay-equity exercise were done with machine-readable data, it would then be quite simple to run a pay line and calculate how many years of wage adjustments would close the gap. It would obviously take longer to meet this standard, especially if the legislated pay-equity fund of 1 percent of payroll annually is not increased. But the acknowledgment of the true extent of undervaluation of women's work is important – even if its correction takes time.

Another much-needed reform would be to allow large and medium-sized establishments that have not yet employed a pay-equity plan *to skip the job-evaluation exercise and move directly to explore the possibility of closing a wage gap established by gender predominance and salary data.* This technique requires that an establishment contain enough male and female job classes to produce wage lines that reflect a pattern of undervaluation. If the government developed guidelines similar to those used in the Canadian Human Rights equal-value complaints, this approach could become quite popular because it would avoid costly job-evaluation exercises.

The fourth amendment needed to salvage the pay-equity process would involve the quick *passage of some clear regulations about what constitutes a gender-neutral pay-equity exercise.* The concept is already in the act, and the government should give it substance. The decisions from the Pay Equity Tribunal could guide this process, but the goal must be to establish legally binding regulations that accompany the Pay Equity Act. The Pay Equity Commission has from time to time released guidelines that do not even bind the Pay Equity Hearings Tribunal, let alone employers.

BEYOND PAY EQUITY

There are many other strategies that could be employed to reduce the wage gap. A legal strategy closely related to pay equity would employ the equal-pay provisions contained in the Employment Standards Act that relate to women who are doing "substantially the same work" as men. As noted earlier, this remedy is currently complaint based, but it could be made proactive. Employers could lift equal-pay problems out of their pay-equity exercises before proceeding. The data used in an equal-pay complaint is the same as the data used for pay equity. If it can be established that the work done in a female job class is substantially the same work as that done in a male job class, the wage adjustment would be the wage rate for that particular male job – not the lowest of several "possible comparators."

Surely one of the most important strategies for reducing the province-wide gender-based wage gap would be *to raise the minimum wage.* Given the concentration of women in low-paid, non-unionized service sector jobs, this would undoubtedly be an effective strategy. An assessment of how an increased minimum wage would close the wage gap should be undertaken immediately. Since a significant increase in minimum wages was a *prominent* part of the NDP's campaign platform, this strategy is long overdue.

Another way to increase women's wages would be to *strengthen the Ontario Labour Relations Act,* along with the practices of the Labour Board, to enable broader-based and easier unionization. It is clear that union membership dramatically improves women's wages. For instance, the average weekly earnings for unionized jobs held by Canadian women workers in 1986 was $388 a week, compared to $242 a week for jobs held by unorganized women workers. This differential is even more striking in the service sector, where most women are employed. In 1986 the average weekly earnings for unionized service occupations was $277 a week, while that for non-unionized service jobs was only $153.[11]

Union organizers have a number of age-old complaints: lack of available information about the workplace they are organizing; the regular separation of full-time and part-time bargaining units; the ability of employers to introduce endless opposition petitions at certification hearings; and the broad interpretation of "freedom of speech" allowed an employer during an organizing drive. Even if certification is made easier, ways must be found to increase the bargaining strength of small bargaining units. One approach would be to allow the units in the multiple locations of the same employer to be added together to create a single bargaining unit. Another idea would be to have the collective agreements of numerous small units expire at the same time so that joint bargaining could take place. This could mean strike action at a number of locations simultaneously, a powerful weapon in the industrial relations world.

The Ontario Federation of Labour has recently become interested in the establishment of a sectoral wage council similar to those in operation under Quebec's Collective Agreement Decrees Act.[12] Although such systems have been considered by many to be reminiscent of the minimum-wage laws of the Depression, they do offer an interesting model for the extension of collective bargaining. It is possible that wage councils would benefit employers as well as workers in that they would ensure that the wage costs of competitors were essentially eliminated as a factor of competition. Furthermore, unions might be more interested in spending money to organize small workplaces in highly competitive sectors if they could be assured that the units would exist long enough to make organizing worthwhile.

CONCLUSION

The NDP must develop a unified and multi-pronged strategy if the wage gap is to be closed. Amendments to the Pay Equity Act, the use of the Employment Standards Act, raising the minimum wage, and finding ways to broaden and strengthen collective bargaining must all be employed. The wage gap must be studied and monitored to ensure that it is not being closed at the cost of lowering men's wages. If an annual decrease is not clearly demonstrated, additional measures will have to be taken until the wage differential between men and women has disappeared. For decades women have had as high an educational attainment as men, their rate of unionization is rising rapidly, and their tenure in the labour market is growing to match that of the male labour force. Soon economists will run out of explanations that presume to justify the gap. If the NDP is to really make a difference, it should start to close the gap now.

NOTES

1 Manitoba (1985), Ontario (1987), Nova Scotia (1988), Prince Edward Island (1988), and New Brunswick (1989) have passed pay-equity statutes. All, except Ontario's, cover only the public sector.

2 *New York Times*, 27 July 1989, 1.

3 Patricia McDermott, "Pay Equity in Ontario: A Critical Legal Analysis," *Osgoode Hall Law Journal* 28, no. 2 (Summer 1990): 381–407.

4 Haldimand-Norfolk (29 May 1991) 0001–89 (P.E.H.T.) at paragraph 146.

5 Debra Lewis, *Just Give Us the Money* (Vancouver: Women's Research Centre, 1988), 120.

6 Carl Cuneo, "The State of Pay Equity: Mediating Gender and Class through Political Parties in Ontario," in J. Fudge and P. McDermott, eds., *Just Wages: A Feminist Assessment of Pay Equity* (Toronto: University of Toronto Press, 1991).

7 Ibid., 12.

8 Ibid.

9 Ontario Ministry of Labour "Extending Pay Equity by Proportional Value and Proxy Comparison," February 1991).

10 Ibid., 2.

11 Statistics Canada, *Canada's Women: A Profile of Their 1986 Labour Market Experience*, Catalogue no. 71-205 (1988), 10.
12 Ontario Federation of Labour, *The Unequal Bargain* (Document 4, 33rd Annual Convention, 20-24 November 1989), 7.

PART FOUR

New Directions for Social Democracy

10 Beyond the Wagner Act, What Then?

JOHN O'GRADY

THE TOLLING BELL

Collective bargaining between workers and employers in privately owned workplaces is in retreat. Leo Troy has estimated that "Canadian private sector [union] density shrunk from 25.7% to 20.7% ... over the period 1975 to 1985."[1] The decline has been absolute as well as relative. Troy estimates that in 1975 there were 1,549,200 private sector, trade union members in Canada. By 1985, that number had fallen to 1,495,900.[2]

Structural shifts in employment explain part of this decline in private sector unionization. Yet they cannot explain the entire decline, for no segment of the private sector has been untouched. Even within the traditional base of CIO unionism – the manufacturing sector – the evidence of contraction is compelling.

In 1980, the peak year prior to the recession of 1981–83, there were 2,053,000 workers in the manufacturing sector. Unions could claim 43.2 percent of these workers as members. By 1987, manufacturing employment had almost returned to its pre-recession peak, standing at 2,040,000. However, union membership among these workers, fell to 36.9 percent. A decade earlier, unionization in the manufacturing sector had stood at 45.2 percent.[3]

For some unions the decline has been especially severe. Their decline has been absolute, not relative. Tragically, their decline has brought with it reduced resources for organizing. For those private sector unions that escaped absolute membership losses, vigorous new

Table 10.1
Absolute Declines in Membership

	1978	*1988*
United Steelworkers	183,585	166,001
United Rubberworkers	16,755	13,383
United Electrical (UE)	19,001	12,000
Intntl Ladies Garment	21,522	14,500
Amal Clothing & Txtl	36,512	30,000
Woodworkers (IWA)	59,783	50,000

Sources: CALURA, 1978; BLI, 1988.

organizing barely keeps pace with membership losses caused by plant closures or downsizing. During the period 1982–88, private sector unions in Ontario added 70,535 members to their ranks.[4] Over the same period, however, they lost approximately 40,000 members to complete plant closures, a further 8,000 members to partial closures, and 30,000 to 60,000 to reduced operations.[5] Moreover, these data exclude permanent job losses caused by technological change as well as permanent job losses in factories with fewer than fifty workers. It is reasonable to believe that for the private sector labour movement as a whole, the number of permanent job losses at least equalled, and probably exceeded, the number of members added by organizing.

According to data compiled by Noah Meltz, the rate of unionization in Ontario's private sector is now lower than that in New York and Michigan, only marginally higher than the rate in Illinois, and just somewhat higher than the rate in Ohio.[6]

Only a successful shift in union strategy or a major change in the legislation governing unionization and collective bargaining can reverse the slide. If present trends in unionization and employment patterns continue, the rate of private sector unionization will be 16 to 17 percent by no later than the end of this decade. Free trade, deregulation, and new technology may accelerate this decline.

Those who look to traditional organizing to reverse the erosion of collective bargaining in the private sector will find little basis for optimism in the record of the 1980s. During the years of recovery and expansion – from 1982 to 1988 – Ontario's employment base grew by an average of 114,000 workers each year. In the same period, the number of new workers brought into the province's unions through organizing averaged only 17,664 per year.[7] For every worker that was added to the membership rolls of Ontario's trade unions in the 1980s, more than six were added to the non-

Figure 10.1
Union Membership As a Percentage of Non-agricultural Paid Workers

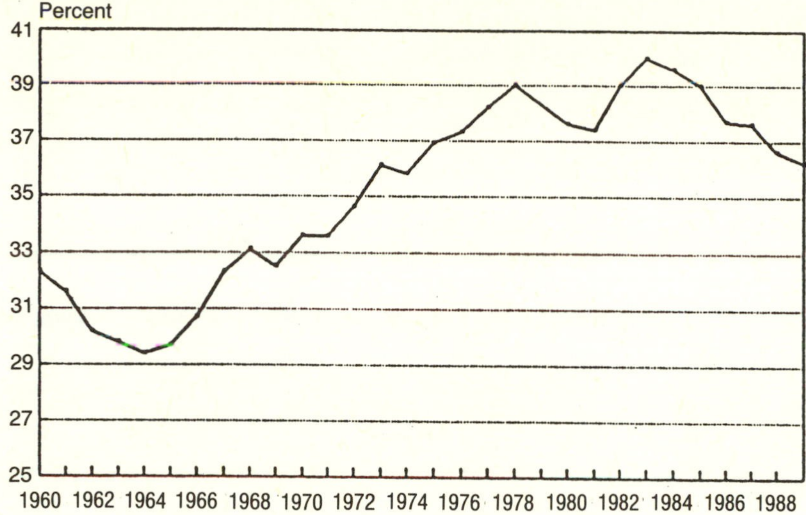

Source: BLI, *Collective Bargaining Review*, September 1989.

union majority. In 1975, 42.1 percent of unionized workers in Canada were employed in the public sector. By 1985, that proportion had increased to 56.4 percent.[8] Collective bargaining, it is clear, is being progressively confined to the public sector, to the regulated private sector, and to a narrowing base in industry and construction.

The public sector in Canada represents approximately 20 to 30 percent of total employment.[9] For the past two decades, the overall rate of unionization in Canada was driven by the expansion of both employment and organizing activity in the public sector. With over 80 percent of the public sector now organized, few expect these trends to continue. It is not surprising, therefore, that the overall rate of unionization has now begun to decline.

Simply halting the decline in Ontario would require that organizing be raised from the 17,664 average of the 1982–88 period to at least 31,000. The recovery of lost economic leverage would require that new organizing reach levels of 40,000 or more. At no time has organizing in Ontario ever achieved either of these levels. Moreover, the current recession will reduce both organizing prospects and the resources that unions can commit to these campaigns.

A wedge is being driven between the unionized minority and the non-union majority. Collective bargaining, as we practise it in Canada, has an extremely uneven impact on the labour market. Arguably, collective bargaining works reasonably well for about

Figure 10.2
Union Membership and the Growth of Paid Employment

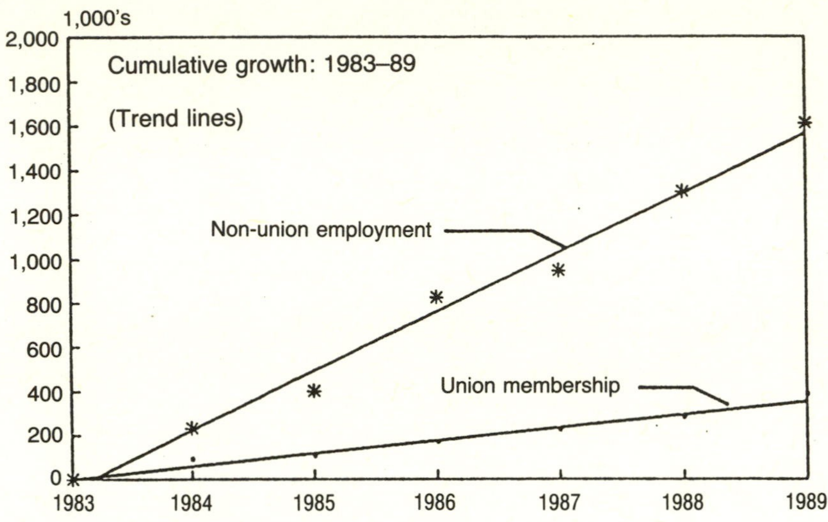

Source: BLI, *Collective Bargaining Review*, September 1989.

one-quarter of workers in Canada – mostly workers in the public sector, the regulated private sector, and the large-scale manufacturing sector. Collective bargaining provides rather less protection to perhaps another 10 percent of workers – mainly workers in the private sector and the periphery of the public sector, such as employees of funded agencies. For the remaining two-thirds of workers, collective bargaining affords no direct economic protection and increasingly less indirect protection. Stagnant real wages in much of the private sector will persuade an increasing proportion of the non-union two-thirds of the labour force that the gains achieved by unionized workers in the public sector, the regulated private sector, and the large-scale manufacturing sector are achieved at the expense of this non-union majority. Those workers who are outside the scope of collective bargaining – the decisive majority – provide a ready social base for anti-social democratic politics. Their numbers are increasing, both absolutely and relatively.

This paper has a straightforward argument: within the framework of the existing labour codes in Canada – the codes that were inspired by the American Wagner Act – it would be naive to expect the decline in unionization to be reversed. If collective bargaining is to again have a central role in the private sector labour market, then we have no choice except to move beyond the Wagner Act.

OUR AMERICAN COUSIN

When Mackenzie King's wartime cabinet brought the Wagner Act to Canada as Privy Council Order 1003, Canada joined the Philippines as the only other non-American jurisdiction to base its collective-bargaining regime on the New Deal model. For Canadian trade unionists, PC 1003 was seen as a major victory. It brought to bear the legal principles that now constitute the very fabric of our industrial relations system: certification by cards or by majority vote, exclusive bargaining-agent status, defined bargaining units, protection against "unfair practices," and an enforceable obligation on employers to bargain in "good faith."

For many, the Wagner Act is virtually synonymous with the New Deal. What is often forgotten, however, is that the act was only half a deal. The original New Deal model was set out in the National Industrial Recovery Act (NIRA). Section 7(a) of the NIRA included provisions that subsequently evolved into the procedures that we now identify as the Wagner Act model.[10] However, the NIRA never envisioned that this Wagner Act model of collective bargaining would have much currency outside of the large industrial employers. The majority of working men and women – who then, as now, would be employed outside these large industrial workplaces – were to find their economic protection in other mechanisms established by the NIRA. Sectoral mechanisms involving labour, employers, and government were to regulate working conditions. Competition was to be limited through a system of licensing. That these mechanisms were intended to re-regulate the labour market is clear from the vigour of planned implementation. Within one year of the NIRA's adoption in June 1933, some 400 codes were in force. A further 300 codes were awaiting proclamation when the US Supreme Court struck down the NIRA in May 1935. The Wagner Act, which Roosevelt signed in July of that same year, emerged from the rubble of judicial reaction.

Like every labour code, the Wagner Act establishes the framework within which economic power will be legitimated and exercised in the labour market. When the act is viewed from this perspective, its distinguishing features are its definition of bargaining units and its collateral presumption that most collective bargaining will occur at the level of the workplace. The definition of "appropriate bargaining units" is fundamental to the way in which the Wagner Act model allocates economic power in the labour market. The model presumes that bargaining will *not* occur at a sectoral or regional level. Indeed, the act did not even require that a common collective agreement apply to workers in different plants owned by the same employer. Collective bargaining in the Wagner Act model was to be decentralized to the smallest practical unit, namely, a single workplace. In fact, the fragmentation of bargaining leverage was carried further by the sanctioning of separate bargaining units for office and plant employees and often for part-time and full-time employees.

This splintering of economic leverage by radical decentralization had two effects. The first consequence was that certification of unions by workplaces made it almost certain that, within every sector, some workplaces would remain outside the formal ambit of collective bargaining. In the first two decades after the Second World War, the flow of influence within sectors was undoubtedly from the unionized workplaces to the non-union workplaces. In the 1970s and 1980s the balance in the United States shifted and the direction of influence reversed.[11] A similar pattern may emerge in Canada as a result of both de-unionization within the manufacturing sector and the impact of free trade with the United States (and possibly Mexico) on decisions regarding plant location.[12]

The second consequence of fragmented collective bargaining was that trade unions would have enormous difficulty in organizing workers in small establishments. The unavoidable fact is that the Wagner Act model simply does not work in small establishments. It was never intended to regulate that segment of the labour market.

SMALL WORKPLACES

The small-workplace sector poses a particular problem for collective bargaining and for trade unions. Small workplaces are exceedingly difficult to organize and costly to represent. Moreover, in most circumstances, especially in the private sector, collective bargaining has quite limited scope for improving employment conditions in this area.

We should not confuse small workplaces with small employers. Many large employers oversee a large number of comparatively small workplaces. Our Wagner Act industrial relations model, however, directs that certification *and collective bargaining* take place at the level of the workplace unless both union and employer move the relationship to the level of the enterprise as a whole. If small workplaces were a marginal or declining feature of our economic landscape, these facts would not be cause for great concern. However, the recent evidence suggests that there is a shift to small workplaces. The proportion of workers employed in establishments with fewer than twenty workers increased from 16.28 percent in 1978 to 24.01 percent in 1986.[13]

Table 10.2
Distribution of Labour Force by Size of Workplace in Ontario

	1978 (%)	*1986* (%)
Micro-sector	16.28	24.08
Under 5	6.02	12.13
5 to 19.9	10.26	11.95
Middle sector	14.68	14.69
20 to 49.9	8.28	8.29
50 to 99.9	6.40	6.40
Macro-sector	69.04	61.23
100 to 499.9	14.87	14.07
500 and over	54.17	47.17

Source: Statistics Canada, Business Microdata.

A structural shift of almost 8 percentage points in as many years is highly significant.[14] It is indicative of new modes of work organization. Hence, the shift to smaller workplaces is related to other labour market phenomena of the 1980s: the increased reliance on part-time employees, casual employees, homeworkers, contracting-out, and out-sourcing.

Small workplaces pose four distinct problems to trade unions and to the extension of Wagner Act collective bargaining.

1. Employer resistance to certification bids by unions is far more effective in small workplaces.

Employer resistance to unionization takes three forms. The first is dismissal of union organizers and supporters. This, of course, is unlawful under the Ontario Labour Relations Act (OLRA). It is also, however, effective. The Ontario Labour Relations Board (OLRB) may award reinstatement with back wages, but the median time taken by the OLRB to reach a decision is six months – long enough to put an organizing campaign in the deep-freeze.[15] Experienced organizers know that the impact of dismissing an organizer and the union's inability to achieve expeditious reinstatement are far more intimidating in a small workplace.

The second type of employer resistance is the encouragement of anti-union petitions under section 7(2) and 103(2) (j) of the OLRA. A petition is typically circulated after a union has signed up workers and applied for certification. A worker who has signed a union card may also sign a petition. Indeed, many do so in order to protect themselves, since they rightly presume that their employer will know who signed the anti-union petition and who did not. The effect of a petition signature is to cast doubt on the union card. It may cause the OLRB to order a vote if the solid card count thereby falls below 55 percent: Petitions are almost entirely a private sector phenomenum. Indeed, this is surely the most persuasive evidence to support the presupposition that petitions are almost invariably employer inspired. The petition process undermines organizing in all workplaces. However, it is especially effective in small workplaces.

The third type of employer resistance is the employer's use of its section 64 rights, which assure to an employer its "freedom to express its views." Such "persuasion" is generally more successful in small workplaces. Managers always have the ability to influence a handful of workers. In a small workplace this influence can affect the standing of the union's application in terms of the requisite sign-up percentage.

2. The cost of representing workers in small workplaces is itself a major obstacle.

Many of the costs of negotiating a collective agreement are fixed, regardless of the number of employees affected. A staff representative is likely to find that a bargaining unit of fifteen or twenty workers consumes as much time as one that is four or five times that size. While many unions would like to organize more workers in small bargaining units, the dues base of these bargaining units would never enable the union to recover its organizing costs. Moreover, these costs have risen significantly in tandem with the increased litigation associated with employer resistance to unionization. Even if unions were to "write off" these organizing expenses as part of the social cost of being a trade union, it remains likely that the dues base in small bargaining units would be insufficient to cover the normal costs of representation, notably those costs relating to negotiating a collective agreement and enforcing that agreement through grievance arbitration.

3. The cumulative impact of collective bargaining is largely nullified by the high attrition rate of small employers.

Collective bargaining is an incremental process. Its impact is felt by workers only over a period of time. Every union negotiating committee secures language in a collective agreement that, though it may be weak, provides a basis for further improvements. This incre-

Table 10.3
Percentage of Firms Measured in 1978 That Survived to 1986

Micro-sector	49.86
Under 5	46.25
5 to 19.9	63.87
Middle sector	66.74
20 to 49.9	66.38
50 to 99.9	67.72
Macro-sector	71.78
100 to 499.9	69.32
500 and over	78.26

Source: Statistics Canada, Business Microdata.

mentalism, however, presumes that the bargaining relationship will endure. However, the Statistics Canada Business Microdata show that between 1978 and 1986 half of the firms employing fewer than twenty workers ceased operations. Not surprisingly, the data show that the survival rate of small workplaces is markedly less than the survival rate of large establishments.

What these data imply, surely, is that in the small-workplace sector, the bargaining relationship must be elevated to a level above the workplace if collective bargaining is to have a material impact on employment conditions.

4. Small workplaces are associated with more competitive product markets than are larger workplaces. Consequently, a unionized employer is at a marked disadvantage in comparison with its non-union competitor.

The objective of collective bargaining is to regulate the labour market – in other words, to take wages out of competition. In the small-workplace segment of the economy, this regulation of the labour market can only occur at the sectoral or at the regional level. Faced with highly competitive product markets, employers in the small-workplace sector have little scope for improving working conditions and a strong incentive to resist unionization in the first place.

From a societal perspective, regulation of the labour market is essential for two reasons. First, an entirely competitive or unregulated labour market generates inequality. It thereby imposes additional burdens on the state's redistributive programs. Second, and of equal importance, an unregulated labour market undermines the development of human resources. It does this by opening the door of wage suppression as an alternative to investing in skills.

In the small-workplace sector, the Wagner Act model of collective bargaining is of limited use in regulating the labour market. When it comes to organizing and to collective bargaining, small is definitely *not* beautiful.

FIXING THE OLRA?

The first question we must ask ourselves is, can the Ontario Labour Relations Act be fixed? By this I mean, can unions and social democrats address the falling rate of private sector unionization *within* the framework of Wagner Act collective bargaining?

Let us first list the steps that should be taken to improve access to collective bargaining within the existing statutory framework:

- Bring the OLRA into conformity with the certification procedures under the Canada Labour Code by prohibiting petitions after a union has made an application for certification.
- Discontinue the requirement that workers pay $1 when signing a union membership card, thereby eliminating the opportunity for management counsel to prolong the certification process by allegations of "non-pay." Elimination of the $1 requirement would reduce litigation expenses and might result in more applications being certified automatically as opposed to being put to a vote.
- Further confine the ability of employers to influence their employees against unionization by imposing greater restrictions on the employer's section 64 "freedom of speech rights."
- Prohibit the implementation of the dismissal of union organizers until after the OLRB has decided on the merits of a union's "unfair practice" allegation.
- Allow the union to determine whether a bargaining unit should include part-time employees. (Current practice allows either union or employer to exclude part-time and similar employees. In practice, if it is in the interests of one party to include such employees, it is usually in the interests of the other to exclude them.)
- Eliminate the fear of *de facto* dismissal for striking by prohibiting the use of replacement workers during a strike.

Of all the desirable changes to the OLRA, the Ontario labour movement has clearly identified reducing the scope for anti-union "petitions" as the one that would contribute most significantly to the expansion of collective bargaining. In 1988–89, the OLRB's *Annual*

Table 10.4
Applications for Certification OLRB, 1988–89

	Filed	*Granted*	*Withdrawn*	*Dismissed*
Private sector	407	272	58	71
Public sector	218	169	30	20
Construction	313	208	74	42
Total	938	649	162	133

Source: OLRB, *Annual Report*, 1988–89.

Report tells us that 938 applications were filed for certification. Of these, 313 were in the construction sector and 218 in the public sector. There were 407 applications for non-construction, private sector units. Of these, 58 (or 1 in 7) were withdrawn. Petitions probably figured in most of these withdrawals. A withdrawn application is not, however, a dead application. Such applications are frequently resurrected (i.e., a new application is filed) when the union has restored its card count to the requisite 55 percent plus one and thereby again puts itself in the position to be certified without a vote. The only procedural effect of a "legitimate" petition – other than litigation costs and processing time – is that it may force an applicant union into a vote situation. A petition cannot kill an application outright. In 1988–89, 56 representation votes were conducted and unions won 28 of these.

On the basis of the OLRB's data we can formulate conservative and liberal estimates of the impact of eliminating petitions. The conservative estimate would add to union ranks *all* of the workers in the 28 bargaining units where votes rejected the union. The average bargaining unit in which a vote was held had 47 members. This yields an estimate of 1,316 workers – roughly a 7 percent increase in overall organizing results outside the construction sector. A more liberal estimate would give unions a large percentage – say two-thirds – of the withdrawn, private sector applications plus the units lost in votes. This would result in approximately 3,065 new union members – about a 15 percent increase in organizing results outside the construction sector. The actual results, should this change be made, would probably fall between these estimates.[16]

If the trajectory of decline is to be reversed, there must be a quantum increase in the number of workers unionized from the average of 17,664 in the 1982–88 period to 30,000–40,000. It is difficult to see increases of that magnitude stemming from changes in the existing framework of collective bargaining. Indeed, where elements of this reform package have been implemented – as in the federal jurisdiction – they have not led to increases in organizing on the scale that is needed. Reform of the OLRA along the lines proposed by trade unions and their allies will be helpful. That these reforms will reverse the trajectory of decline is highly doubtful. Certainly none of these reforms will deal with the high cost of representation or the limited impact of collective bargaining within the small-workplace sector. It is not surprising that many unions have been forced to adopt *de facto* policies of avoiding small bargaining units. Even with the adoption of reforms to the OLRA, such policies would continue.

Reform of the OLRA within the confines of the Wagner Act model will not meet the labour movement's need to reverse its decline. Nor will reform within the Wagner Act framework meet the broader need to regulate the private sector labour market and thereby reverse the trend towards increased labour market–based inequality.

WIDER-BASED BARGAINING

There are various ways of dealing with the problem of regulating the private sector labour market. Paul Weiler frames the problem as how to govern the private sector workplace.[17] He identifies various candidates for filling the "representation gap" caused by the decline of private sector unionization. The first solution entails greater reliance on the civil courts, mainly in regard to protection against dismissal. The second solution looks to administrative law mechanisms, especially in the areas of pay equity, employment equity, and health and safety. The third solution would rely on employers to implement progressive, human resource management policies. A fourth solution would be to adapt the "work councils" that emerged in Europe following the Second World War to the North American environment. Weiler's premise, which I share, is that the status quo is unlikely to endure. In a democratic society, the private sector labour market will be regulated. The real questions are how and to what degree. If there is no credible collective-bargaining-based solution, then other solutions will be canvassed, even by the labour movement's political allies.

If collective bargaining is to play a key role, let alone the leading role, in regulating the private sector labour market, then the constraints of the Wagner Act model must be overcome. Foremost among these constraints is the act's presumption that bargaining will take place at the level of the workplace. It is this radical decentralization – or more accurately, radical fragmentation – that effectively precludes the extension of collective bargaining to small workplaces in the private sector. Much of the retail sector, the financial sector, and the business services sector effectively are outside the scope of Wagner Act collective bargaining. In the non-profit sector and the para-public sector, child-care centres, clinics, and small social agencies are equally likely to fall outside the ambit of collective bargaining. Only by moving the bargaining relationship to a level above the workplace will collective bargaining be feasible for employees in small workplaces. What is required, clearly, is a legislative commitment to *sectoral* or *regional* bargaining models.

The mechanism of *juridical extension*, which operates in Quebec and several civil code jurisdictions, is one instructive example that goes beyond the Wagner Act model. Under Quebec's Collective Agreement Decrees Act, either party to a collective agreement may apply to have the economic terms of that agreement extended to other employers in the same sector and within the same region. The mechanisms of extension in the Quebec legislation are not germane to this discussion. In many respects, they are highly dated. What is relevant is the principle of extending some of the terms of a privately negotiated collective agreement to parties who were not associated with the initial agreement.

Juridical extension has had an uneven history in Quebec. At its peak, in 1960, the system governed employment conditions for some 267,000 workers – roughly 15 percent of the non-agricultural labour force. Approximately half to two-thirds of these workers were also covered by collective agreements. Indeed, even today collective agreement coverage extends to more than 50 percent of workers governed by decrees. Quebec's Beaudry Commission reported that in 1982 some 112,639 workers were governed by decrees. Significantly, the average size of workplaces covered by decrees was six to eight employees. In Quebec, the evidence suggests that juridical extension has facilitated the extension of collective bargaining to some sectors and has retarded its decline in others. The Quebec labour movement favours (as would any labour movement) mandatory sectoral bargaining and (by implication) compulsory unionism. Juridical extension falls between mandated sectoral unionization and the radical decentralization of the Wagner Act model.[18]

One could readily see a form of juridical extension being established in Ontario through a special "small workplace" chapter in the OLRA, analogous to the separate chapter dealing with the construction sector. Juridical extension could significantly strengthen both collective-bargaining leverage and unionization in chain operations in the retail, financial, and fast-food industries. One could also see a form of juridical extension being applied to individual shopping malls or possibly to the mini-industrial parks that are now so typical of the computer-related industry. And finally, one could see juridical extension being usefully applied to low-wage sectors such as office cleaning, garages, child-care centres, security and parking operations, and restaurants.

Rightly understood and shrewdly adapted to Ontario's circumstances, juridical extension could provide a collective-bargaining-based solution to the problem of regulating the private sector labour market. As well, it could provide trade unions with the statutory framework they require to reverse the trajectory of decline in the private sector.

The labour movement in Ontario, especially in the private sector, is in retreat. The decline in private sector unionization rates is more than merely disturbing; it is a crisis – a crisis for both the labour movement and its social democratic allies. To reverse that decline will require both vision and leverage. The vision that is needed is about the social role of the labour movement; it is also about *not* reducing trade unionism to collective bargaining, or collective bargaining to the procedures spawned by the Wagner Act. Leverage, however, is about power; it is about the ability to act. Within the confines of the Wagner Act model, the labour movement lacks the leverage to reverse its decline, regardless of its vision. Without leverage, vision is irrelevant; it will be reduced to nostalgia. One is reminded of the line in Osborne's play: "They spend their time mostly looking forward to the past."

Some believe that the labour movement's decline can be reversed by situating the trade union movement within a broader, progressive, social coalition. Such a strategy may indeed provide important underpinnings for a social vision. The labour movement's fate, however, is inextricably bound up with the fate of collective bargaining. The changes in our social and economic structure that have undermined the Wagner Act model of collective bargaining will undermine both the labour movement and the coalitions of which it is a part.

The Ontario labour movement has had almost fifty years of the Wagner Act. This model, however, is running out of gas. The labour movement in Canada has been successful, in comparison with its American counterpart, in using political leverage to consolidate and strengthen its collective-bargaining base. The opportunity to again use that leverage is being presented to the Ontario labour movement at the same time that its private sector arm has entered a sharp decline.

Without doubt, the first task of a social democratic government in its reform of labour law will be to address the changes needed in the OLRA. Those changes will focus on the certification process, the duty to bargain, and restrictions on the use of replacement workers. When that legislative task in finished, we will have pushed the Wagner Act model to its limits. We will then have come to a fork in the road. Either we must put our further emphasis on administrative law solutions or we must look for new forms of collective bargaining. The question that both trade unionists and social democrats will have to ask within the next year is, after the Wagner Act ... what then?

NOTES

1 Leo Troy, "Is the U.S. Unique in the Decline of Private Sector Unionism?" *Journal of Labour Research* 11, no. 2 (Spring 1990): 125

2 Ibid., 134. Troy's comparisons are based on CALURA data.

3 Noah Meltz, "Changing Industrial Structure and the Implications for Industrial Relations in Canada" (Paper presented to the Industrial Relations Section, Sloan School of Management, MIT, March 1990), 11

4 Based on data compiled in Anil Verma and Noah Meltz, "The Underlying Sources of Union Strength: Certification Activity in Ontario, 1982–88" (Paper presented to the twenty-seventh annual meeting of the Canadian Industrial Relations Association, Victoria, 1990). The figure 70,535 excludes the construction sector, as OLRB data seriously under-reports workers affected by a certification in the construction sector. The 70,535 figure also excludes certifications that involved displacement of an incumbent union.

5 Based on data supplied by the Employment Adjustment Branch, Ontario Ministry of Labour. Job losses are disaggregated by three categories: permanent closures, partial closures, and reduced operations. The first two are indicators of structural change. "Reduced operations" reflects significant cyclical influences. The actual numbers for the period 1982–88 are as follows:

Complete closures	51,387
Partial closures	9,992
Reduced operations	71,835

If the year 1982 is omitted to eliminate the statistical "bump" of the recession, the number of permanent job losses caused by reduced operations for the period 1983–88 was 36,934. Data available for the years 1989–90 indicate an 83 percent rate of unionization among reported job losses.

6 Noah Meltz, " Interstate vs. Interprovincial Differences in Union Density," *Industrial Relations* 28, no. 2 (Spring 1989): 152–3.

7 Verma and Meltz, "Underlying Sources of Union Strength." For the period 1982–83 to 1988–89, the average number of workers outside of construction affected by new certifications was 20,467. Adjusting for certifications that displaced an incumbent union reduces this number to 17,664.

8 Troy, "Is the U.S. Unique?" 134

9 Ibid., 116. Troy provides a useful comparison:

	1975 (%)	1985 (%)
France	18.7	27.9
West Germany	21.9	23.3
Italy	20.4	23.1
Netherlands	15.5	19.9
Sweden	33.2	33.1
Canada	29.8	29.9
US	18.3	16.3

Narrower definitions estimate the Canadian public sector at closer to 20 percent.

10 Section 7(a) of the NIRA, it must stressed, did *not* spell out the procedures we now associate with the Wagner Act. However, the tribunals that were established under the authority of section 7(a) rapidly adopted policies that were subsequently incorporated in the Wagner Act. See Wm. E. Leuchtenburg, *Franklin D. Roosevelt and the New Deal, 1932–1940* (Chicago: Harper Torchbooks, 1963).

11 This is the central argument of Thomas Kochan, Harry Katz, and Robert McKersie in *The Transformation of American Industrial Relations* (New York: Basic Books, 1986).

12 Richard Freeman has observed pointedly that "the close institutional and economic ties between Canada and the United States and between Canada and the United Kingdom and Japan makes the rapid de-unionization of those countries the most important foreign development likely to impact the Canadian labour scene." See Richard Freeman, "Canada in the World Labour Market" (Unpublished, October 1988).

13 Labour is measured in "adjusted labour units," roughly equivalent to a "job."

14 In its 1989 edition of *The State of Small Business,* Ontario's Ministry of Industry and Trade uses the same database but computes a less significant structural shift. Its 1986 calculations are as follows: micro-sector – 17.3 percent; middle sector – 15.9 percent; macro-sector – 66.7 percent. The data relied on in the ministry publication are not

fully cited. The data used in this article are taken from Statistics Canada, "Business Microdata Integration and Analysis," 4 May 1988 (File: 139660), 73.

15 Peter G. Bruce, "The Processing of Unfair Labour Practice Cases in the United States and Ontario, " *Relations Industrielles* 45, no. 3 (Summer 1990): 497. Bruce also documents the lengthening period of litigation:

Median Time Lapse for Disposition of OLRB Section 66 Cases Formally Heard

1983/84	137 days
1984/85	146 days
1985/86	183 days
1986/87	187 days

Noah Meltz's data show up the following comparison, which suggests that there may have been a greater incidence of employer resistance to unionization in the late 1980s:

Period	No. of Certifications (Applications)	No. of OLRA Contraventions (Filed)	Contraventions per Certification (Ratio)
1977/78 to 1979/80	3,102	1,467	.47
1987/88 to 1989/90	2,973	2,472	.83

The above table indicates not only that increased employer resistance may have occurred, but that unions incurred significantly greater litigation costs per certification application. (The data are based on Noah Meltz, private correspondance.)

16 Ontario Labour Relations Board, *Annual Report, 1988–89*, tables 6 and 9. The total number of workers in certified units outside of construction in 1988–89 was 19,982. Decertifications claimed 1,165 union members.

17 Paul C. Weiler, *Governing the Workplace: The Future of Labour and Employment Law* (Cambridge, Mass.: Harvard University Press, 1990).

18 The information on juridical extension in Quebec is drawn from unpublished work by Geoffrey Brennan. This work is being done as part of a study commissioned by the Ontario Federation of Labour. The study will be published later in 1991.

11 A New Social Welfare Agenda for Canada

LEON MUSZYNSKI

THE WELFARE STATE AND ECONOMIC ADJUSTMENT

By many different measures social conditions in Canada have deteriorated over the past two decades. Inequality has increased and society has become more polarized.[1] Poverty has increased especially among women and children.[2] Dependency on social assistance has increased and hunger and homelessness are now visible signs of social marginalization not seen in Canada since the Great Depression. As we head into a recession in the early 1990s, it is certain conditions will only get worse.

Most of this deterioration can be linked to changes in the labour market. The most visible among these is high and persistent levels of unemployment, especially evident in dramatic regional disparities in employment opportunities in Canada. But there are other even more important factors: real-wage declines; the growth of part-time, temporary, and low-wage employment (bad jobs); the phenomenal rates of turnover of firms and workers, with closures and layoffs disrupting communities and leaving many (especially older) workers unemployed; and persistent discrimination in wages and jobs against women, visible minorities, and the disabled.

I will argue that unemployment, wage erosion, and labour market inequality are policy choices that flow from a particular form of a political economy of economic adjustment. The political philosophy underlying this strategy is reflected in a variety of initiatives in Canada that are a reversal of the postwar commitment to a Keynesian high-employment, high- and stable-income welfare state. These include privatization, deregulation, the erosion of minimum wages, tax reform, and cutbacks in social transfers and labour market programs. Through these policies, governments have quite purposefully put downward pressure on wages in order to increase flexibility in Canadian labour markets. This flexibility is seen as a key factor in Canada's ability to compete internationally. The central elements of this political economy are its rejection of the positive role of government in the political management of economic and social change, and the reassertion of the market as the driving force of society.

THE LOGIC OF FEDERAL SPENDING RESTRAINT

It is at the federal level that this philosophy of governmental disengagement has been most effectively articulated. Since 1984 many statutory social programs have been significantly restricted or reduced. The most notable declines in federal spending have been in Established Programs Financing (EPF), which is the federal funding of provincial health and education, and federal training and job creation allocations. In real terms, federal EPF funding has declined by 13 percent from 1984/85 to 1990/91. Federal funding for the Canadian Jobs Strategy, the omnibus program supporting training and job development, has declined by 36 percent in Ontario over the same period. On the face of it, it is difficult to understand the logic behind these cutbacks in a period when skills are widely considered to be critical for economic success. But this is not simply misguided policy on the part of the federal government. The strategy can be seen as part of a concerted effort to reduce worker security and power in the labour market. Business and government believe this is the essence of any future ability to compete within the context of the Canada-US Free Trade Agreement (FTA), declining tariffs, and the globalized economy.

UNEMPLOYMENT INSURANCE

There is no more pronounced demonstration of this strategy than in the recent changes to the Unemployment Insurance Act and the new Labour Force Development Strategy (LFDS). The LFDS is a good example of how the federal government has become adept at obscuring the real impact of what it is doing by couching changes within the context of a progressive principle. The principle here is that in Canada we spend too large a share of our labour adjustment dollars on income maintenance rather than on developmental programs such as training. It is a principle upheld by business and labour alike. This theme has been reiterated in many different reports by the Organization for Economic Co-operation and Development (OECD), the Economic Council of Canada, the Canadian Labour Market and Productivity Centre, the Ontario Premier's Council, and the Social Planning Council of Metropolitan Toronto, to mention just a few. However, to rectify this imbalance the federal government is attempting to save over $1.3 billion by making unemployment insurance (UI) benefits much more difficult to receive through a longer qualifying requirement, and by penalizing workers who quit jobs. They have also reduced the wage-replacement ratio to 50 percent from 60 percent. These savings will be redirected to other more "developmental" activities such as training. By appealing to the universal desires to reduce the appallingly high amount we spend on unemployment insurance and to invest more in training, the federal government is trying to obscure the fact that in an unstable labour market a major source of income security for the unemployed *is being reduced* and many people will suffer. One likely result will be to shift many workers who do not qualify for UI benefits onto welfare, as every other change of this nature has done in the past.

The main reason for high UI expenditures is high unemployment, particularly in the Atlantic provinces. The main issue of UI reform is whether government is willing to keep unemployment low. The 1971 amendments were premised on the assumption that not only was it possible to keep unemployment rates below 4 percent, but it was the responsibility of the federal government to do so through effective application of national economic policy and labour market programs. This was entrenched in the specific provisions in 1971 that gave the federal government responsibility for both regional benefits and for any benefits that were the result of an increase in the rate of unemployment above 4 percent. The recent changes, which finally cleared the Senate in late 1990, after being hung up there for a year, absolve the federal government of any responsibility for direct funding of UI and for keeping unemployment low.

For well over a decade now the federal government has been unable to keep the national rate of unemployment down to the low levels that were expected when the 1971 revised UI program was put in place. The cynical philosophy that guides UI reductions is that high unemployment is inevitable and the best thing government can do, particularly because of its high deficit, is to cut its losses. This view of unemployment is unnecessary and ultimately harmful to us all.

The logic of the recent revisions lies to a large extent in the context in which they were proposed. A close look at the federal UI strategy reveals a remarkable similarity between the proposed new Canadian UI program and what exists in the United States, especially in regard to the new twenty-week qualifying period. This point has not been lost on those who have continually argued that Canada's social programs will suffer under the regime fostered by the free trade agreement because the United States will see our more generous social programs as unfair subsidies.

This attack on UI is not new. Since the 1971 revisions, there have been numerous changes, the most notable in 1978, which substantially reduced the protection provided to unemployed workers by the program. Liberal governments pursued the same strategy as today's Tory government, often just as vigorously, of reducing UI protection in times of rising unemployment. It is useful to understand how this strategy for UI reform fits into the overall income security reform strategy of the present federal government.

In 1985 the federal government appointed the Commission of Inquiry on Unemployment Insurance, headed by Claude Forget. The Forget Commission report released in December 1986 recommended sweeping changes to the UI program that would result in restrictions on eligibility and the elimination of regional benefits. Similar proposals were put forward in the 1985 report of the Macdonald Commission (the Royal Commission on the Economic Union and Development Prospects for Canada) within the context of a free trade strategy. In addition to restricting eligibility, the basic premise of these proposals was that the non-social insurance aspects of UI should be replaced by a new national income or wage supplementation program. Much of the framework outlined by these reports has now been adopted. Unfortunately, many of the positive recommendations of the reports, such as the dramatic expansion of labour adjustment programs, were ignored.

THE ATTACK ON TRANSFER INCOME

This unemployment insurance strategy can be seen as one part of a larger effort to significantly alter the entire income security framework that was established in Canada between 1940 and 1971. Various periods – the 1940s, 1950s, and even more so the 1960s – witnessed a flurry of income security expansion: the initial introduction of UI in 1940, family allowances in 1944, Old Age Security in 1951, the Canada Assistance Plan, the Canada Pension Plan, and the Guaranteed Income Supplement in 1966, and in 1971 the dramatic expansion of UI. These were some of the remaining elements of the Beveridge-style Keynesian welfare state that was outlined by Leonard Marsh in the 1940s. Despite a large unfinished social policy agenda, this strategy was effectively abandoned in the mid-1970s. No significant new welfare state development has occurred since the early 1970s.

Canada's income security system is made up of a complex set of public and private programs. Most analysts, if not the general public, now recognize that income security programs are delivered through a combination of transfers and taxes. There are many examples of poor integration and contradictory tendencies; what transfer policy does on the one hand (e.g., family allowances) tax policy undermines on the other (e.g., the child-care deduction). Current changes are often difficult to detect, even for those schooled in income security policy. For example, the universal demogrant – family allowance – has been partially de-indexed so that its real value will decline every year by at least 3 percent as long as inflation continues above that level. A similar formula has been applied to the refundable child tax credit and to many other aspects of the tax/transfer system.

More recently, in the 1989 federal budget, universality was dealt the death knell by the imposition of a "clawback" on family allowances and on Old Age Security. Universal child and retirement benefits are being squeezed and in a decade will be virtually meaningless in terms of supplementing the incomes of families with children and of the elderly.

The reality for Canadians is that the limited social dividends they have now are in serious and purposeful decline. This is an important part of the strategy to restructure Canadian labour markets.

On the fiscal level, tax reform has hit low- and middle-income earners the hardest and given windfalls to rich individuals and corporations.[3] The maintenance of the grossly unfair deduction for contributions to registered retirement savings plans in the context of an overall shift to fairer tax credits highlights this fact. Even more important is the reduction in personal income marginal tax rates and a decline in the relative importance of generally progressive income taxes as a source of government revenue. While there is little doubt that the federal manufacturers sales tax needed to be scrapped, the new goods and services tax (GST) is a highly regressive new tax initiative that will play a larger revenue-generating role for the federal government in the future than what it replaces.

DANGERS OF AN INCOME SUPPLEMENTATION STRATEGY

Labour flexibility is widely seen as essential to an ability to compete internationally within the global economy. Globalized markets and new technologies demand more flexibility in the deployment of labour. But how flexibility is achieved varies, depending on the relative power of capital and labour. One idea of flexibility is "numerical" in the sense that workers' wages should fluctuate and employers should be able to adjust the size of their work forces quickly in response to competitive pressures by changing levels of production or shifting to new products.[4] This approach to flexibility is prevalent in the context of weak labour movements and industrial relations structures that reinforce traditional management prerogatives with respect to layoffs. The flexibility sought by Canadian employers is for the most part a numerical flexibility. This means that the dominant approach of employers is to reduce wages, or weaken organized labour's wage demands, and to lay off workers with impunity.

The alternative flexibility is "functional" and is more common in economies and firms where labour is highly skilled, organized, and more powerful, and where there is a smaller discrepancy between the top and bottom range of wages. Workers who are highly skilled can easily move from job to job in response to changes in production, and with more wage equality there is less need to protect rigidly defined job definitions. This has been the foundation of the successful Swedish approach to industrial relations and their high productivity achievements.[5]

The income security strategy of the federal government fits well with business's desire to increase labour flexibility in Canada. But it is designed to increase numerical flexibility rather than functional flexibility. The strategy is in large part based on the prevailing relations of power in the workplace.[6]

An integral part of the tax/transfer reform strategy, under the guise of deficit reduction, is to reduce protection provided to people at all income levels and to introduce some form of guaranteed income (or income supplementation plan), probably by using the refundable sales tax credit as the basic foundation. Those who know about the history of income security reform efforts in Canada will recognize the recurring themes here.

The most important concept embodied by the term "guaranteed income" is income supplementation. While income support (i.e., social assistance) is provided to people with no other means of assistance, and income continuity (i.e., social insurance) is provided to people who lose their wages through unemployment, retirement, or disability, income supplementation is provided to people to supplement low incomes, however derived. The first income supplementation scheme in Canada, family allowances, was provided to families to compensate for the unrelatedness of wages and family size. We now have a wide variety of income supplements provided through the tax and transfer systems. None, however, in itself guarantees an adequate income – hence the idea of a more generalized guaranteed annual income or national income supplementation program.

There are three main reasons for the introduction of an income supplementation program: to improve the incomes of the working poor, to expand labour supply by increasing the incentive to work or to stay in a low-wage job (removing the poverty trap), and to make wages more flexible. The two mechanisms for the delivery of a guaranteed income are a social dividend or demogrant paid out to everybody and then taxed back from higher-income earners, like our family allowance program or the more generally preferred negative income tax, which, like our child tax credit, is paid out only to those with lower incomes. Although they sound dramatically different, the social dividend and the negative income tax are basically the same thing. One pays out in advance and relies on the tax system to recoup some of the benefits; the other essentially taxes the benefits before they are given out. What matters is the basic guarantee levels that are set, the break-even points of income where people lose the benefits, and the rates at which income from other sources is taxed back.

A high guarantee level is required to assure adequacy, and a low tax-back rate is required to assure a strong incentive to earn extra income. But this combination means that the break-even point will be very high (i.e., it will be paid to very high income earners) and will cost a lot. As a consequence, all serious proposals for an income supplementation program have been guided by a cost containment strategy and have incorporated the major negative aspects of the existing system, such as high tax-back rates, low guarantee levels, the maintenance of questionable categorical distinctions between people (such as those who are expected and not expected to work), as well as poor integration of the tax and transfer system.

The key reason for support of income supplementation by business (reiterated consistently in the editorials of the *Financial Post*) and by the Macdonald Commission relates to the third objective – the desire to improve the flexibility of labour. There is a real danger in this vision of how to deal with problems in the labour market. In an economy that operates at less than full employment and that has a weak labour movement, an income supplementation program would likely make wages downwardly flexible. By reducing tax-back rates that now apply to welfare, labour supply would increase. This would increase competition in the labour market, particularly at the low end of the wage scale, and would tend to lower wages. It would also more effectively induce wages to adjust downwards in periods of high unemployment because there would be less resistance on the part of workers to take lower-wage jobs, since the loss of income due to wage erosion would in part be compensated by the income supplement provided by government.[7]

As a form of wage subsidy, an income supplementation program would over the long run potentially create an incentive to employers to restructure jobs to take advantage of any supplementation provided to individuals. There is evidence that this has happened with UI insofar as it has supplemented incomes, and it would not be surprising to find the same dynamic with a new supplementation program. Another problem would be the potential for employers to split full-time jobs into part-time jobs in order to take advantage of the reduced wages and increased flexibility associated with part-time workers. Low-level income supplementation would make up for the loss of income to individuals shifting from full- to part-time work and would reduce their resistance to change. The negative effects of income supplementation would be highest in the context of high unemployment. Clearly, the danger is that income supplementation may simply accelerate the push towards a low-wage economy.

A basic assumption of business and the federal government is that Canadian wages are too high and that we have an inflexible labour market. This is the implicit rationale for welfare state erosion – the need to compete in an increasingly competitive global labour market. This strategy of course is folly. We could choose to compete in those industries that require cheap labour, such as in shoes and clothing, and may even benefit in the short run by increased employment, but the benefit to the country as a whole in the long run would be limited. We could never hope to compete with low-wage countries that produce these same products, particularly in a world with declining tariff barriers and especially under the Canada-US Free Trade Agreement.

THE ALTERNATIVE VISION

An alternative vision of economic and social development does exist. The alternative to competition based on downward wage flexibility is one based on the idea that we can improve our standard of living through increases in functional labour flexibility and continuous productivity increases. This is the intuitive appeal to progressive forces of the basic premise of the Ontario Premier's Council's strategy.[8] (The reports of the council are discussed later in this chapter and elsewhere in this book.) The premise of the council's work was that we don't get richer by expanding our low-wage, low value-added production, but by raising the proportion of the labour force in high value-added production. The important idea is that economic growth, productivity increases, and even the ability to compete internationally are not incompatible with higher levels of income and increased employment security for workers.

It is here that the welfare state plays a crucial role. Rather than a constraint on the market, the welfare state can be part of the solution in that it can build social productivity through investments in education, training, and health, and encourage social citizenship and solidarity through universal income security, high-quality social services, and effective labour adjustment mechanisms.[9] Such a vision sees the positive role that income security (and regulations such as the minimum wage) has on the economy in inducing productivity improvements. A high-wage, high-employment strategy is the context in which the struggle against poverty and inequality has to be mounted. This vision also sees the traditional separation between economic and social policy as inappropriate. There are limits to which the state can redistribute; it is much more effective to assure that the distribution of income, primarily through wages, is equitable in the first place.[10] High levels of investment in training and education are critical components of such a strategy. Reform within the employment system has to embrace pay equity and employment equity as well.

What follows represents the major components of an alternative income security and labour market policy strategy. This strategy reinforces high wages and the development of social solidarity. While I have concentrated on the deeds (and misdeeds) of the federal government, since it is responsible for much of the income security system, it should be emphasized that provincial governments have considerable scope for regulation of labour markets and, therefore, can on their own undertake important initiatives that move us towards an alternative to wage erosion and labour market insecurity.

The Income Security System

The first element of reform focuses on the need for strong social insurance programs for the maintenance of income in unemployment, disability, and old age. Any progressive income security alternative must begin with a defence of unemployment insurance.

Unemployment Insurance. Unemployment insurance is the largest single income security program in Canada. Despite its many drawbacks UI remains an important source of security for workers, especially in the context of an economy that faces considerable labour market adjustment and continued high unemployment. As social insurance, UI provides non-stigmatizing income continuity, and sometimes supplementation, to people who suffer primarily because of the economy's failure to achieve high levels of employment.

Many of the problems of UI would be considerably less important if there were a greater commitment to economic and labour market policies that reduce unemployment and expand education and training options. High unemployment and the failure to develop more comprehensive income security reform in Canada account for the distortion of the UI program. In the absence of alternatives, UI has had to assume many income security functions it would be better to leave to other programs. Given the lack of alternatives, UI plays an important, albeit inadequate, income security role for Canadian workers. UI should not be immune to reform. However, reform might focus on more democratic administrative arrangements at the community level or with labour, as well as on alternative uses.

Pensions. The system of income security for the elderly in Canada consists of the universal Old Age Security, the Canada/Quebec Pension plans, private occupational plans, private savings, and, when all of this fails to produce an adequate income in retirement, the income-tested Guaranteed Income Supplement. The most vulnerable group in old age is single women, whose independent pension rights are inadequate because of their lack of labour force attachment or because of intermittent attachments.

Some improvements have been made in reducing poverty in old age over the past decade. Increases in the Guaranteed Income Supplement in particular have been effective in reducing measured rates of poverty. But the pension system in Canada is still based on the idea that people will secure adequate income in retirement through their own means. This simply reproduces in old age the inequalities that exist in the labour market. Private pensions cover only a minority of people in the labour force. Many workers, especially women, are poor in retirement because they do not have occupational plans. The main solution to the pension problem is well known: expand the Canada/Quebec Pension plans (C/QPPs). The main political barrier to this strategy is the way it would trample on the rights of the major private financial institutions in the country that profit by access to the savings of workers.

Disability Insurance. The existing system of disability income replacement is an irrational, wasteful, and unfair patchwork that operates through workers' compensation, the C/QPPs, compensation for victims of crime, private individual and group long-term disability insurance, auto insurance, the tort liability system, UI sickness benefits, and, when all else fails, social assistance. Proposals for a comprehensive disability income program have been put forward by the federal Special Parliamentary Committee on the Disabled in 1981, the Macdonald Royal Commission in 1985, the Forget Commission on Unemployment Insurance in 1986, the Joint Federal-Provincial Study on a comprehensive disability income plan in 1985, and more recently by the Ontario Social Assistance Review Committee in 1988.

A truly universal disability insurance plan would merge all existing plans to eliminate duplication, inequity, and the inefficiencies of multiple administrations. It would also provide an indexed income replacement up to a maximum and could be funded through a combination of employer-employee contributions, a tax on gasoline and motor vehicles, a tax on hazardous activities, and general government revenue. It would also allow for an integrated and systematic approach to rehabilitation, a key element that would help stabilize costs. Some analysts believe that this kind of rationalization could result in a system of equal or lower cost overall than the existing system and in considerably improved coverage.[11]

The reason for the lack of action on disability income reform is similar to the reason we do not have pension reform. The alternative is there for a government willing to take on the powerful private insurance industry and legal profession, the only real beneficiaries of the status quo. In Ontario it is essential that any provincial effort to reform the auto insurance industry is made in the context of a rationalized income security system for the disabled.

Income Supplementation. It must be acknowledged that even if a high-wage strategy were pursued, wages, particularly for entry-level jobs, would not be enough to provide adequate incomes to all Canadians regardless of family size. Supplementing incomes remains an important short- and long-term objective for social policy. But income supplementation can be achieved in a wide variety of ways that do not reinforce low wages. Particularly useful income supplementation programs in this regard would include child benefits, housing and medical assistance, and assistance to single mothers, families, and women. Of these, child benefits – family allowances and the child tax credits – are of central importance. An enriched child-benefit system forms one cornerstone of a policy to eliminate child poverty, supplement family incomes, and make it possible for women, especially single mothers, to be in the labour force. Child benefits are important because they attack the problem of child poverty directly by giving money to families with children. They provide a cash supplement to the incomes of families whether or not they are in the labour market. Because they are given to people who are employed, they furnish an important supplement to low wages with no or few financial disincentives.

International comparisons have shown the importance of child benefits in keeping down poverty rates for children. Those countries that have more generous child-benefit systems than Canada have significantly lower rates of poverty among single-parent families.[12] The critical elements in any child-benefit package are that benefits be either universal and generous or income-tested and pitched to middle-income earners as well – or a combination of both. Such benefits would significantly increase the incomes of families working at low wages, have no financial disincentives, and have no stigma attached.

Unfortunately, Conservative policies have substantially reduced child benefits in Canada through partial de-indexation. This reduction in child benefits has several implications: (1) it will increase child poverty; (2) it will make it more difficult for women, especially single parents, to have adequate incomes; (3) it will undermine work incentives and make welfare relatively more attractive than low-wage work; and (4) it will in the long run create a greater burden of social assistance dependency in Canada.

Policies that the provinces could pursue on their own to supplement the incomes of people whose incomes are vulnerable include improved child-support arrangements, a new child-support or court-ordered maintenance payment program, extended day care, and improved parental leave. With such a strategy in place, and the labour market doing the job it should, it is doubtful that there would be a need for a more generalized non-categorical approach to income supplementation. There would also be little need for welfare or income support. Nevertheless, welfare reform constitutes the next major component of income security reform.

Welfare Reform. The purpose of welfare reform is to make social assistance a truly residual and transitional program meant to assist people in serious life changes achieve independence. The best articulation of this alternative vision of welfare was made by the Ontario Social Assistance Review Committee (SARC) in its 1988 report *Transitions*. Under a reformed system that includes employment, education, other transfers, and services, we may envision welfare as a significantly different program. The major difference would be that long-term dependency needs would be met by other programs outlined above, while the short-term needs would be met by a variety of income and in-kind supplements. Welfare would become a program of transition. People who require assistance because they have no other means of support would be assumed to require it for relatively short periods of time as they get their bearings and plan for the future. The primary beneficiaries of transitional assistance would be young, single people and women in transition because of a marriage break-up. Ontario should proceed post-haste with the implementation of the SARC proposals.

Labour Market Policy

The first priority for labour market policy is to raise the minimum wage. Since 1975, the minimum wage in Canada has declined in real value by up to 30 percent, depending on the province. The minimum wage is a policy tool that is controlled by provincial governments for the majority of the labour force. At the very least, it should be regularly increased in accordance with changes in average wages in some constant ratio (50 to 60 percent) to the average wage.

The Premier's Council's second report, *People and Skills in the New Global Economy* (June 1990), provides a useful framework for an approach to labour market policy. The report encompasses education, training, and labour adjustment as supports for the idea of a move towards a high-wage, high-productivity economy. The main theme of the council's approach was the need for Ontario to pursue an education- and skills-based adjustment strategy.

Central to the report's analysis was the recognition of the failure of federal training and adjustment policy – under the guise of the Canadian Jobs Strategy – to meet the challenges posed by restructuring in Ontario. The council argued that Ontario should move into areas of labour market policy that have been the exclusive or prime responsibility of the federal government. This bears consideration by the new Ontario government. The well-documented failure of federal labour market and, especially, training policies and the vulnerability of Ontario with free trade demand a unique Ontario approach to labour market training and adjustment.

In the training area, the most significant proposal was for Ontario to establish a Training and Adjustment Board. This would allow business and labour a direct role in managing training and adjustment in Ontario. Sectorally based committees made up of labour and management would be a key mechanism for initiating training, while regional committees and an apprenticeship board would also direct training to appropriate needs. The key assumption underlying the proposal is that a management-, labour-, and community-controlled training body would be more effective than a government-driven one. This system has its roots in the philosophy of Sweden's Labour Market Board.

The Premier's Council also advocated specific changes in labour adjustment policies. These included improved advance notice, mandatory adjustment committees at the level of the firm, and a wage protection plan for workers who lose severance pay and wages in cases of closures and bankruptcies. The philosophy behind these policies was that worker security was compatible with labour flexibility. To the extent that workers are highly skilled and multi-skilled and have a high degree of security of income and employment (although not necessarily with the same employer), they will be more likely to favour positive adjustment and change. As Block argues, a universal welfare state where worker security is taken for granted is a society where flexibility and productivity are most likely to be achieved.[13]

CONCLUSION

Progressive forces badly need a vision to present to Canadians of the real alternative to welfare state erosion. This vision has to embrace a credible idea of economic renewal. Without such a vision, efforts to expand the welfare state will be perceived as naive. Secondly, progressives too often find themselves unequivocally defending programs that have contradictory effects. The alternative vision should tap into widespread sentiments that the existing system reinforces dependency, but it should do so without blaming the victims of the system. This can be done by building on the idea that an income security system should be a springboard rather than a trap. The best way to do this is to focus on improvements in the labour market and to create programs that encourage independence, high levels of skills, and high wages. Finally, a key lesson from the Swedish experience is that a strong, universal welfare state is of central importance in building cross-class political alliances in favour of welfare state efforts and redistribution. In Canada there is both a critical need and opportunity to build alliances between women, labour, the disabled, families, and other groups who benefit in one way or another from the welfare state. To the extent that all Canadians can identify with the welfare state, they will be likely to support a broad range of welfare efforts.

NOTES

1 See Economic Council of Canada, *Good Jobs, Bad Jobs: Employment in the Service Sector* (Ottawa: Supply and Services Canada, 1990).

2 See Morley Gunderson and Leon Muszynski, *Women and Labour Market Poverty* (Ottawa: Canadian Advisory Council on the Status of Women, 1990).

3 Leon Muszynski, *Is It Fair: What Tax Reform Will Do to You* (Ottawa: Canadian Centre for Policy Alternatives, 1988).

4 For a discussion of these notions of flexibility, see Ontario Premier's Council, *People and Skills in the New Global Economy* (1990), section 3.

5 For a discussion of how flexibility is achieved in different industrial relations settings see Paul Osterman, *Employment Futures* (New York: Oxford University Press, 1988).

6 See Leon Muszynski and David Wolfe, "New Technology and Training: Lessons from Abroad," *Canadian Public Policy* 15, no. 3 (September 1989).

7 For a discussion of the economic effects of income supplementation, see Mario Iacobacci, *The Labour Market Effects of Earnings Supplementation Schemes in Canada: A Focus on the Incidence of Low-Wage Employment* (Ottawa: UI Analysis Directorate, Strategic Policy and Planning, Employment and Immigration, November 1987).

8 See Ontario Premier's Council, *Competing in the New Global Economy* (1988), and *People and Skills in the New Global Economy* (1990).

9 See Fred Block, *Revising State Theory* (Philadelphia: Temple University Press, 1987), chap. 9.

10 For an elaboration of this position, see Robert E. Goodin and Julian Le Grand, eds., *Not Only the Poor: The Middle Classes and the Welfare State* (London: Routledge & Kegan Paul, 1985), concluding chapter.

11 See Leon Muszynski, "Alternatives to Welfare Policy," *Options* 9, no. 2 (March 1988).

12 T. Smeeding, Barbara Boyle Torrey, and Martin Rein, "Patterns of Income and Poverty: The Economic Status of Children and the Elderly in Eight Countries," in J. Palmer, T. Smeeding, and B. Boyle Torrey, eds., *The Vulnerable* (Washington: Urban Institute Press, 1988).

13 See Fred Block, "Rethinking the Political Economy of the Welfare State," in Fred Block et al., eds., *The Mean Season* (New York: Pantheon, 1989).

12 Deficits – Fact or Fiction? Ontario's Public Finances and the Challenge of Full Employment

HAROLD CHORNEY

INTRODUCTION

Since the NDP came to power in Ontario, the government has been under intense pressure because of the public sector deficit. There are indeed constraints issuing from the deficit, but as I hope this essay will show, they are largely political rather than economic. The premier and the treasurer have been courageous in resisting the siren calls of conventional and, one might add, conservative wisdom. One hopes they will be prepared to continue along the road to rededicating Canadian public policy to the humane and economically rational objective of full employment and stable, ecologically balanced, equitable economic growth. Social democracy requires nothing less than this commitment. If there is one lesson to be learned from our past, it is that sound finance and fiscal conservatism are fundamentally incompatible with a just and equitable society and therefore with social democracy itself.

Fiscal conservatism is more than just politically and morally inappropriate for social democrats – and for progressive liberals for that matter. It is also based on misguided and false economic logic. It is therefore economically wasteful of potential productive output and thus of human lives. It is no coincidence that periods where the dogma of sound finance and balanced budgets hold sway are also periods of profound human disruption and suffering and unstable economic growth. In order to see why that is so, it is necessary to explore at some length a number of common misconceptions that exist about public sector debt and deficits. But first we must assess the actual situation in Ontario as we find it in 1991.

THE PUBLIC SECTOR DEBT AND DEFICIT IN ONTARIO

Despite all the outcry over the increase in public sector deficits in Ontario, the ratio of the provincial debt to the gross provincial product (GPP) – the only meaningful way to measure indebtedness – was and continues to be among the lowest in Canada. No other Canadian province has such a consistently low debt to GPP ratio. Part of the explanation lies in the fact that until the current recession, Ontario had been blessed with relatively lower rates of unemployment and higher than average rates of economic growth. It is the relative strength of the Ontario economy that explains the absence of serious public sector debt.

Problems with public sector debt usually arise after periods of slow growth and higher unemployment. Governments generally respond to a downturn with policies of austerity and high interest rates rather than policies of stimulation. An even worse situation arises when governments deliberately use unemployment and high interest rates as weapons against inflation. This classical monetarist policy prescription has been followed, for example, by the federal government since the recession of 1981–82.[1] It became the policy choice of the Bank of Canada in 1975. The results have been a prolonged period of higher unemployment and a chronic obsession with a stubborn public sector deficit that refuses to disappear.

The recession of 1981–82, although severe, was followed by a much more rapid and substantial recovery in Ontario than in other parts of the country. By 1987 Ontario's unemployment rate had fallen to 6.1 percent. The national rate rose from 7.5 percent in 1980 to 11.0 percent in 1982 and 11.8 percent in 1983. By 1987 it still stood at 8.8 percent, a full 1.3 percentage points above the rate that prevailed before the recession.

Throughout the decade from 1980 to 1989, unemployment averaged 9.3 percent for Canada, 7.4 percent for Ontario, and 11.3 percent for Quebec. As of August 1991, unemployment stood at 10.5 percent nationally, 9.9 percent in Ontario, and just over 12 percent in Quebec.[2] Toronto's rate was 10.8 percent and Montreal's, 12 percent.

The current recession has caused a considerable increase in the public sector deficit in Ontario.[3] The 1990 Ontario budget projected an actual operating surplus of $30 million in the 1990/91 budget

Table 12.1
Debt to Gross Provincial Product, Ontario, 1973–91

1973/74	13.9	1983/84	18.0
1974/75	13.2	1984/85	17.5
1975/76	15.2	1985/86	17.9
1976/77	14.8	1986/87	17.4
1977/78	15.2	1987/88	16.5
1978/79	15.8	1988/89	15.7
1979/80	15.2	1989/90	14.6
1980/81	14.8	1990/91	15.0
1981/82	16.2	1991/92	18.3
1982/83	17.4		

Note: Data for the fiscal years 1973/74 to 1980/81 are based on the ratio of funded debt to GPP and are taken from the 1982 Ontario budget. Data for fiscal years 1981/82 to 1990/91 are based on the ratio of total debt to GPP and are taken from the 1990 and 1991 Ontario budgets. Funded debt includes bonds, debentures, notes, and treasury bills but excludes Ontario Hydro debt. Total debt appears to be a larger figure and may include several broader categories of debt.

year. In fact, the actual result will probably be a capital deficit of more than $3 billion. The 1990 budget was premised on unemployment averaging 5.6 percent throughout 1990, with the national rate averaging 7.8 percent. In reality, the Ontario rate averaged 6.3 percent and the national rate, 8.1 percent.[4] The rise in unemployment, the unexpected increase in social assistance expenditures, and the decline in revenues on account of the recession have caused the deficit to increase substantially. As well, it would appear that certain expenditures associated with largely non-business-cycle expenditures, such as health care, have been greater than expected.

Despite the rise in the deficit, the increase in the ratio of debt to GPP has been less dramatic (See Table 12.1). Even if the deficit rises by some $9.7 billion in the 1991/92 fiscal year as projected in the budget and the GPP shrinks by 3 percent over 1991, the ratio of total debt to GPP will still be only 18.3 percent by the end of 1992. This is a rate that is within the range of the debt to GPP ratios over the past decade and compares well with the previous recession, given the rise and fall in the ratio in response to the rise and fall of the business cycle itself.

It is clear from Table 12.1 that the financial position of Ontario is very sound and in no way threatened by the increase in debt due to the current economic recession. This reality of financial solidity is reinforced when one compares the Ontario situation with that of her sister province, Quebec, where the debt to GPP ratio is considerably higher. Furthermore, it must be understood that as of the end of the fiscal year 1990/91, 97 percent of the provincial debt, exclusive of Ontario Hydro debt, is owed to Ontario and Canadian savers. These include the Canada Pension Plan Investment Fund, the Ontario Teachers' Pension Fund, the Public Service Pension Fund, and the Ontario Municipal Employees Retirement Fund.

In the current fiscal year, it will probably be necessary for Ontario to finance much, if not all, of the new debt from sources other than these traditional sources, but the net new additional debt, some $9.7 billion, of which $4.3 billion is for capital expenditures, is still likely to be almost entirely financed within Canadian capital markets. In other words, Ontario will continue to owe its debt to Ontario and Canadian taxpayers. As such, the burden of the debt is largely illusory. It may well have adverse income distributional implications, but because the financiers of the debt pay taxes in Canada and spend most of their incomes within Canada, much of the payments on the debt simply return in future rounds of expenditure and taxation to the Ontario economy. Beneficiaries of interest on the debt, because they feel richer on account of it, may spend or invest more in the economy. To the extent that the interest is subject to taxation, it will be partly recaptured in government tax revenues.

Furthermore, while it is true that future generations will inherit the debt, these same generations will also inherit the bonds and the incomes that flow from them. As well, they will inherit and benefit from the productive assets, including human capital, that are financed by current government expenditures. To the extent they are burdened, they are also enriched. Indeed, society is enriched because the debt permits expenditures, many of them of a capital nature that would not occur in a time of economic downturn unless they were debt financed. Of course, it would be much better if these expenditures were financed at much lower interest rates because of the rentier nature of the interest payments and the income distributional consequences. For all those who purchase it, the debt of the Canadian and Ontario governments represents a real and tangible asset. It would even be better again if some of the expenditures were financed by zero interest loans, such as is possible when the central bank buys the bonds and monetizes the debt. In order to better explain the impact of austerity and sound finance, let me try to clear up a number of misconceptions about debts and deficits.

DEFICITS AND DEBT: CLEARING UP SOME CONCEPTUAL CONFUSIONS

The most common misconception about the deficit and government debt is the notion that the impact of a public deficit is exactly comparable to one's own personal financial situation when one is in debt. After all, as the logic goes, you can't go on being in debt forever. In fact, however, as far as countries are concerned, there is a fair bit of evidence that this is not true. If we examine the indebtedness of countries like Britain, the United States, and Canada, we discover that they have debts that accumulated over centuries.

In the case of the US, for example, there is a historical ebb and flow to debt reflecting economic and military events. The ratio of gross debt to the size of the economy, or GNP, rose significantly during the American Revolution, the Civil War, and the two world wars. The ratio also rose, though less steeply than during the Second World War, during periods of economic downturn and high unemployment.

The experience of Britain since the end of the eighteenth century is not radically different. The Napoleonic Wars, the First World War, and the Second World War were all periods associated with significant increases in indebtedness. The economic depressions of the late nineteenth century and those of the 1930s and 1980s were also periods when indebtedness rose sharply.

The Canadian situation follows this pattern. The ratio of debt to GNP in such periods was much greater than at present, and the national economy survived. Indeed, following the Second World War, during which enormous debts associated with military expenditures had accumulated (i.e., dead-weight debts unsecured by comparable assets), there was a period of rapid economic growth. In 1946, at the end of the war, the ratio of net federal public debt to GNP was over 100 percent. Today it is about 60 percent. Because military expenditures involve the production of goods and services that ultimately are destroyed or rarely have peacetime application, the debt associated with these expenditures can be considered deadweight. Debts incurred to finance the production of assets, on the other hand, are not a burden and should not be regarded as such. This is particularly important when debts are incurred as part of a policy to promote fuller employment.

The situation in the provinces is not that different from the experience of the federal government. Ontario, for example, during the Depression of the 1930s had a much higher ratio of debt to GPP than it does today. The ratio was over 60 percent in comparison to a ratio of less than 15 percent in 1990. The ratio steadily fell in the 1940s as full employment returned during the Second World War. It has stayed within the current range of low ratios since the 1950s.[5]

Since much of government expenditure on health care and education, for example, is essentially investment in human capital, it is sensible not to finance all of these activities out of current expenditures. It is irrational to cut back on the expenditure on these programs when a business-cycle downturn occurs because this only delays necessary investments and ensures they will cost more in the future. In fact, capital-works projects will be cheaper during business-cycle downturns because of lower labour and material costs.

When investment intentions in the private sector are weakened because of a downturn, it only compounds the problem to cut back on the public side. The great error made by contemporary neoconservative economists and many politicians in all three major parties is to misunderstand the partnership between the public and private sectors of the economy – specifically, this partnership's key role in producing economic value. Privately produced economic value is not possible without the necessary infrastructure and human capital produced by the public sector. The great strength of social democracy is that it recognizes this symbiotic relationship and nurtures it. To do otherwise is to weaken the productive potential of the economy. What is morally good – the creation of full employment – is also economically beneficial.

Another common error is to confuse the public sector deficit with the foreign trade deficit. In fact, these are quite different concepts. They are only connected if part of the public sector deficit is financed by government borrowing in foreign capital markets or if domestic financing of the debt forces private borrowers to go abroad for funds. In either case, interest payments to foreigners and capital inflows from abroad become part of the balance of payments. In such circumstances, domestic interest rates and exchange rate risk can become important factors in attracting funds.[6]

In the case of Ontario Hydro, which finances $5.2 billion of its $7.9 billion of direct debt in the United States, the issue of dependence on foreign borrowers is a significant one. Here, issues such as exchange rate risk and impact on the Canadian balance of payments are important. Since Ontario Hydro investments are directly and more obviously linked to future cash-generating activities than other public expenditures, many of the concerns raised about public sector indebtedness are often waved aside. But in reality there is not much difference between much of the expenditures of the public sector financed through debt creation and those of Ontario Hydro. Both kinds of expenditures create the possibility of future cash flow benefits. The difference is that Ontario Hydro's are more directly obvious than are investments in education, health care, basic infrastructure, and human capital. Given the high dependence of Ontario Hydro on American savings, it may well be time to re-evaluate the role of Canadian capital markets in financing Hydro investment. In any case, for the purposes of this essay, the financing of Hydro investment is a separate issue.

Some economists might also argue that funds borrowed from abroad free up domestic savings for other activities or that domestic borrowing by the public sector drives private borrowers abroad. In regard to the latter assertion, the argument turns on whether or not there is a fixed supply of loanable funds. In fact, loanable funds are themselves the product of central bank policy and fiscal policy and are therefore not fixed stocks but flows, subject to the flow of economic activity, including public sector activity, which generates incomes and savings from which loanable funds are drawn. In any case, the federal Canadian debt is over 82 percent domestically held.

In recent years much has been made of the tendency for Japanese investors to buy Canadian treasury bills and long-term bonds. While it is true that there has been a greater interest shown by these foreign investors in our debt instruments, the total amount of foreign holdings in comparison to the total debt – 18.6 percent – is still quite small and manageable. In Ontario, exclusive of Hydro, the percentage is negligible – less than 3 percent. Some private sector critics and some Treasury officials have warned of an erosion of Ontario's credit rating because of the rise in public sector debts. Aside from the fact that it is unwise and essentially undemocratic to make policy decisions according to the will of private concerns that are not part of the electorate and that in certain cases are non-Canadian, in reality an erosion of Ontario's AAA credit rating to AA+ would cost the province only $25 million in extra annual interest payments.[7] This is a modest cost in comparison with the lost output and human suffering that would result from austerity policies that would please the credit-rating agencies.

THE DIFFERENCE BETWEEN THE DEBT AND THE DEFICIT

When we use the terms debt and deficit, it is important to establish very clearly what level of government we are speaking about and what accounting basis we are using to measure the debt and deficit. A deficit, of course, is simply the difference between government expenditures and government revenues. When expenditures exceed revenues in a given year, there is a deficit. When revenues exceed expenditures, there is a surplus. The year-to-year accumulation of surpluses and deficits yields the outstanding debt or surplus. Any retirement of debt (i.e., any redemption of a loan outstanding) reduces the total debt outstanding. The deficit (or surplus) can be calculated for the federal government alone, for the provincial government(s), for the hospital sector, for the Canada and Quebec Pension plans, and for local levels of government. As well, the deficit or surplus can be calculated for federal, provincial, and local enterprise. The consolidation of all these accounts yields the overall consolidated public sector deficit or surplus. The notion of the consolidated public sector deficit or surplus thus involves examining each aspect of the public sector independently and arriving at a financial balance for each sector and then aggregating the result.

Often the public is unaware that the Canada and Quebec Pension plans and the hospital sector, for example, are important parts of the public sector from a financial point of view. The net financial balance in each of these sectors as well as in the provincial and municipal sectors have to be taken into account if we are to have a sense of the total picture insofar as national public debt is concerned.

In the case of Ontario, the consolidated public sector debt consists of debt issued for provincial purposes, deposits with the Province of Ontario Savings Office and other deposits, Ontario Hydro direct debt, Ontario Hydro debt guaranteed by the province, and a residual category, other public sector debt, which is an estimate of debt in the form of bonds, debentures, and notes, excluding sinking funds and own holdings incurred by provincial agencies and by local government, university, and hospital sectors. The public sector deficit that is the subject of so much public concern is the portion of the annual addition to the stock of debt that occurs because direct expenditures exceed revenues in the operating budget of the government. Expenditures in this case include interest paid on outstanding debt exclusive of Ontario Hydro debt. A certain proportion of the debt is held by the province itself or by its own institutions and ought to be deducted from the total when its economic impact is assessed.[8]

Thus, whenever someone cries in alarm about the mounting deficit, it is critical to inquire, what deficit is being spoken of? Is it the federal deficit, the provincial deficit, the local government deficit? Does it include the accounts of the hospital sector, the pension funds, government enterprises? Does the measure net out the holdings of debt by other public sector institutions?

For example, as of the end of 1987, the Bank of Canada held over $20 billion of the total federal debt. The proportion of the total federal debt held by the bank represents the proportion of the debt that the bank has monetized. In other words, each year the central bank purchases a portion of the net deficit and pays for it by expanding the money stock. Significantly, the proportion the bank purchases and holds in this way has declined from the 20 to 30 percent range during the 1960s to under 10 percent during the 1980s. Data for 1989 show that only 7.6 percent of the total of the federal government debt was held by the central bank. This reflects the bank's belief in the monetarist doctrine that monetizing any significant portion of the debt is automatically inflationary. In fact, the evidence for this is not convincing in all circumstances. There were a number of years where 20–30 percent of the debt was monetized but inflation rates remained low. Since the mass of the debt has greatly increased in recent years, monetarist economists would argue that the proportion of the debt that should be monetized should decrease in order to preserve monetized debt as a constant proportion of the money stock. But when the debt is measured against the money stock defined as currency outside the banks and chartered bank deposits, the ratio, as seen above, has dropped sharply in recent years. Thus, there is considerable room for the central bank to monetize more of the debt and thereby reduce interest rates to stimulate employment growth. There are undoubtedly upper limits to what proportion of the debt can be monetized before inflation is generated but we are nowhere near those limits today.

From an accounting point of view, inter- and intra-governmental holdings of debt should be identified when the economic significance of the debt is assessed. As well, these debts ought to be compared with the assets that the government holds in terms of buildings, land, and capital infrastructure. All too often, these assets are not properly accounted for at current values as opposed to original acquisition prices or even, in certain circumstances, at nominal token dollar values. In Ontario's case, for example, although expenditures are broken down into current and capital expenditures, no account is taken of public assets that are offset by public debt. If this were done, the total public debt of some $40 billion would pale in comparison to the total value of Ontario assets.

It is fairly meaningless therefore to speak about the deficit as an absolute dollar figure. While talk of Canada's $30-billion deficit has a certain shock value, very little indeed is revealed about the state of the economy. The only meaningful way to assess the debt is to measure its size in relation to the overall size of the economy – the gross domestic product in the case of Canada and the gross provincial product in the case of Ontario. When this is done, it is possible to understand that despite the growth in the ratio of federal debt to the GDP, it is still not anywhere near the peak that occurred in the postwar period. Nor for that matter is it yet equal to the secondary peak that occurred in the early 1930s. Indeed, the ratio today of

Table 12.2
Net Federal Public Debt As a Percentage of GNP*

Fiscal Year	*% of GNP*	*Fiscal Year*	*% of GNP*
1926/27	45.6	1970/71	20.6
1931/32	50.6	1971/72	20.5
1936/37	66.6	1972/73	19.9
1941/42	48.3	1973/74	18.5
1946/47	106.6	1974/75	16.8
1951/52	48.0	1975/76	18.3
1956/57	35.7	1976/77	19.0
1957/58	34.7	1977/78	22.0
1958/59	36.0	1978/79	25.1
1959/60	35.6	1979/80	26.1
1960/61	35.6	1980/81	27.6
1961/62	35.7	1981/82	28.2
1962/63	34.7	1982/83	34.3
1963/64	34.8	1983/84	39.6
1964/65	32.4	1984/85	44.8
1965/66	28.9	1985/86	48.8
1966/67	26.1	1986/87	52.3
1967/68	25.4	1987/88	53.1
1968/69	23.7	1988/89	53.4
1969/70	21.2	1989/90	55.0

Source: Hon. Michael Wilson, minister of finance, "Public Debt: The Fiscal Plan," Budget Papers, February 1988, Table 11; the Budget, 1990; the Budget, 1991.

* Period 1926/27 to 1960/61 shows percentage of debt to gross national product; period 1961/62 to 1989/90 shows percentage of debt to the gross domestic product.

about 60 percent is only 25 percent above the ratio in 1952, when it stood at 48 percent. In 1952 inflation was 2.4 percent, unemployment 2 percent, and the real rate of interest 2.2 percent. Despite a mass of debt in relation to GNP that is only 25 percent higher, the ratio of interest payment on the debt to GNP has doubled from 2.6 percent as compared to over 5 percent today. Clearly, it is not the relative size of the debt that counts as much as it is the real rate of interest.

The situation in Ontario is even less of a problem. The ratio of the debt to the GPP will be less than 20 percent even after the large deficit expected for 1990/91 and the larger one budgeted for 1991/92. Interest on the debt in 1990, when it stood at $39 billion, was 10.3 percent of total revenue, or 1.5 percent of the GPP. Assuming an increase in the debt of $9.7 billion and average interest on this portion of the debt of 9 percent, the interest to GPP ratio should be about 1.8 percent. Interest rates are clearly far too high in real terms and should be reduced so that the real rate of interest is no more than a percentage point or a point and a half. In other words, a nominal rate of only 1.5 percentage points above the rate of inflation is a reasonable real rate of interest given the record of real interest rates over the past sixty years.

THE BURDEN OF THE DEBT AND OTHER DEBT ILLUSIONS

One of the more complicated debates concerning the deficit revolves around the issue of the "burden" of the debt.[9] One of the brief accomplishments of the Keynesian era was the puncturing of the myth that a rise in state indebtedness paralleled a rise in private indebtedness. In the first instance, the argument turns around the question of to whom the debt is owed. In the case of an individual, the debt is owed to outsiders and therefore its repayment constitutes a burden on future income streams. This burden has a present value that can be compared with the benefit to be gained by getting into debt. Clearly, individuals make the decision (to the extent that becoming indebted is ever a voluntary decision) on the basis of comparing the present value of the benefit acquired with the loan against the cost imposed by future repayment of the debt. Can we then compare the situation of an individual with that of a country?

The answer to this question is not simple, but the short answer is definitely no. Unlike the case of an individual, there is very little chance of a country such as Canada or a province as large and economically diverse as Ontario becoming insolvent. Indeed, as William Krehm has pointed out, current accounting practices greatly overestimate the size of the accumulated government debt and at the same time grossly underestimate the value of government assets.[10]

One must make a distinction between a secured and an unsecured debt. Debt unsecured by assets are dead-weight debts. Such debts do impose a burden upon an economy. By contrast, debts secured by assets are normally an investment in the future wealth of the economy and are counted as such. Government debt represents investment in public assets. The total wealth of our public sector, including our network of roads, expressways, rapid transit systems, hospitals, airports, ports, power plants, public buildings, universities, schools, crown lands, and natural resources, represents enormous wealth-producing assets. As Krehm points out, the government's public accounts value lands, buildings, works, and equipment at the "nominal value of one dollar." This is clearly absurd.

It is also absurd to believe that one could lose faith in the net worth of Canada's or Ontario's collective assets without first having lost faith in the total value of the private sector itself. To understand this in simple terms, just divide the total value of the accumulated public debt in Canada (net of any debt held by public bodies) by the population of the country. Currently this figure works out to a few thousand dollars. Then ask yourself, would you be willing to buy one twenty-five millionth of all the assets belonging to Canada, including crown lands, for this price? I should think that there would be very few people who would regard this offer as anything less than a bargain.

Attempt the same calculation for the province of Ontario. Debt per capita in Ontario amounts to some $4,400. Divide the total value of Ontario's assets, including natural resources, provincial infrastructure, roads, hospitals, schools, universities, government buildings, crown lands, freeways, civic buildings, and local and provincial public works, and ask yourself whether one ten-millionth share in them is worth $4,400. The obvious answer is that their present value as assets far exceeds the present debt. It is nonsense to claim, as Mulroney does, "that the country is bankrupt." Factually this is untrue.

The only sense in which the situation of a private individual is comparable to that of a country is that in both cases the future cost of debt repayment can be measured against the future stream of benefits. So long as the present economy is operating at less than full employment and current debt represents an investment in jobs, both present and future benefits are enhanced. Every hospital, road, environmental improvement, and educational institution that is neglected today simply guarantees a more expensive burden for the future. Some conservative economists argue that the benefits of deficit-financed expenditures are exactly offset by the discounted present value of the cost of repaying the debt. However, this argument underestimates the degree to which the cost of the present unemployment of resources constitutes a burden for the future. In general, the conservative argument about the burden of the debt usually assumes away the most critical issue – namely, the fact that the economy is suffering from unemployment, and government borrowing therefore does not constitute a reduction in private economic activity.[11] The argument also tends to ignore the fact that those who own the financial assets and receive the future stream of earnings associated with them regard them as highly desirable. After the stock market crash in 1987, the flight to government debt instruments as "safe havens" was remarkable in this respect.

There may well be income redistribution questions involving who receives the interest payments associated with the debt and, for that matter, the incidence of taxation on the interest income associated with the holding of the debt. In regard to redistributive effects, one question relates to transfers of income through interest payments to those who loan the government money by buying its debt instruments, such as bonds and debentures. The incidence of taxation refers to the way in which the tax system recoups some of this income transfer.

To the extent that our tax system recaptures some of the increases in income and wealth, the money paid in interest payments to bond holders simply returns in the next round as tax receipts. In other instances, repayment is postponed because of tax shelters such as RRSPs; tax expenditure decisions along these lines ought to be subject to critical scrutiny. One could argue that too much income is sheltered in RRSPs. If the people who receive a large measure of their income from interest income also tend to be among the upper-income classes, these questions become important from an equity point of view. Nevertheless, whatever the redistributive effects and the incidence of taxation, the fact that the bulk of the debt is held internally and that the economy is not at full employment makes the burden argument less than convincing.

In the case of provinces, a more genuine problem involving the debt burden relates to leakages of revenues to non-residents. This is particularly so for provinces that have borrowed heavily in the European and Japanese markets when foreign currency values were low. In the absence of protective hedging against the rise in values, these provinces are forced to pay off loans at excessive values. However, this does not appear to be a problem in Ontario. The province itself has borrowed almost all of its money from internal sources. Only Ontario Hydro has borrowed heavily in foreign markets, and here almost all of the foreign borrowings have occurred in the United States. While the Canadian dollar is currently overvalued in relation to the American dollar, the likelihood of severe exchange rate risk for Ontario Hydro is probably small.

The fact that some provinces have resorted so heavily to foreign markets speaks loudly about the underdeveloped nature of Canadian capital markets and the inflexibility of the Bank of Canada in developing a significant market for the borrowing needs of the Canadian provinces. What would be wrong, for example, in allowing the provinces access to their relative share of the central bank's debt acquisition capacity? From the point of view of fiscal federalism and sound economic management, the proposition would seem to have much to recommend it. In Ontario, for example, this would permit provincial authorities greater flexibility in financing an increase in the deficit during an economic downturn. Since Ontario accounts for about 40 percent of the national gross domestic product, under the regime I am proposing it would be entitled to 40 percent of the share of debt-financing capacity provided by the Bank of Canada to help service the debt-financing needs of the provinces.

The amount of debt financing available to the provinces as a whole would be roughly one-half of the total debt-financing capacity of the Bank of Canada, given the fact that the discretionary spending power of the provinces, as a whole, is close to that of the federal government. The total amount of debt financing made available by the bank would be constrained by the operational rule that the relationship between monetized debt and the money stock be compatible with low inflation. Based on past evidence, this would appear to be somewhere in the 15 to 20 percent range. In other words, at no time could monetized debt in proportion to a broad measure of the money stock, say M2B, exceed this range. Obviously, this would not solve the total capital needs of the provinces or the federal government. But it would help matters considerably. The exact amount available would depend upon negotiations between the provincial and federal governments. Such an arrangement would improve the efficacy of fiscal policy in Canada, permit greater co-ordination of policy between the federal and provincial governments, and improve the operation of capital markets in the country. As well, it would help overcome the barrier that a federal state structure has placed in the way of the operation of effective fiscal policy in Canada. If other reforms permitting provincial input into the governance of the central bank and making interest rate policy more sensitive to regional concerns were implemented, for the first time in its history the Bank of Canada would become a truly federal institution.[12]

CONCLUSION

Space limitations do not permit a more comprehensive review of the issues involved in public sector debt and deficits as they apply to a province like Ontario.[13] But for the purposes of this essay, social democrats should note that Ontario is well placed to absorb the rise in its public sector deficit because of the current recession. Rather than impose austerity and thereby prolong the recession, the province ought to step forward and reverse the tide of neo-conservative dogma that has damaged Canada's economic prospects so dramatically in the past decade. Through a careful policy of planned investments in social and capital infrastructure, environmental improvement, and education and the development of an industrial policy aimed at durable job creation, the province could help reverse the recession and alter expectations about the economic future. By doing so it would be following a course that is both prudent and courageous. It would light the way ahead not only for Ontario but for the country as a whole.

NOTES

I would like to acknowledge the research support of SSHRC and the assistance of Richard Nimijean, Deppy Papandreou, Ana Gomez, Andrew Molloy, and Nicole Bernier.

1 I discuss this problem at length in "The Economic and Political Consequences of Canadian Monetarism" (Paper presented to the British Association of Canadian Studies, University of Nottingham, 12 April 1991).
2 All the data are from Statistics Canada, *Labour Force Survey.*
3 This is no surprise since Ontario lost 226,000 jobs between March 1990 and March 1991 – 74 percent of all jobs lost nation-wide; Statistics Canada, 5 September 1991.
4 See Floyd Laughren, treasurer of Ontario, 1991 Ontario Budget; Robert Nixon, treasurer of Ontario, 1990 Ontario Budget; Ontario Finances, Quarterly Update, 31 December 1990, Third Quarter (Ministry of Treasury and Economics); and Richard Mackie, "Ontario's deficit expected to grow: Treasurer fears 1991 budget shortfall to be much larger than $2.5 billion," *Globe and Mail*, 31 January 1991, B3.
5 See Harold Chorney, *The Deficit and Debt Management: An Alternative to Monetarism* (Ottawa: Canadian Centre for Policy Alternatives, 1989), 92.
6 L. Laliberté, "Foreign Investment in the Canadian Bond Market, 1978 to 1990," *Canadian Economic Observer*, June 1991.
7 I have calculated this on the not unreasonable assumption that the rise in indebtedness would cause a fall of one notch in the credit rating of the province; that this fall in the credit rating would mean an additional 1/4 of 1 percent in interest rates on the debt; that the rise in the deficit would be of the order of $8 billion; and that according to the budget roughly $2 billion of already existing debt would have to be refinanced in the coming year. See Robert Nixon, treasurer of Ontario, 1990 Financial Report, 28.
8 The details of Ontario's debt and deficit are explained at length in Robert Nixon, treasurer of Ontario, 1990 Financial Report, 13ff.
9 For a discussion of the burden of the debt argument from a neoconservative point of view, see James Buchanan, *Public Principles of*

Public Debt (Homewood, Ill.: Irwin, 1958); for a non-scholarly polemic, see The Progressive Conservative Party of Ontario, *Today's Deficits Are Tomorrow's Taxes* (Toronto, 1991); for a Keynesian point of view, see Abba Lerner, *The Economics of Control* (New York: A.M. Kelley, 1970), Alvin Hansen, *Economic Policy and Full Employment* (New York: McGraw-Hill, 1947), Ruben Bellan, *Unnecessary Evil: An Answer to Canada's High Unemployment* (Toronto: McClelland and Stewart, 1986), Hugh Dalton, *Principles of Public Finance* (London: Routledge & Kegan Paul, 1961), and James Ferguson, ed., *Public Debt and Future Generations* (Chapel Hill: University of North Carolina Press, 1964).

10 William Krehm, "The Deficit As Mirage," *Policy Options* 6 (June 1985): 36–40.

11 See E.J. Mishan, "How to Make a Burden of the Public Debt," in Ferguson, *Public Debt and Future Generations.*

12 See Harold Chorney and Bernard Bouska, "Regionalizing Monetary Policy, An Alternative to Monetarism: Learning from the Japanese Example" (Paper presented to the Eastern Economics Association, Baltimore, 4 March 1989). Reprinted in COMER Papers (Toronto: Committee on Monetary and Economic Reform, 1991).

13 See the following works by Harold Chorney: *The Deficit and Debt Management* (forthcoming); "Keynes et le problème de l'inflation: les racines du retour à une saine gestion financière," in G. Boismenu et G. Dostaler, *La théorie générale et le Keynesianisme* (Montreal: ACFAS, 1987); *The Deficit: Hysteria and the Economic Crisis* (Ottawa: Canadian Centre for Policy Alternatives, 1984); and "The Power of Reason and the Legacy of Keynes," *Canadian Journal of Political and Social Theory* 8, no. 3 (Fall 1984): 162–8. See also Robert Eisner, *How Real Is the Federal Deficit* (New York: Free Press, 1986); Robert Heilbroner and Peter Bernstein, *The Debt and the Deficit: False Alarms/Real Possibilities* (New York: W.W. Norton, 1989); D. Conklin and T. Courchene, *Deficits: How Big and How Bad?* (Toronto: Ontario Economic Council, 1983); H. Minto and P. Gross, "The Growth of the Federal Debt," *Canadian Economic Observer*, June 1991; and J. Rock, ed., *Debt and the Twin Deficits Debate* (Toronto: Mayfield Publishing, 1991).

13 Labour and the Environment: A Look at BC's "War in the Woods"

ELAINE BERNARD

INTRODUCTION

Over the last decade, with the growth of the environmentalist movement and increased public concern about the environment, there have been a number of dramatic confrontations between workers and environmentalists. From the "Redwood Summer" campaign of resistance to and sabotage of logging efforts in Northern California to the blockade of Red Squirrel Road in Temagami, Ontario, the confrontations have increasingly been discussed in terms of jobs versus the environment. In Canada, the resource and energy industries, in particular, have been at the centre of these dramatic confrontations. The "wars is the woods" in British Columbia and Ontario have made national and at times even international headlines.

A priority for Bob Rae's New Democratic government will be to establish a process by which land-use conflicts can be resolved and a long-term forest management plan developed to reforest and to protect the remaining "old growth" and wilderness areas. The conflict between workers and environmentalists threatens the very core of party unity and support. Organized labour has been the bedrock of support for the New Democratic Party in Ontario, especially in small, single-industry communities and the industrial heartland. The environmental movement, on the other hand, is one of the most rapidly growing social movements worldwide – a movement that demands the redefinition of much of the legal foundations of our society, including private property and ownership rights. Environmentalist insist that government implement a new method of social accounting to set societal priorities.

BC's WAR IN THE WOODS

The new NDP government in Ontario, in attempting to develop a process to resolve the land-use conflicts in Ontario, may find the BC experience instructive. While British Columbia is far from forging a long-term solution, there have nevertheless been some important initiatives from labour, environmentalists, native people, and the NDP on forest land use and conservation. As a case study, the ongoing battle in the BC forests illustrates both the opportunities for and the barriers to constructing a program to address the needs of working people in a key sector of the economy. Many of the issues at stake in the BC war in the woods, from jobs versus environment to who should bear the cost of industrial readjustment, are central to any discussion of a labour strategy in the context of global economic restructuring.

British Columbia's land-use conflict is a product of the increased pressure of international competition in forest products. Seeking a competitive edge, the forest companies have targeted the province's highly profitable old-growth forests (i.e., forests in a natural state, with trees over 200 years old) for logging. With an estimated seventeen years before the economically recoverable coastal old growth runs out, at current harvest rates, Meares Island, the Carmanah Valley, and the Stein Valley have all been the scene of dramatic confrontations. Loggers and forest companies have been pitted against native people and environmentalists.

Politically, such land-use issues are critical for labour and its political ally, the New Democratic Party. The war in the woods threatens the coalition that the NDP and labour see as vital for an NDP electoral victory. It is internally divisive for labour and could potentially drive a wedge between public sector and forestry workers. Provincially, the conflict has tended to divide the urban population centres of the Lower Mainland and lower Vancouver Island from the interior of the province and central and northern Vancouver Island. But most significantly, the anger and frustration caused by the valley-by-valley confrontations over logging threaten to unravel the vital bonds of unity between labour and many of the other social movements in the province.

FORESTRY AND FOREST MANAGEMENT

The forest industry is vital to the entire country. Canada is the world's number one exporter of forest products, with $22.5 billion worth of products in 1988 and sales values at $40 billion. An estimated one million workers are employed in this industry, either directly or indirectly.[1]

In British Columbia, forestry is the largest revenue-earning industry with product sales of $11.5 billion.[2] In total percent, the timber products sector is estimated to generate 17.5 percent of total provincial employment and 25.5 percent of the gross provincial product.[3] In addition to the province-wide significance of this industry, many BC communities are particularly dependent on the province's forests, with seventy communities having been identified as dependent on this single industry.[4]

Forests are, of course, not inexhaustible. The goal of forest management is to apply a scientific approach to maximizing timber production on a continuous basis. The concept of "sustainable timber yield" is offered as a threshold that permits maximum harvesting while ensuring constant supply. Yet this is a most inexact science. With poor data on projected forest growth, equally poor data on existing forests, and a variety of apprehensions about the possible effects of global climate change, air pollution, pests, and disease, the very concept of sustainable yield is full of uncertainty.

In spite of such uncertainties, with rare unanimity, environmentalists, loggers, and native people have all criticized the provincial government and the forest industry for their waste and mismanagement of this vital resource. All three groups have engaged in "whistle blowing" on wasteful practices by companies and have called the provincial government to task for failing to enforce its own industry regulations.

For the industry, the main issue is to assure a supply of industrial softwood for delivery to processing mills at a competitive cost. In recent years, increased competition from South America, changing demand in the wood products market, and declining quantities of accessible old-growth timber have pushed forest companies to seek to maximize profits through increased volume production. Consequently, the remaining old-growth forests have become particularly attractive. In pursuing profits through a volume strategy, logging activities have grown in excess of sustainable annual allowable cut. In 1987, for example, the national sustainable annual allowable cut was estimated to be 166 million cubic metres. Canada cut approximately 175 million cubic metres, of which 90.5 million cubic metres,[5] or over half of the total volume, came from British Columbia.[6]

THE UNIONS

The International Woodworkers of America–Canada, which represents the woodworkers, is also interested in a stable supply of softwood. The union hopes that smoothly running mills and processing plants will provide economic stability for its members. In the words of IWA-Canada president Jack Munro, "Our jobs are at stake in the biggest industry Canada has."[7] Feeling the jobs-versus-environment crunch acutely, the IWA-Canada adopted a lengthy position paper entitled *Forest Policy* at its 1989 annual convention. The union's forest policy included an endorsement of "the recommendations of the United Nations' Commission on the environment and development [the Brundtland Commission]," and a four-point "sustainable forest strategy," which calls for the creation of a rational land-use planning process, including a fair conflict resolution mechanism; community and worker input into planning and monitoring of forest activities; research and development into new harvesting methods, silviculture, and job creation; and environmentally sound logging practices within work plans that pay as much attention to regeneration as they do to harvesting.[8]

NATIVE PEOPLE

Native people have asserted that large areas of the coastal old-growth forests are subject to native land claims. The provincial government has refused to negotiate these claims, and native people fear that logging will destroy the physical evidence of their early habitation of these areas as well as much of the cultural and commercial value of the land in dispute. Significant components of West Coast native traditional culture are tied to these forests. Specific sites and natural features are associated with harvesting rights and religious rituals. Native people are adamant in their position that land claims must be resolved in disputed areas before any further economic activities take place.

THE ENVIRONMENTALISTS

Like the other groups mentioned so far, environmentalists hold strong opinions on the forestry issue. In regard to old-growth forests, they emphasize the importance of maintaining the remnants of complete coastal rainforest ecosystems such as those in the Carmanah Valley and in interior wilderness areas like the Stein Valley. They criticize the current practices of forest companies, which they believe to be short-sighted, wasteful, and non-sustainable.

In line with the emphasis on the preservation of wilderness, one group, the Valhalla Society, released in December 1988 a proposal that entails more than doubling (from 5.2 to 13.1 percent) the amount of land protected in the province.[9] The Council of Forest Industries (COFI) characterized the proposal as a "shopping list" that it fears does not represent "the totality of their demands." The industry estimates that the proposal would affect 10 percent of the current industrial forest, thus jeopardizing over 25,000 jobs – 8,500 direct forest industry jobs and 17,000 jobs in related industries.[10] In spite of opposition from COFI, the Valhalla Society proposal has received considerable support from environmentalists and other groups in the province.

THE SOCIAL CREDIT GOVERNMENT

BC's Social Credit provincial government has not been sympathetic to environmentalist concerns, notwithstanding its marketing strategy which promotes "Super, Natural British Columbia." While tourism is BC's second-largest industry, with revenues of $3.5 billion in 1988 (tourism is responsible for approximately 5,000 new jobs annually, and wilderness tourism has been growing by 15 to 20 percent annually), the provincial government has been hesitant to create additional parks and wilderness reserves.[11] British Columbia has been characterized by political scientist Martin Robin as "the company province"; its economy has long been dominated by extractive natural resource industries. Clearly, there are those who fear that additional wilderness or park reallocation of land would place significant hardship on extractive industries.

The BC government opposes single-use options and the reallocation of land, as advocated in the Valhalla proposal, preferring instead a multiple-use model. Such a model, the government claims, would permit, with proper management, the integration of several resource uses simultaneously – timber, mining, grazing, fishing, and recreation.

"SHARE THE FOREST"

"Share the Forest," a political movement that popularizes the multiple-use approach, has emerged over the last few years with the purpose of wrestling the public away from the growing environmentalist sentiment. Share the Forest engages in language appropriation reminiscent of the abortion debate, where "pro-choice" stood against "pro-life." The movement criticizes environmentalist groups as "preservationist" and "anti-development," arguing that they are fundamentally against all logging and development and that they do not care about workers and their communities. Environmentalists are accused of successfully lobbying and agitating for the withdrawal of prime old-growth areas from logging, leading to the loss of forest industry jobs and the destruction of forest-dependent communities. In line with the corporate strategy outlined in "The Greening of the Boardroom," an article that appeared in the *Globe and Mail*'s *Report on Business Magazine* in July 1989, Share the Forest seeks to use the language of the environmental movement to mobilize community support for logging and the forest companies, arguing that today's corporate leadership is environmentally conscious.

One of the major problems with the multiple-use concept is that many of the proposed uses are mutually exclusive. Multiple-use advocates suggest that special preserves, such as the giant sitka spruces of the Carmanah Valley, can be saved while logging continues on the slopes. Environmentalists would dispute this, insisting that the survival of such preserves depends on the continued existence of whole ecosystems and watersheds.

POLITICAL ALTERNATIVES

For the NDP and its labour allies, a comprehensive plan for sustainable forests is a prerequisite to ending the war in the woods. But lacking the power and resources of a provincial government, the NDP, at this point, is not in the position to negotiate the drawing of the map. "Drawing the map" is a BC euphemism for determining which areas will be preserved and which can be logged, at what rates, and with what technology. Until such a plan is negotiated, the valley-by-valley confrontations seem inevitable and will likely escalate in their intensity.

But drawing the map requires more than scientifically assessing existing forest resources and determining a harvesting and reforestation strategy. It also means negotiating a new provincial social contract and a long-term economic plan for the forest industry. The current provincial Social Credit government is ideologically opposed to such planning, preferring instead to let market forces, dominated by a few forest multinationals, direct the industry and by extension the economy of the province.

The environmentalists, through the Valhalla proposal, have indeed attempted to draw the map. But their proposal simply outlines the areas they feel must be preserved. It is not, and was not meant to be, a comprehensive plan for forest management and for the industry, and it does not attempt to deal with the issue of native land claims. Yet, by providing a map, the Valhalla Society has shown that the environmental movement is willing to work towards a province-wide strategy.

A recent detailed analysis of the Valhalla proposal by students and faculty in Simon Fraser University's Natural Resources Management Program (NRMP) finds that the proposal would not be as costly – either in terms of lost jobs, loss of provincial revenues, or removal of land from harvesting – as COFI or even the Valhalla Society itself had predicted. The report stated that with no offsetting policies the Valhalla proposal would increase protected land area in the province from 5.2 percent to 11.7 percent (well within the Brundtland recommendations, which were endorsed by the IWA); reduce net area available for timber harvesting by 4.7 percent; reduce the annual allowable cut by less than 4 percent; affect 2,554 direct jobs in the forest industry; and reduce government revenues by $52.9 million, which is less than 2 percent of resource revenues and 0.5 percent of provincial revenues from all sources.[12]

According to the NRMP report, a number of improved forest practices could considerably reduce, even offset, the job and revenue loss of the Valhalla proposal and the waste in current BC forestry practices. Improved silviculture alone could potentially offset the impact of the Valhalla wilderness withdrawals. Jobs and revenues could greatly be increased through improved timber utilization, especially by increasing lumber recovery at the milling stage, and through improved wood processing, especially if higher manufacturing is encouraged in the solid wood industry. It has been projected that an investment of $600 million in secondary manufacturing could increase industry revenues by $1.8 billion and create 3,900 jobs.[13]

While not attempting to draw the map, Vancouver Island native leaders have initiated an important step in drawing labour, environmentalist, and community groups together in a collaborative process to discuss aboriginal land title and rights, land-use conflicts, and resource development. At a conference at Tin-Wis hosted by the Nuu-chah-nulth Tribal Council in February 1989 and attended by representatives of native nations, environmentalists, labour representatives, the NDP, and community groups, an accord was drawn up emphasizing the need to draw these groups together in a broad-based coalition to work on a "people's" alternative to current government policies. The resulting Tin-Wis Accord states:

1. We commit ourselves to active support for the recognition by all non-Native governments, of Aboriginal title and rights, and for the immediate

commencement of governmental and community processes to negotiate treaties between Native nations and non-Native governments. We recognize that these rights have not been and cannot be extinguished.

2. We further commit ourselves to develop and implement a process of learning and sharing within and between Native and non-Native communities and organizations, with a goal of developing trust and a shared vision about how we can justly and sustainably share in this earth. This includes a process of learning about the full meanings of terms like democracy, community, local control and ownership.
3. In accordance with the above, we further commit ourselves to develop and implement mechanisms for Native people, trade unionists, environmentalists, women, youth and others to work together on a regional basis to resolve resource development and environmental issues and conflicts, and to further the process of developing a "peoples" alternative to the policies of the present government.

These representations will become effective when the organizations concerned sign this Accord, and submit credentials demonstrating their ability to represent their full constituency.

The tasks of the steering committee will be to:

a) further the coalition building process;
b) plan further gatherings or actions; and
c) develop a collective plan of action which will deepen commitment to, and mobilize support for, the above principles.

Both the BC Federation of Labour and the NDP conventions have endorsed the Tin-Wis Accord and have continued to participate in this important coalition. While the Valhalla Society has started the process of drawing the map, the Tin-Wis Accord has initiated the process of coalition building.

Building on these two initiatives, provincial NDP leader Mike Harcourt has proposed an "Environment and Jobs Accord between Aboriginal people, forest companies, forest workers, environmental groups, and the province of B.C." Harcourt sees the three goals of an accord as being (1) to create stability and economic security for forest communities and forestry workers by increasing significantly the value of sustainable forest production through new jobs in value-added and secondary manufacturing industries and through improved forestry methods, such as intensive silviculture; (2) to double BC's park and wilderness areas from less than 6 percent to 12 percent; and (3) to settle outstanding aboriginal land claims.[14] Significantly, Harcourt's accord raises the vital issue of "compensation of forest workers and communities in relation to lands alienated for conservation activity."[15]

Harcourt's accord has clearly attempted to find common ground by embracing the Valhalla Society's proposal of doubling the park and wilderness area, the native people's central demand for the settlement of outstanding land claims, the woodworkers' concern for job and economic stability, and finally, a touch of the broad-based process adopted in the Tin-Wis Accord (though with the significant addition of the forest companies in the equation).

To date, Harcourt has been careful not to take on the forest companies directly. While he has called for improved silviculture and increased research and development, he has not said who will be responsible for this and who will pay. Harcourt has stated that he would introduce new legislation to protect workers who blow the whistle on bad forestry practices. He would also tighten up forest environmental and health and safety standards. But much of the future vision is left to be worked out through a proposed "Royal Commission on the Forest."[16]

Such a commission could play an important policy role if it was organized along the lines of Justice Thomas Berger's Mackenzie Valley Pipeline Inquiry, with significant community and native involvement.

THE REAL WAR

While BC's war in the woods is far from over, the tentative steps taken by labour, environmentalists, native people, and the NDP towards developing both an alternative strategy for resolving land-use conflicts and a program for sustainable forest management are encouraging. But the real battle will be the struggle to develop an alternative economic strategy to the Socreds' and forest companies' current demand for more logs and greater profits. This ultimately means challenging the power of capital and the market's unrestricted rule over resource use and development. To quote 1989 CBC Massey lecturer Dr Ursula Franklin, "If someone robs a store, it's a crime and the state is all set and ready to nab the criminal ... but if somebody steals from the commons and from the future, it's seen as entrepreneurial activity and the state cheers and gives them tax concessions rather than arresting them. We badly need an expanded concept of justice and fairness that takes mortgaging the future into account."[17]

For the woodworkers in particular, this means recognizing that the forestry industry is too important to their livelihood and to the entire province to be left to the mismanagement of the forest companies. Through massive technological change and new forestry practices, tens of thousands of jobs in the forestry industry have been lost over the last two decades. While the companies through publicity campaigns like "forests forever" have tried to show their concern for the workers and for wilderness preservation, at the same time they are attempting to lay the blame for loss of forestry jobs on the land-claim demands of native people and the conservation demands of the environmentalists. Through initiatives such as the Tin-Wis coalition, the Valhalla proposal, the woodworkers' forest policy paper, and the NDP's environment and jobs accord, a new coalition is being forged, one that will not scapegoat working people, whether natives, environmentalists, or woodworkers, but instead develop a sustainable forest policy that will not pit environmental concerns against job security. Such a forestry policy is a cornerstone of British Columbia's future.

THE OPTION FOR ONTARIO

In Ontario, the NDP caucus set out its forestry policy in a December 1983 paper called "The Last Stand." This position paper calls for "a complete re-evaluation of Ontario's forest resource inventory" and "a complete overhaul of current forest management planning systems." It urges government to "formulate and implement a comprehensive wood utilization policy based on consultation with labour and community-based groups as well as industry."[18]

While this planning process will necessarily take a long time, especially if it is to both be comprehensive and have wide participation and involvement, there are some immediate steps the government should take to begin the dialogue. As a show of good faith and a first step, the government should stay or drop any outstanding charges against environmentalists who were involved in the blockade of the Red Squirrel Road. This is routinely done with charges laid during picket-line scuffles once strikes are settled. The government should assist unions, environmental groups, native people, and communities to develop alternative plans and programs for the forests and forest-dependent communities. In British Columbia, the fact that there is a diversity of groups developing their own programs and alternatives has not been a problem; it has, in fact, added to the process of clarification and coalition building in that discussion has focused on concrete and specific plans, such as the Valhalla proposal, rather than on destructive speculation about "the real agenda" of various groups. Finally, it is important to outline an immediate program for old-growth protection.

The BC experience is instructive insofar as it shows the need for the NDP to play an active role in coalition building around the issue of land-use conflicts. It cannot simply be left to the bureaucrats or technicians to find a "scientific formula" setting out the right mix of cutting and reforestation to meet the universally shared goal of sustainable yield. Ending the land-use conflicts in Ontario's woods means wielding a new social contract between workers and the community, including environmentalists and protectionists. Success will depend on the ability of the Ontario government to involve the labour movement, environmentalists, native people, and community groups in constructive dialogue on the province's forest resource.

NOTES

1 F.L.C. Reed, "Forest Resource Conflict and Its Resolutions: The Context for a Policy Review," NSERC Industrial Chair in Forest Policy (Faculty of Forestry, University of British Columbia, 5 June 1989).

2 Natural Resource Management Program (NRMP), Simon Fraser University, *Wilderness and Forestry: Assessing the Cost of Comprehensive Wilderness Protection in British Columbia* (Burnaby: Simon Fraser University, January 1990), 3.

3 Romain Jacques, *The Impact of the Forestry Sector on the Economy of Canada and Its Provinces: An Input-Output Approach* (Ottawa: Canadian Forestry Service, 1988).

4 NRMP, *Wilderness and Forestry*, 12.

5 Reed, "Forest Resource Conflict," 2.

6 NRMP, *Wilderness and Forestry*, 7.

7 Jack Munro and Jane O'Hara, *Union Jack* (Vancouver: Douglas and McIntyre, 1988), 206–7.

8 IWA-Canada, *Forest Policy* (Third Annual Constitutional Convention, 4 October 1989, and National Executive Board, 13 December 1989), 1, 3, 4.

9 Valhalla Society, *British Columbia's Endangered Wilderness: A Proposal for an Adequate System of Totally Protected Lands* (New Denver: Valhalla Society, 1988).

10 NRMP, *Wilderness and Forestry*, 4; and Council of Forest Industries, Press release (Vancouver, 5 December 1988).

11 NRMP, *Wilderness and Forestry*, 3.

12 Ibid., 90–1.

13 Ibid., 91, 92.

14 Press release, "Hartcourt Puts Forward Environment and Jobs Accord as Alternative to Socreds' Shortsighted Carmanah Bill" (Victoria, 14 June 1990).

15 Press Release, "An Environment and Jobs Accord for B.C." (Victoria, 14 June 1990), section 4.8.

16 Press Release, "Eight Points to Sustainable Forests" (10 October 1989).

17 Ursula Franklin, *The Real World of Technology* (Toronto: CBC Enterprises, 1990), 122.

18 Task Force on Forestry, "The Last Stand," Report of the Ontario New Democratic Party Caucus (Toronto, December 1983), 25.

PART FIVE

Conclusion

14 The Way Ahead for Ontario

DANIEL DRACHE

INTRODUCTION

The globalization of production and the search by corporations for ever-larger markets are imposing tough conditions of adjustment on Ontario's labour movement. Labour now finds itself at a crossroads. One road, the one we have been taking, will surely lead to labour's demise. Another suggests a different agenda, one governed by principles of labour empowerment. These opposing workplace-oriented strategies and management's dogged determination to slim the work force are forcing the labour movement to look for alternatives to this new international order.

Will the deep-rooted tension between the drive for competitive efficiency and the search for well-being and security ignite something much larger and more significant in the hearts and minds of working people? Today, there are grounds to be optimistic. The victory of the Rae social democratic government may well mark the turning-point in a decade of far-reaching neo-conservative politics. What the NDP victory points to is the fact that Ontario's working men and women have a right to a greater share of Canada's wealth and to the more equitable distribution of their province's income. As well, they are entitled to an ever-increasing political say over their daily lives and at their place of work. For an NDP government, these goals are not unrealistic, but the way ahead is fraught with difficulties and many practical problems remain to be overcome. If global competition is not going to drive living conditions down to their lowest common denominator, new policies are needed.

SHAPING COMPETITIVE ADVANTAGE: THE CORE ISSUE

In recent years two broad approaches have emerged on the left as responses to the globalization of markets. The first approach stresses the need to regulate trade relationships both to achieve balanced trade relationships with the country's principal partners and to avoid the severe dislocation that free trade inevitably produces. This rejection of a hyperliberal export-driven strategy requires that government shape market forces through a range of policy instruments rather than rely on the market to determine the country's competitive advantage. Government has to take measures to insulate the economy from the swings of the business cycle; it must decide whether it is in the country's interest to export and determine the extent to which its economy can be competitive by riding the back of the global economy. In this policy option, government must be willing to manage the economy, target trade, and stabilize labour markets.

The second approach implicitly involves accepting the pressures of globalization. Under this strategy, government would manage the construction of the country's comparative advantage, trying to find ways to respond to the new pressures of competitiveness. The key conceptual idea is that government should encourage a restructuring of the economy towards high value-added, skills-intensive production. This strategy focuses on the importance of the country's institutional underpinnings to a strong export performance, particularly with respect to technology diffusion, skills training, capital markets, industrial relations, and the like. An alert government can shape the country's competitive advantage by relying on its "natural" comparative advantage, flexible specialization, and technological upgrading.

This debate over constructing comparative advantage hinges on how an economy chooses to deal with the problem of "flexibility." Many economists and political scientists have used the term "post-Fordist" to refer to the radical changes occurring in the organization of work and the structure of employment due largely to leaner management strategies. The central element is the corporate world's search for systemic flexibility at the level of organization of production, flexibility in the hierarchy of skills of the labour force, in worker mobility within and between firms, in the formation of wages, and in the extent and degree of social security coverage. As well, the contemporary managerial obsession with flexibility is synonymous with something more grand. Business is convinced that increased capital mobility, used in tandem with portable technologies, can create a new science of management. Thus, it wants to encourage other dramatic changes in work and employment practices in line with its immediate objective to cut costs and restore profit levels.[1]

With work organization, wage formation, and collective bargaining all on the table, Canadian social democrats will have to make fundamental decisions about the new economic order. Without a theory of competition, a social democratic administration will find itself handicapped. It may not like the idea of competitiveness because the concept of competition is one of the central ideas in the tool kit of neo-classical economics and has become the single-minded concern of large and small business everywhere. But it has no alternative if it expects to develop compatible policies on efficiency and welfare so that it can respond to far-reaching structural change without betraying its roots. Social democratic policy-makers need a theory that tells them where the jobs will come from. Will income flexibility generate more income and social inequality? Does society promote flexibility by relying on the stick of market discipline or by adopting active labour market policies? Are companies made more flexible by developing the skills of their workers or by creating a large stratum of contingent workers to whom a company has no long-term commitment?[2] While the range of outcomes is highly varied, unions, governments, and firms are facing two competing choices about the future.

If the Rae government and its allies, the unions, choose to stay in a defensive posture with respect to restructuring capital/labour relations, business will continue to rely on the old Fordist principles of work organization; this situation would be only marginally improved by the adoption of new technologies. Certainly, Canada's union movement can expect more two-tier wage contracts and the de-indexing of wages more generally. In such a situation, unions will be further weakened and the decentralized nature of Canada's system of collective bargaining will lead to more concession bargaining. For governments, private sector ordering will become even more the norm than it is today.

If, on the other hand, the government and unions opt for an offensive strategy to exploit the advances in information-based technologies, they have to be prepared to entertain the possibility that Canada's industries can be modernized, that the new technologies can become an alternative to Fordist top-down management practices, and that future joint bargaining on wages and welfare with firms or industry-wide groupings can lead to solidaristic wage policies and a stable wage hierarchy. If labour and government choose the second path, they will have to develop new institutional arrangements so that large-scale restructuring can effect the wholesale reorganization of economic space on different premises. The challenge is to get business to accept government's broad policy goals while it pursues its own short-term interests. For governments seized with the imperative of restructuring, the task is not unrealistic, even if fraught with theoretical and practical difficulties.

NEW REALITIES AND NEW CHALLENGES

In an era of increased capital mobility, what has changed is that nations have less control over their future. The difference is that the nation-state has been rendered more porous and less able to act as a buffer between the national economy and the globalizing forces of production. As countries open their economies to trade, regional and local economies are directly exposed to international price competition. As well, in an interdependent world, states have less and less recourse to many of the traditional instruments of Keynesian stratecraft – tariffs and monetary, fiscal, and investment policy – that used to allow countries to protect their domestic industries from foreign competition. Finally, business everywhere has been given more rights to invest and divest and, thereby, has more power as a social actor. As corporations become larger and indeed even more powerful, driving down costs becomes the single most important priority for business and the state.

Under these conditions, it is not surprising that high unemployment has already become a permanent feature of industrial economies. Despite the fact that over the past decade thousands of jobs have been created in the service sector, there has been no let-up in the trend towards de-industrialization. If anything, this trend has intensified. Industries today are producing more goods with far fewer workers than a decade ago. Industrial production continues to be one of the pillars of the economy, even if economists are predicting zero job growth.[3] (See Table 14.1.)

Both the labour shedding that has taken place since the 1982 recession and the move towards smaller work forces point to the profound changes affecting labour markets. (See Figure 14.1.) Industrial societies everywhere are faced with the emergence of labour-surplus economies for the foreseeable future. The growth of long-term unemployment along with the tightening of UIC (Unemployment Insurance Commission) rules and benefits have prepared the ground for a new pay and employment structure, particularly for young people and for women in the service sector. The Economic Council of Canada has found that these targeted groups are being

Table 14.1
Ontario Economic Outlook

	1989	*1990*	*1991*	*1992–94 Average Annual*
Real growth (%)	3.2	0.7	0.5	2.9
Job creation (000s)	87	−1	0	100
Unemployment rate (%)	5.1	6.1	7.3	6.9
Inflation (%)	5.8	4.9	6.1	4.1
Housing starts (000s)	93	63	54	n/a
Business investment (% change)				
Plant	8.6	−8.2	−7.6	n/a
Machinery and equipment	3.1	−6.6	−3.3	n/a

Source: Ontario Ministry of Treasury and Economics.

channelled into low-paying, "bad" jobs in a highly segmented labour market. Unless corrective action is taken, this will become the norm for the next generation of workers.

The globalization of trade is, in part, responsible for the attack on employment conditions. In the past, only a few select services were traded. Today, the service sector is billed as the next investment/trade frontier. Foreign business wants new rights to deliver business services and to invest in banking and finance. In public services, foreign multinationals want to deliver health, educational, and social services now provided by governments. This quantum change in capital mobility poses new problems for labour movements as well as for aspiring social democratic governments. Finance capital wants to be able to invest and divest with the minimum of restriction and reshape labour standards to fit the lowest common denominator of its investment needs. In particular, social security programs are no longer to reflect national standards that formerly were intended to protect society from the uneven hand of the market. In their place, a new concept of citizenship has emerged, one with an operative logic that gives less weight than ever before to the twin goals of security and welfare. Not only are people expected to be more self-reliant but they must work longer and harder. A person is considered a productive member of society if he or she contributes to the country's commercial success. Individuals who succeed in putting themselves on a competitive footing are promised that they will move up the employment/wage curve. Those who supposedly lack the resolve to take risks will slide down the curve.

For the majority of women who find employment in service sector jobs, these tough new labour market conditions present immediate

Figure 14.1
More Production, Fewer Workers

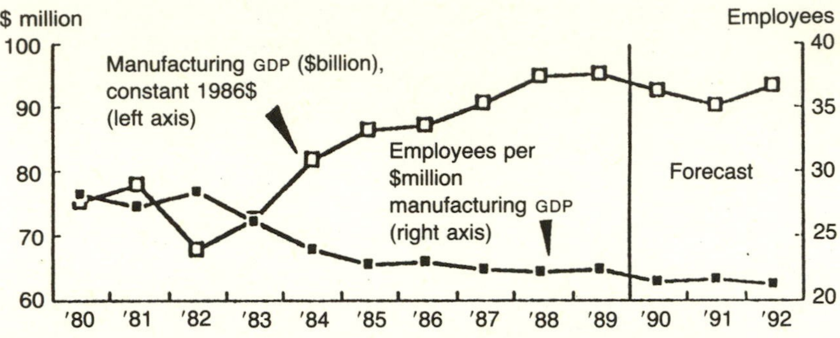

Source: Statistics Canada, Canadian Manufacturers Association forecasts for 1990–92.

difficulties. Frequently, these women work at subsistence wages without the protection of collective bargaining. They have to rely on labour-standards legislation for the most minimum benefits with respect to hours and conditions of employment as well as other employment security measures.

Employment-standards legislation provides a range of statutory entitlements – minimum wages, maximum hours of work, overtime rates, maternity leave, mass termination notice, and statutory holidays – to both male and female workers. Conceived as an adjunct to the collective-bargaining process, the legislation has not been effective in ensuring that women receive "a decent wage or secure employment."[4] Since the largest number of workers who rely on employment standards are women, "no one other than women concerned themselves with the adequacy of the statutory floors" that this legislation established. The gender bias of this statute meant that when large numbers of women entered the work force, their work would be undervalued by the market and their subordinate position more pronounced, particularly in the feminized sectors of the economy.

Now, with women comprising close to 50 percent of the labour market, the feminization of labour poses a threat to an underlying assumption of collective bargaining: that the labour force is made up of full-time employed male workers bargaining for a family wage. Clearly, this norm no longer fits reality. Women's participation is permanent, not temporary, even if many women work part-time in insecure employment situations. For unions the immediate challenge is to find ways to extend collective bargaining to the feminized sectors of the labour force, which historically have not had access to the collective-bargaining mechanism.

The current shakedown in labour markets and employment practices increasingly also has other direct consequences for the institutional mechanism of wage formation. Labour's status and the collective-bargaining process are in a period of transition. Collective bargaining used to be predicated on the idea that the members of major industrial unions would share in productivity growth on a regular basis. For more than a decade, business has attacked this central premise, and in many sectors workers have suffered dramatic losses at the bargaining table.[5] Canadian workers have been locked in a losing battle against the strong and persistent inflationary price movements. Now, after ten long and difficult years and despite the current recession, have trade unions reached the end of this long economic cycle of wage concessions and givebacks? Possibly.

The widespread practice of concession bargaining has made many forget that when workers do not share in productivity growth on a regular basis, wage pressures will eventually build to the point where they can no longer afford to wait for the inevitable recovery. They will have to strike, legally and illegally, with increasing frequency when they feel cheated of their just due. The visible failure of wage increases to keep pace with productivity gains for the better part of a decade can only provoke greater militancy and stubbornness at the bargaining table. In Canada, we are rapidly approaching such a flashpoint. Labour's patience is wearing thin. Radical changes in the production paradigm, the organization of work, and the structure of employment have brought matters to a head. While management wants to adopt a system of lean production relations, labour finds the new paradigm highly threatening.

To say that an economy faces a restructuring problem is to admit that a large number of its industries in the traded goods sector have an uncompetitive cost structure. Where this uncompetitive cost structure is the result of wage inflation, it may be possible to re-establish competitiveness through currency devaluation, as Sweden did at the beginning of the 1980s. Where the uncompetitive cost structure is the result of higher capital costs, it may be possible to correct the structural weaknesses by channelling capital to industry on more favourable terms. The restructuring problems faced by Ontario, however, go beyond these macroeconomic factors.

Ontario's industries are confronted by two sources of competitive pressure. At one end of the spectrum there are producers in newly industrialized countries relying on standard technology and low-cost labour. At the other end there are producers in other advanced economies using a different production model. It is this different production model that must be explored.

When the United States achieved its hegemony in international markets, it did so by pioneering a new production model called Fordism. The new methods of production associated with the Fordist work revolution dramatically altered production costs in the traded goods sector and allowed American producers to swiftly capture European markets. A similar pattern is now evident. The production model that has emerged in Japan and is diffusing through the non-union sectors of American manufacturing is fundamentally different in the way it organizes production and manages labour. The Toyota production model is invariably associated with lower unit costs and higher productivity quality. Moreover, companies adopting the "lean" production model appear to put themselves on a trajectory of productivity growth that widens their advantage over competitors who rely on traditional Fordist production methods.

Two facts seem clear. First, the restructuring problem must be addressed within the sphere of production. The restructuring problem can be solved neither through macroeconomic policy nor through trade policy. Second, the Toyota production model and its American clones fundamentally undermine established collective-bargaining practices. Indeed, most private sector employers seem to be convinced that the new production model is best introduced in a new, non-union plant. For Ontario and Ontario's labour movement, the challenge is how to deal with this fundamental shift in the production paradigm.

A RETURN TO COMPETITIVE CAPITALISM: CAN ONTARIO COMPETE?

Competing in the New Global Economy, a report from the Premier's Council of Ontario, addresses the global shift towards exploiting these new production practices. The report proposes policies that are, at once, job-creating and wealth-creating. For the social democratic left, this attempt to escape the neo-conservative ditch and rethink Ontario's future economic and industrial direction needs to be examined critically.

The report sets out to question one of the cherished ideas that Ontarians have of their province. Ontario is seen by many to have a strong and diversified economy that has made it the industrial heartland of Canada. But behind this image of well-being is another reality. Ontario's economy has as many weaknesses as strengths. It exports more then $60 billion of goods annually, but fifty firms account for 75 percent of the total and most are foreign owned. Ontario has the lion's share of Canada's auto industry, but this important sector is facing massive reorganization, soft markets, and a direct challenge from Mexico as the future growth pole of the North American auto industry. Ontario also has the lion's share of Canada's high-tech, high-growth industries. But here, too, the writing in on the wall. The majority of firms are small, and the sector is fighting to stay afloat because Ontario's mature industries prefer to import the latest technology from the United States rather than source it here in Canada. The prognosis for a turnaround is not particularly good. This sector faces increased competition at home and declining market shares in the large American market. The light, labour-intensive industrial sector is also a disaster waiting to happen. In the space of fourteen months, two out of every ten jobs have vanished from Ontario's textile, food-processing, and furniture industries. In this recession, more than half of all the layoffs are permanent compared with only 21 percent in the 1982 recession. The simple fact of the matter is that there are more firms failing than new ones being born. Most analysts now agree that the jobs lost in these sectors will be gone forever.

So, which of Ontario's industrial sectors have done well? Its resource industries comprise the one sector where Ontario has a competitive advantage and the one sector that was supposed to increase its exports as a result of the Canada-US Free Trade Agreement (FTA). But here also its mining and forest-based industries face an unparalleled crisis. Environmentally, Ontario's forest industry is a virtual disaster zone. Inefficient production methods, a declining resource base, and corporate greed have combined to mortgage the future of this key sector. Since 1980, industrial timber cutting has been the leading cause of primary forest destruction. According to the 1990 Worldwatch Institute report, roughly only half of Canada's primary forest remains.[6] Ontario's resource industries now face tough new competitive pressures from developing countries that have higher-grade resources to sell at lower prices. This too has led to more reckless price-cutting policies than ever.

WHERE THE PREMIER'S COUNCIL WENT WRONG: RETHINKING INDUSTRIAL POLICY

This picture of a province fighting for its economic life raises questions about the relevancy of the Premier's Council's principal recommendations, those that urge the province to come to terms with the dramatic downturn in Ontario's and Canada's industrial fortunes.[7] According to the council's view of industrial strategy, Canada should generate a high standard of living for itself by exploiting "the opportunities arising from technological advances." The information revolution in the microelectronic, computer, telecommunication, and information technologies has the capacity to transform the global economic scene. Mind work, intelligence, and the information revolution are now more important to a country's future well-being than its natural resource endowment. In many industries, information inputs account for three times the actual direct labour costs. Groups like the Premier's Council of Ontario have shown that the link between the role of science and technology is one of the driving forces in the emerging global economy. The council, in particular, points to the ways Canada can turn a high-tech, high value-added strategy to its national advantage.

The Premier's Council's working premise is that Canada's long-term prosperity now depends disproportionately on its developing cumulative gains in productivity sufficient to increase its share of global markets and transform consumption norms. Therefore, the primary goal of state policy must be to increase the output of each person-hour worked. Workers have to be better trained – and work smarter and harder – to produce products that require both more skill and ingenuity in their manufacture. For its part, corporate management needs to rethink its reliance on a steep organizational hierarchy and acknowledge the advantages of labour-management cooperation over confrontational tactics.

While this model emphasizes open-ended trade rather than free trade of the kind championed by the FTA, its appeal is highly seductive. It holds out the possibility that forward and backward links with many countries will be created through the establishment of leading-edge firms that, in time, will evolve into viable multinational enterprises. The benefit of going global comes from the fact that a web of supporting firms and jobs will be created in Canada. The strategic aim is not to add a lot of jobs but to create "good" jobs, jobs capable of generating wealth while boosting the size of the GNP. And it is to be hoped that the economic growth will be dispersed in an equitable manner. The aim of government policy, then, is to produce tough, resilient industries capable of supporting a whole range of employment in their own as well as other sectors of the economy.

Not surprisingly, therefore, the key recommendation of the Premier's Council advocates the creation of Canadian businesses that can compete successfully in the high-growth, high value-added sectors of the international economy. The council is of the opinion that if Ontario can create a dozen new indigenous multinational world-scale firms in addition to the likes of Northern Telecom, Noranda, and Magna International, its industrial structure would equal that of Sweden's and it would need not face a de-industrialized future as a has-been region in North America. These fifteen or so multinationals could each be a world leader with its own specialized niche. Their combined muscle could propel Canada successfully into the new world order of the twenty-first century.

The high-tech route is not the best choice for Canada or Ontario. However appealing the theory, it cannot be implemented because the existing economic realities present too many hurdles. The fact is that there are very few indigenous Canadian firms with the capacity to establish themselves as leading-edge enterprises in a worldwide setting. Most of Canada's top exporters are branch plants, and the greater part of their so-called exports are little more than the sale of parts between the branch plant and the parent. Of course, it is possible that with a commitment to go "global," new firms would come along to fill the bill. But this requires a great deal of co-ordination and intelligent government support. This is not on the horizon. But even if Canadian government policy did succeed in creating more multinationals, nothing would prevent them from becoming as footloose as American multinationals. They would want to be free to invest and divest with the minimal amount of government restriction. They would want to be able to produce goods cheaply wherever it benefits their corporate strategy. Thus, as Canadian capital becomes larger and more mobile, all the evidence suggests that "threshold" companies will pick up and move to the United States, Europe, Mexico, or wherever.

The most dynamic Canadian multinationals, such as Dominion Textile, Northern Telecom, Magna International, and Bombardier, have already shifted jobs, production, and research and development out of Canada. This tendency can only accelerate as Canada's world-class firms increasingly try to shake off their origins as they develop global marketing and production strategies. Their priority is to learn to live in a borderless world economy in which governmental regulations will no longer cramp their innovative vitality. They see the nation – and their national base – as becoming less important to their marketing strategy. With customers worldwide, they want to be as close as possible to their biggest, most dynamic markets. In practical terms, this means setting up production facilities in the United States. Merely letting a few industries compete can only adversely affect Canada's chances of successfully building a stronger industrial base.

The Premier's Council strategy has not addressed the pervasive weaknesses of Canadian industrial practices and therefore has not formulated a realistic set of recommendations to counter them. Its critical error is to reinforce the dominance of a few competitive sectors at the expense of the rest, leaving Ontario no workable alternative to the multinationals' inevitably holding sway over the production of goods and services. Under this scenario, employment standards, union viability, and wage levels would necessarily be pushed to the lowest common denominator. This is because a society that puts competitiveness ahead of any other single concern can only use traditional methods to deal with the new challenges – by dismantling many labour standards, savagely cutting real wages and fringe benefits, or imposing rigid controls over union activity.

The lesson should have been learned. If productivity is confined to a few highly specialized trade-oriented sectors, only the privileged and best-situated workers will benefit. At present, a handful of firms now account for 70 percent of Ontario's trade with the United States: three auto producers, two steel and aluminum companies, two metal mining enterprises, and four pulp and paper giants. As we know, the job and wage gains have diffused very poorly throughout the economy.

Creating more multinationals is not going to do anything to reverse the bleak future confronting the thousands upon thousands of small indigenous enterprises or protect the job security of their employees. With Ontario's industries facing an increasingly volatile world and a work force threatened with persistent job loss, what kinds of policies are needed to maximize Ontario's leverage?

REJECTING THE FREE TRADE STATUS QUO

Prior to the election of the Rae government, a reasonable industrial strategy was considered to be one that permitted companies to operate in unco-ordinated "free markets," free to satisfy their bottom-line needs. Such anarchic activity, it was thought, creates a long-term, viable competitive edge for Canada internationally and Ontario in particular. Canadian governments have long championed this idea of letting a combination of market forces, geography, and private sector actors shape Canada's domestic needs as well as its external trade relationships.

Certainly, the rationale behind the signing of the Canada-US Free Trade Agreement was the prospect of enhanced market access and greater economies of scale, with the integration of the two economies as the final result. The premise justifying the creation of a North

American common market is that this larger market for private economies would generate more prosperity for Canadians.

But this narrow neo-liberal focus on the alleged gains from new economies of scale for Canadian manufacturers and a greater number of Canadian multinationals is in fact not likely to lead to more jobs and better employment prospects. Indeed, in the first year of the FTA's reign, job loss in the goods-producing and manufacturing sectors has been dramatic. The reasons for this are twofold: first, in a more competitive environment, manufacturers must slim down their work forces, and second, in a North American common market, it frequently makes no sense for formerly protected firms to stay in business, at least not in Canada. An ever-increasing number of Canadian-based firms are faced with one of three unpalatable choices: closing down, relocating to the United States, or merging with a larger enterprise. While the free trade/free enterprise model, in theory, is capable of leading to greater economic output for the whole of the North American common market, the benefits will not necessarily flow to Canadians, given the disparate size of the two economies. For labour, this kind of growth model is not an option for economic renewal but an open invitation to industrial decline and lower living standards.

Ultimately, the premises underlying the free trade model are flawed because they are posited on the notion that trade is a good in its own right. To quote the corporate sector's favourite refrain, to be required to compete on an uneven playing field is unfair. However, it would be foolish for a smaller, less mature nation to enter into unrestricted trade with a more powerful trading partner. In order for disadvantaged sectors and industries to gain a measure of equality, they often need the benefit of the unequal treatment that only governments can provide. This is the basis of all affirmative action strategies, including the one designed for every industrial policy. Canada's favoured growth model, posited on harnessing the alleged benefits from continental integration, ignores this to its citizens' detriment and its industries' peril. What, then, can the Rae government do to shape market pressures rather than to allow the economy to be shaped by them?

The preferred option of past governments has been to give more subsidies, tax breaks, and other kinds of financial relief to firms. But more handouts will neither change Ontario's policy environment nor encourage firms to experiment with other organizational forms. When a government underwrites a program of skills training or technology diffusion, firms will take advantage of the offer for assistance, but a decade of government reports confirms that a policy of handouts does not lead to sustained increases in productivity or competitiveness at the firm or sector level, if competitiveness is measured by new markets obtained, new products developed, and new jobs created.[8] Business's first choice is always to let the government pay for what is, after all, its principal area of responsibility. The fact is that business is not investing in such critical areas as skills training, technology acquisition, and market innovation.

Indeed, the only way to explain the failure of Ontario firms to adopt best-practice techniques is to contrast the strategies applied here with the restructuring strategies of Sweden, Germany, and Japan (widely different but all successful). In the latter instances, decisions about private sector investment in skills training and research are not left up to the individual firm or enterprise. Under Swedish law, companies, for instance, are obligated to invest a percentage of their profits in training and R & D. In Germany, there is also a clearly established link between high levels of productivity and a culture of training by individual firms. In Japan, companies are "overtly structured as learning organizations."[9] By contrast, in Ontario, where the provision of vocational and skills training is left to the initiative of the individual firm and enterprise, the results are dismal. On average, Canadian employers only provide two hours of training per year per employee compared to the over two hundred hours annually provided by Japanese firms.

Two things can be learned from these widely divergent approaches. First, where business does not pay for training, it will not value its work force or develop a high-trust system of industrial relations practices. Second, business needs an institutionalized funding mechanism before it will behave differently. Voluntary ad hoc measures cannot be relied on to change either business culture or the way labour responds to the pressures to restructure work and employment. For Ontario's social democratic government, more is required. If the province is to follow a different trajectory and break the restructuring logjam, it needs an industrial strategy that will not have a negative impact on the links between productivity, real-wage formation, consumption, and investment. At a mimimum, this requires an informed perspective on the way economic space and industries need to be transformed.

A NEW POLICY FRAMEWORK FOR GOVERNMENT

If the people of Ontario are not to become trade-battered victims, Ontario needs innovative policy instruments to guide the restructuring process. The dilemma any Ontario government faces is that macroeconomic policy remains a strictly federal prerogative. Ottawa sets interest rates, determines taxation levels, and controls the price of the Canadian dollar. The Rae government cannot do much about the policy levers in federal hands. It can try to pressure the Mulroney government and the Bank of Canada to change policy direction and stimulate the economy, but its arguments have only the power of moral and political suasion.

By contrast, Ontario is a powerful actor in its own right at the micro-level. It is responsible for broad areas of social and economic development, such as labour markets, industrial restructuring, pay and employment equity, industrial relations, the financial regulation of institutions, technology transfer to firms and enterprises, worker retraining, as well as export assistance to Ontario-based business. All fall within its jurisdiction. Thus, there are many initiatives the Rae government can and must take to change employment rules and encourage the rationalization of whole sectors and industries. It has little choice; to stand still is to let the market and private sector actors define the restructuring agenda. The alternative is to take steps to redefine the relationship between the state and the economy in such a way as to make the government restructuring policies proactive rather than re-active. The government must find ways to overcome the high degree of institutional inertia that now exists.

The place to begin is with an industrial strategy whose principal aim is to achieve a higher standard of living for Canadians by increasing economic welfare, not simply by increasing the competitiveness of the private sector at the expense of the rest of society.

Boosting productivity would open the door to new opportunities for existing industries; it would make possible change in employment rules and encourage the modernization and rationalization both of firms and of whole industries. The success of such an industrial strategy depends on taking advantage of the potential of the new technologies and non-Fordist forms of workplace organization, issues that have to be negotiated between capital and labour. Because Ontario's economy exhibits a high degree of institutional and technological inertia, nothing less than a policy that encourages productivity will work to strengthen long-term competitiveness and the continued improvement in the standard of living.

Today, new forms of global competition require new institutional arrangements and different kinds of policy levers. Ontario must embark on a course of bold legislative change to reshape its institutional fabric. If Ontario is to live with the pressures for constant change, it has to provide an economic environment that allows enterprises and whole sectors of the economy to change and adapt. Firms need institutional-based alternatives to going global and/or remaining subscontractors to American multinationals. Many studies have made the irrefutable point that corporate culture has a direct impact on employee motivation and on a corporation's business performance. Businesses' strategic vision and commitment to qualitative change are critical to their success in the new economic age.[10] Yet, the only way firms are likely to entertain new workplace practices is if they are faced with an irreversible change in the regulatory environment. An industrial policy worthy of the name has to induce firms to behave differently. They need to adopt different investment strategies, different marketing approaches, and different labour market policies.

Western democracies have had much experience with different kinds of regulatory frameworks that have induced firms to alter their market behaviour and the way they produce. The creation of state enterprises has been one strategic device used to change business practice. Technology policy, affirmative action legislation, and minimum-wage norms are other well-known examples of the way the business sector in many different settings has been required to adopt different investment strategies, different marketing approaches, and different labour market policies. The most dramatic instance of this kind of regulatory instrument was the National Labour Relations Act, better known as the Wagner Act. Its advent in North America and its later equivalent in Western Europe constituted a large step forward for labour and an irreversible change in management practice. It forced employers to bargain with the chosen representative of their workers and with no one else.

Employers no longer had a choice in regard to unionization; they were obliged to bargain in good faith with their employees. This had other immediate consequences. It diminished competition between workers and gave unions a new standing in the workplace. In addition, it provided a measure of representative democracy in that workers were to be left as free as possible to choose a union they could influence. The fact that collective bargaining was regularized in the mass production industries and that unions were accorded a new status meant that wages were no longer determined by brute competition. Wages were still subject to the market but were also partially taken out of competition. This meant that for workers in the mass production industries, productivity and real-wage growth would be roughly linked together and would move in parallel. While the extent and nature of this intervention varied from state to state, it resulted in, among other things, a radically different kind of regulatory framework for dealing with capital/labour relations in all industrial countries. Labour was accorded a new status; Western industrial society achieved both rapid economic growth and social stability in the workplace; and for the first time, the class identity and the consumer identity were inextricably linked together for the better part of three decades.

More recently, Quebec took equally bold steps to force a basic change in its industrial structure by turning to the public sector to effect deep-rooted change in private sector activity. In the 1960s its economy was dominated by foreign-owned enterprises and an English Canadian business elite. The Lesage government created a regulatory instrument to effect a fundamental change in the ownership of the Quebec economy. In the early sixties, it created the Caisse de dépôt et placement du Québec. This legislative initiative allowed the Caisse to buy Quebec firms and support Quebec-based businesses. Business welcomed the Caisse because it was seen as an alternative to the power of the Anglo-Canadian banks. They way it worked was that the Caisse put aside a small proportion of its cash flow to support the growth of Quebec businesses. It worked hand in glove with Hydro-Québec to direct investment towards francophone firms. Over time, this institutional lever gave Quebec's business class control of key sectors of the economy.[11]

The lesson to be drawn from these examples is that governments intent on economic restructuring need a range of new policy instruments to change the investment climate and business culture. An industrial strategy has to stimulate more-fundamental kinds of changes in the social relations of production and in business practices; it must help to plug the gaps in technology, skills training, and capital resources that exist between enterprises. This is the message that the contributors of this volume want to send to the newly elected Rae government. Ontario needs a range of policy instruments to rebuild its battered industries from the ground up.

THREE POLICY PROPOSALS

At the top of the list, Ontario requires a developmental bank, the equivalent of a Quebec-inspired financial instrument, to restructure its battered industries. It needs this kind of powerful policy instrument so that the government will have the means to restructure the economy and the province's industries will have the financial means to adopt new technologies and reorganize production. Such a bank would also provide the Rae government with the instrument it needs to mount regional development programs. The initial funds would have to come from the large pools of capital in Ontario-based pension funds and other kinds of publicly held funds deposited with the government for future use.

A second essential instrument for the government would be a powerful restructuring commission to oversee the entire process of building strong industries throughout the province. The existing restructuring commission lacks authority and clout. The Rae government could upgrade the existing commission and, by giving it new sweeping powers, put it in charge of restructuring Ontario's industrial structure. Or a new agency could be established for this purpose. Whatever the choice, the commission would be responsible for framework policies with respect to sector-specific programs dealing with the needs of labour-intensive industries (food processing, textiles, and clothing), resource-based industries (largely in the north of the province), and mature industries (e.g., auto, steel, and rubber). As well, the commission would have to integrate within a restructuring strategy the proposed legislative changes with regard to education, training, women's rights, and energy.

Finally, the government needs to link labour market adjustment programs and labour retraining schemes to its larger long-term drive to diversify Ontario's exports through co-ordinated industrial planning. The key to any long-term meaningful change is to wean Ontario-based firms from their deep attachment to Taylorism and Fordist principles of work organization. Only then would it be feasible to entertain the possibility that business will forge a qualitatively different relationship with its work force, a relationship based on a high-trust system of industrial relations. Ontario needs a funding mechanism to begin the process of workplace change and renewal that will lead to a private sector commitment to training programs. The government has to introduce an employer's payroll training tax to support high-quality retraining and skills upgrading. The training should be carried out for the most part in the workplace and paid for largely by employers, with government providing supporting funding where necessary. To be effective, training programs need community input as well as participation from business organizations, government agencies, and labour. The institutional framework for skills acquisition and retraining has to be rethought. A framework within which only labour, business, and government make all the decisions is to be avoided. Training has to be defined more broadly to be reflective of community and regional needs.

A social democratic government should need no convincing that economic restructuring entails its making a significant investment. To be an efficient, innovative, and successful competitor in today's world requires large and persistent amounts of long-term investment. Countries or provinces that are committed to supporting both increased welfare and efficient industries have to have superior institutions if they want qualitatively different kinds of outcomes. Creating a modern framework of public policy requires all kinds of investment in infrastructure, in enterprises, in technology – but, above all, in people. It is paradoxical that the indebtedness incurred by the corporate sector when it invests in the future is seen as a necessary good, while that incurred by government to pay for schooling, health care, job training, or technology diffusion is denigrated in the media as deficit creating and harmful to good economic performance. Much of the current obsession with deficits makes little sense from a restructuring perspective. Countries cannot compete if they disinvest in their future and let industries and firms fail for the wont of resources.

In Ontario, Canada's wealthiest province, the NDP was elected on a forward-looking platform of social spending, modernization, and increased social welfare benefits for low-income individuals and families. In the domain of labour market adjustment, it pledged to overhaul and upgrade skills training and acquisition as well as introduce wholesale revision to Ontario's industrial relations system to protect workers from job loss, plant closures, and technological change. It announced its intention to give workers new protection under the Employment Standards Act to ensure that they receive wages, vacation pay, severance pay, and termination pay when firms fail or close down. The NDP also announced its plans to take new initiatives to facilitate the adjustment of workers facing mass layoffs. It promised "rapid and comprehensive assistance to displaced workers" as well as far-reaching revisions to Ontario's pay- and employment-equity legislation.[12] It has made the introduction of a universal system of child care a priority and has promised wholesale changes to Ontario's affirmative action legislation. It also pledged to introduce new initiatives to protect the environment and to impose tough penalties on corporations who befouled the environment. In the area of taxation, it promised a policy of fair taxation and important changes to Ontario's tax regime that would ensure a minimal corporation tax, an inheritance tax, and other reforms. Taking its own figures, it costed the total election package at $4.2 billion over two years.

If it is to make good on its electoral commitments, the Rae government must put in place an industrial economic strategy that will create jobs and rebuild Ontario's battered industries by providing enough stimulus to the economy to get it back on track. Part of the money would be recovered through a strong economic performance and higher levels of taxation revenue. Other parts of the strategy would be self-financing. Schematically, an industrial budget would entail the following core items:

- An $800-million developmental bank financed from pension funds, workers' compensation funds, and the like
- $1.5 billion to renew affordable housing stock and build non-profit apartments
- A 1 percent employers' skills-development, payroll tax
- $5 billion to build a mass transit system to create a dense network of industrial districts in Southern Ontario and the North. The money would be raised on the bond market.
- A $2-billion northern environmental fund to transform the existing forest and mining production techniques into environmentally sustainable ones. Companies would be required to match provincial investment.
- A $1.8-billion interest relief fund targeted at home buyers, farmers, small businesses, and communities to develop and upgrade existing industries and firms.
- $370 million to fund 20,000 new child-care spaces, boost salaries of non-profit child-care workers, and construct new facilities
- A $1-billion technology fund to upgrade Ontario's technological capacity. The fund would be repaid out of corporate profits.

In the final analysis, this kind of an industrial policy would create a new regulatory environment. It would permit the government to plan strategically by being able to initiate change across industries and across whole sectors of the economy. With such a policy in place, small and medium-sized firms could no longer function as autonomous actors outside dense networks of localized forms of development. They would have to pool their resources rather than compete with each other. For labour, this kind of economic strategy is its best hope to create a rising standard of living in secure employment settings. For women, it would mean a new range of services and a commitment to close the gender gap. All of this is within the realm of the possible if the Rae NDP government chooses a different economic trajectory than the current one. The goals of orderly change and increased economic welfare are compatible provided that Ontario industries are put on a different footing and that the business culture is transformed to enable large and small firms alike to produce differently. Only then will enterprises be forced to develop a new relationship with their work forces and seek out qualitatively different labour relations practices.

NOTES

1 For a discussion of the new international order, see D. Drache and M. Gertler, eds., *The New Era of Global Competition: State Policy and Market Power* (Montreal: McGill-Queen's University Press, 1991).
2 R. Boyer, "The Capital Labour Relations in OECD Countries: From the Fordist 'Golden Age' to Contrasted National Trajectories," in J. Schor, ed., unpublished manuscript.
3 Economic Council of Canada, *Good Jobs, Bad Jobs: Employment in the Service Economy* (Ottawa: Supply and Services Canada, 1990).
4 Judy Fudge, "Labour Law's Little Sister: The Employment Standards Act and the Feminization of Labour" (Ottawa: Canadian Centre for Policy Alternatives, 1991).
5 D. Drache, "The Systemic Search for Flexibility: National Competitiveness and New Work Relations," in Drache and Gertler, *New Era.*
6 Lester R. Brown, ed., *State of the World* (New York: W.W. Norton, 1990), 75.
7 This and the next section are drawn from the forthcoming work on work, employment, and collective-bargaining regimes in Canada 1960–90 to be published in 1991 by Harry Glasbeek and myself.
8 For an insightful discussion, see Fred Lazar, "An Essay on Competitiveness and Productivity" (York University, unpublished manuscript, November 1990).
9 Leon Muszynski and David Wolfe, "New Technology and Training: Lessons from Abroad," *Canadian Public Policy* 15, no. 3 (1989): 255.
10 Ronald J. Grey and Ted J.F. Thone, "Differences between North American and European Corporate Cultures," *Canadian Business Review*, Autumn 1990; idem, "Corporate Culture and Canada's International Competitiveness," *Canadian Business Review*, Winter 1990.
11 Jacques Fortin, *Québec le défi économique* (Sillery, Que.: Les Presses de l'Université du Québec, 1990).
12 Ontario Ministry of Labour, "Wage Protection Fund" (Discussion paper, December 1990); idem, "Labour Adjustment: Consultation Paper" (Policy Branch, Ministry of Labour, 24 January 1991).